The Best
AMERICAN
ESSAYS
1999

The Best
AMERICAN
ESSAYS
1999

Edited and with an Introduction
by EDWARD HOAGLAND

ROBERT ATWAN
Series Editor

HOUGHTON MIFFLIN COMPANY
BOSTON · NEW YORK

148321

ISSN 0888-3742
ISBN 0-395-86054-7
ISBN 0-395-86055-5 (pbk.)

Printed in the United States of America

QUM 10 9 8 7 6 5 4 3 2

Contents

Foreword

"CAN A COMPUTER evaluate an essay?" a *New York Times* reporter asked me shortly before we wrapped up this year's book, the fourteenth in the series. The reason for the question: a new computer program called e-rater that will be used to grade essay questions on the Graduate Management Admissions Test. I take it that the "e" stands for essay.

I replied that a computer could very easily score the results of the essay questions, assuming that all anyone wanted to know was whether the writing conformed to standard English usage and reflected a few other elements of style, like syntactic variety, that could conveniently be machine-measured. In fact, most popular word processors already provide some version of this (mine immediately questioned the use of *e-rater*). But could a computer, even one as enlightened as e-rater, detect humor and irony, evaluate metaphor, or discern a writer's tone of voice or attitude? E-rater's developer honestly admitted to the *Times* that it couldn't: "It's not designed to score Montaigne," she said. "It's designed for a specific purpose, to score the kinds of essays we see on standardized tests."

Which brings us to the heart of the matter: what do we talk about when we talk about essays? Montaigne's term for his eccentric and digressive meditations is now employed so broadly and indiscriminately that its traditional literary meaning is all but forgotten. An essay, it seems, is anything we want it to be. Our dailies, weeklies, and monthlies are chock-full of nonfiction prose, but very little of it is either creative or literary. Most of it is informative, functional, or advisory, and that's as it should be. Produced with built-in obsolescence, such writing is made for the month (at best) and not for the years. I worry when I see the honorable word *essay* applied to writing that displays no literary or ruminative characteristics, no mind in process.

I find I must continually remind readers that the essay is a literary genre. Like poems, plays, short stories, and novels, essays are written to survive a particular moment. That doesn't mean they can't be topical: George Santayana's marvelous "Tipperary" was written to mark the end of the First World War, yet even today I find its message powerfully effective. Santayana knew what an essay should do. He doesn't interview five military experts or ten veterans, he doesn't drop newsworthy names, and he doesn't cite any combat statistics, but his thoughts on war and peace are as salient now as they were at the conclusion of that "war to end all wars." The difference between literature and news, as Ezra Pound put it, is that "literature is news that *stays* news."

The essays featured in this year's volume will, it is hoped, leave a permanent impression. Like all memorable essays, they confront life's enduring themes: sexual obsession, child abuse, aging mothers and fathers, spiritual hunger, childhood frolics, loneliness, laziness, violence, destruction, beauty, and waste. The tones of voice are as varied as the topics: nostalgic, meditative, conversational, amused, confrontational, humorous, vitriolic. No matter where they land, they all take off from the first-person singular. They have little respect for sheltered views and prefer, as Barbara Hurd writes in "The Country Below," to find out what's beneath the surface: "We are drawn to what's below." Like many essayists, she is especially attracted to the world of "margins," a word, incidentally, that Ian Frazier ponders in "A Lovely Sort of Lower Purpose." Hurd explores the mystery of margins: "From the safety of whatever boardwalks we have chosen, we linger at the edges, testing the mire with the tips of galoshes, a long stick, a hand. Do we dare? Do we dare?"

Hemingway dared, Joan Didion reminds us in "Last Words," and he met the challenge with a style that will live for as long as literary prose is respected. "This was a man," she says, "to whom words mattered. He worked at them, he understood them, he got inside them." As readers will see, words — and their opposite, the other language of silence — make up one of this volume's interlocking themes. Visiting Proust's childhood home in Illiers-Combray, André Aciman finds that the great novelist's famous residence pales beside his gorgeous fictional memoir; after an account of unspeakable acts, Charles Bowden concludes his essay "without a word. Nobody wants to hear these things." Hilary Masters recalls the strange childhood delight he took in an old copy of *Robinson Crusoe,* a spellbinding story for the world's loners; Patricia Hampl spends a blessed "week in the word"; Mary Gordon visits her ninety-year-old mother, who "does not use language to describe her mental state." Cynthia Ozick considers the well-chosen words of an angry God, while Annie Dillard contemplates God's mysterious silences. Joyce Carol Oates confronts the awful self-silencing that accompanies a brutal, humiliating experience; Daisy Eun-young Rhau sensitively depicts an entirely different sort of self-silencing. Attempting to describe beauty, Scott Russell Sanders faces the "limitations of language." George W. S. Trow appropriately concludes the collection with a tribute to the printed word as he lovingly remembers New York City newspapers in a world before television.

In "Compression Wood," Franklin Burroughs describes what it's like to live in a "world of words." It's a world that can be taken utterly for granted and become so depressingly predictable that "we seem to have words only for thoughts that have already been thought, and for emotions and perceptions that don't quite feel like our own." One proven therapy for this state of mind is literature. As this collection confirms, the daring writer can brilliantly reanimate both the word and the world. It's something e-rater knows nothing about.

The Best American Essays features a selection of the year's outstanding essays, essays of literary achievement that show an awareness of craft and a forcefulness of thought. Hundreds of essays are gathered annually from a wide variety of national and regional publications. These essays are then screened, and approximately one hundred are turned over to a distinguished guest editor, who may add a few personal discoveries and who makes the final selections.

To qualify for selection, the essays must be works of respectable literary quality, intended as fully developed, independent essays on subjects of general interest (not specialized scholarship), originally written in English (or translated by the author) for publication in an American periodical during the calendar year. Periodicals that want to make sure their contributors will be considered each year should include the series on their complimentary subscription list (Robert Atwan, Series Editor, *The Best American Essays*, P.O. Box 220, Readville, MA 02137).

For his encouragement, advice, and generosity over the years I'd like to thank my good friend David Perler. For hands-on assistance with this year's collection, I'm grateful to Daniel Kirchener, who graduates from Harvard this spring — congratulations, Dan! As always, I appreciate the efforts of the Houghton Mifflin staff, especially Janet Silver and Heidi Pitlor, who are a big reason a collection like this one can appear every year. It was an enormous pleasure to do essays this year with Edward Hoagland, one of the finest essayists of our time. A decade before this series got started, he alone saw the need for one. If the American essay is finally receiving the literary attention it deserves, it is largely due to his creative achievements. Our first great essayist, Ralph Waldo Emerson, wrote of *essaying to be;* Edward Hoagland knows exactly what that means.

R. A.

Introduction: Writers Afoot

ESSAYS ARE HOW we speak to one another in print — caroming thoughts not merely in order to convey a certain packet of information, but with a special edge or bounce of personal character in a kind of public letter. You multiply yourself as a writer, gaining height as though jumping on a trampoline, if you can catch the gist of what other people have also been feeling and clarify it for them. Classic essay subjects, like the flux of friendship, "On Greed," "On Religion," "On Vanity," or solitude, lying, self-sacrifice, can be major-league yet not require Bertrand Russell to handle them. A layman who has diligently looked into something, walking in the mosses of regret after the death of a parent, for instance, may acquire an intangible authority, even without being memorably angry or funny or possessing a beguiling equanimity. *He* cares; therefore, if he has tinkered enough with his words, we do too.

An essay is not a scientific document. It can be serendipitous or domestic, satire or testimony, tongue-in-cheek or a wail of grief. Mulched perhaps in its own contradictions, it promises no sure objectivity, just the condiment of opinion on a base of observation, and sometimes such leaps of illogic or superlogic that they may work a bit like magic realism in a novel: namely, to simulate the mind's own processes in a murky and incongruous world. More than being instructive, as a magazine article is, an essay has a slant, a seasoned personality behind it that ought to weather well. Even if we think the author is telling us the earth is flat, we might want to listen to him elaborate upon the fringes of his premise because the bristle of his narrative and what he's seen intrigues us. He has a cutting edge, yet balance too. A given body of information is going to be eclipsed, but what lives in art is spirit, not factuality, and we respond to Montaigne's human touch despite four centuries of technological and social change.

Montaigne's *Essais* predated by a quarter-century Cervantes's *Don Quixote,* which was probably the first novel. And the form of composition Montaigne gave a name to would not have lasted so long if it were not succinct, diverse, and supple, able to welcome ideas that are ahead of or behind the blurring spokes of their own time. But whereas a novelist is often a trapezist, vaulting from book to book, an essayist is afoot. Not a puppetmaster or ventriloquist, he will sound recognizable in his next appearance in print. There is a value to this, though Don Quixote as a figure outshines any essay. Imperishably appealing, he is an embodiment, not speculation, and we can simply call him to mind, much as we remember Conrad's Kurtz, in *Heart of Darkness,* and Dickens's Oliver Twist, although the regimes up the Congo River and in London aren't now the same.

An essayist's materials are drawn primarily from his or her own life, and he knits a skein of thoughts and impressions, not a made-up tale. An epic drama such as *King Lear* is thus not his province even to dream about. His work is humbler, and our expectations of him are less elastic than of novelists or poets and their creations. *They* can flame out in a flash fire, surreal or villainous, if the story is compelling or the language smacks a bit of genius. We accept different behavior from Céline or Genet, Christopher Smart or Ezra Pound, than from Dr. Johnson. Norman Mailer can stab his wife and William Burroughs can shoot his, and somehow we don't blanch. They "needed to," one hears it said. Their imaginations must have got the better of them. But if an essayist had done the same it would have queered his legacy. He is supposed to be the voice of reason. Though modestly chameleon as a monologuist (and however much he wants to recalibrate it), he is an advocate for civilization. He doesn't murder a foe in the street, like the sculptor Benvenuto Cellini, or get himself slain in a tavern brawl, like the playwright Christopher Marlowe, or gutshot, like John Ruskin, in a duel. A murderer or madwoman quarantined in a book on the bedside table can provide excitation and cautionary reading, but an essayist, being his own protagonist, should be faceted rather like a friend. We might give him our keys and put him up in the guest room. He won't be stealing the silverware and debauching the children, and, after sleeping on our problems, he will sit at the breakfast table in the morning sunshine and tell us what we ought to do. Or, at the outside, if — like the master essayist Charles Lamb — his sister has slaughtered his mother, he will devote the next thirty-odd years to piecing together a productive existence for himself and her, not despairing like an aficionado of the Absurd.

Essayists are not Dadaists, and in the endgame that may be in progress — with our splintering attention span, our hiccuping religions, staccato science, and spinning solipsism — they may prove useful. *Do* we human beings have a special spark of divinity? And if so, as we mince our habitat and compress ourselves into ever tighter spaces, having always claimed that there couldn't be too much of a good thing, how many of us *are* finally going to constitute a glut of divinity? Judeo-Christianity hasn't said. Nor did "the Laws of Nature and of Nature's God," which Thomas Jefferson invoked at the beginning of our Declaration of Independence. Or Emerson's rapturous prescription in *Nature* in 1836 (Emerson being the other founding father of essay writing in America) that an intelligent observer should become "a transparent eye-ball . . . part or particle of God," amid nature's ramifying glory. Now, man threatens to become a divinity doubled, redoubled, and berserk ad nauseam. However, the essay's brevity, transparency, and versatility should suit this age of reconsideration.

Essays are a limited genre because the writer will suggest that life is more than money, for example, without inventing Scrooge; that brownnosing demeans everybody, without the specter of Uriah Heep. Candide, Starbuck, Injun Joe, Moll Flanders and Becky Sharp led lives more far-fetched than an essayist's, whose medium is mostly what he can testify to having seen or read. Working in the present tense, with common sense his currency, "This is what I think," he tells the rest of us. And even if he speaks about alarming omens, we feel he'll be around tomorrow, not leap headlong into life and burn to a crisp at thirty-two or twenty-eight, like Hart Crane or Stephen Crane, or wind up forlorn in a railroad station fleeing his wife, as Tolstoy did when dying. The limitations are reassuring as well as tethering.

James Baldwin didn't metamorphose into an arsonist or a rifle-man when he warned against race war in *The Fire Next Time*. And George Orwell deconstructed colonialism in essays considerably more nuanced than *Heart of Darkness* — supplementing though not supplanting Kurtz's immortal line "The horror! The horror!" In a way, it's easier to visit a headwaters area of the Nile or Congo and find conditions not substantially improved since indepen-dence when you've read Orwell as well as Conrad on human nature, because these nuances prepare you better for disillusion. Conrad's picture was so stark, surely never again would the world see comparable scenes!

Ripples sway us — traffic tie-ups on a cloverleaf, on-line stock swings, revenge-of-the-rain-forest viral escapees — at the same time that our proud provincialism is called upon to bend the mind around Islam's surging claims, Latino vigor and disorder, chaos in Africa, and a Chinese-puzzle future. In a famine belt along the upper Nile, I've seen child-sized raw-dirt graves scattered every-where beside a poignant web of paths of the sort that starving people pace. A scrap of shirt or broken toy was laid on top of each small mound to personalize the spot; and hundreds of bony, wob-bling children who had survived so far ran toward me (a white-haired white man) to touch my hands in hopes that I might somehow be powerful enough to bring in shipments of food to save their lives. Their urgent smiles were giddy or delirious in skulls already outlined under tightened skin — though they were fatalis-tic, almost docile, too, because so many adults had told them for so many weeks that there was nothing to eat and so many people whom they knew had died. I interviewed the Sudanese guerrilla general who was in charge of protecting them about what could be done, but he was delayed a little that afternoon because (I found out later from an Amnesty International report) he had been torturing a colleague by pounding a nail through his foot.

Now, essayists in dealing with the present tense are stuck with the nuts and bolts of what's going on. And what do you say about that endgame on the Nile, which I believe was a forerunner, not an anomaly? I expect an epidemic of endgames and disintegration in other forms. Essayists will become "journeymen," in a new definition for that hackneyed term: out on the rim, seeing what's in store. The cataract of memoirs being published currently may be a prelude to this — memoirs of a cascading endgame. Yet essayists are not nihilists as a rule. They look for context. They feel out traction. They have a stake in society's survival, breaking into the plot line of an anecdote to register a reservation about somebody's behavior, for instance, in a manner that most fiction writers would eschew, because an essayist's opinions are central, part of the very protein that he gives us. Not omniscient like a novelist, who can create a world he wants to work with, he has the job of finding coherence in the world that we already have. This isn't harder, just a different task. And he usually comes to it in middle age, having acquired some ballast of experience and tested views — may indeed have written several novels, because of the higher glamour and freedom of that calling. (For what it's worth, I sold my first novel at twenty-one and wrote my first essay at thirty-five.)

"Art is not truth. Art is a lie that makes us realize truth," as Picasso said; and to capture within an imagined story some petal of human longing and defeat is an achievement irresistibly appealing. Essayists, by denying themselves that license to extravagantly fudge the facts of firsthand observation, relegate themselves to the Belles Lettres section of the bookstore, neither fiction nor journalism, because they *do* partly fudge their reportage, adding the spice of temperament and a lifetime's favorite reading. And if an enigma seems a jigsaw, they will tend to see a picture in it: that life therefore is not an oubliette. The fracases they get into are on behalf of democracy, as they see it (Montaigne, Orwell, and Baldwin again are examples), and their iconoclasm commonly leans toward the ideal of "comforting the afflicted and afflicting the comfortable," which journalists used to aspire to. Like a short-story writer, an essayist is after the gist of life, not Balzacian documentation. And, like a soothsayer with a chicken's entrails, he will spread his innards out before us to discern a pattern. Not just confessional, however, a good essay is driven by the momentum of an inquiry, searching out a point, such as *are we divine?* — an awfully big one for a lowly essayist, but it may be the question of the coming century.

Essayists also go to the fights, or rub shoulders on the waterfront, get divorced ("Ouch," says the reader, "that was like mine"), nibble canapés, playing off their preconceptions of a celebrity or a politician against reality. They will examine a prejudice (is this

piquant or ignoble, educated or soggy?) or dare a pie in the face
for advancing an out-of-fashion idea. Or they may simply saunter,
in Thoreau's famous reading of the word: *à la Sainte Terre*, to the
Holy Land, or *sans terre*, at home everywhere — maybe only to the
public library to browse among dead friends. Although a novelist
can blaze along on impetuous obsessions and we will follow if
Scheherazade has set her cap to catch us *(and then what happened?)*,
an essay is a current of thoughts corduroyed with sensory impressions, an author afoot, solo, with no movie sale in the offing or
hefty hope of fame. Speaking his mind is likely to be a labor of
love, and risky because if a work of fiction flops, at least it's nominally somebody else's persona that has been boring the reader.

A solo voice welling up from self-generating sources, or what
Thoreau once called an "artesian" life, has not been the dominant
mode of expression for the past half-century, so most of the best
essays have had to find a home in magazines of lesser circulation,
like *Harper's*, the *Village Voice*, the *American Scholar*, *Outside*, *Yale
Review*, or the *Hungry Mind Review*. The first-tier publications had
corporate styles and personalities, each one insisting upon its
editorial "we." But recently publishing has met with such a swirl of
confusion that even flagship magazines have been losing money
or grandiosity and wondering what tack to take. Essays are reap-
pearing in unexpected places, in *National Geographic* as well as *The
New Yorker*, and on the airwaves and in newspapers, as corrective
colloquy or amusing "occasionals." Paralleling the flood of memoirs that are coming out, the essay form is in revival. And the two
genres do overlap, though for essays a narrative is not an end in
itself, as it can be in a memoir.

A sense of emergency, I suspect, is powering the popularity of
memoirs, the urge for quicker answers than we get from reading
novels: What's happening? How shall we live? Nature, which Jefferson and Emerson regarded as central to the health of society,
is lately treated as a kind of dewclaw on our collective consciousness. This will, I think, begin to change in the face of ecological
catastrophes, and essayists will be in on the action again — as they
have attacked so many problems before, from slavery to political
tyranny, in the struggle to preserve civilization from itself. (War is
a "human disease," Montaigne said.)

The most civil of the literary arts, yet also a "book of the self," "spying on the self from close up," essays are versatile enough that in the same piece, "Of Experience," in which Montaigne says that "death mingles and fuses with our life throughout," he tells us that he can't make love standing up and speaks considerably about his kidneys, urination, and bodily "wind." Wholehearted, supple, an essayist over time may tell you everything you might want to know about him and stretch that measurement a bit, the way a friend or spouse or partner gradually does, until nothing about the living package of that person turns you off. If you know the anguish, joy, and bravery somebody has experienced, you can also share their episodes of shame and indigestion.

Like you, an essayist struggles with the here and now, the world we have, with sore and smelly feet and humiliation, a freethinker but not especially rich or pretty, and quite earthbound, though at his post. Like Thoreau later on (according to Emerson's report), Montaigne says that at a dinner party, "I make little choice at table, and attack the first and nearest thing." He is not much for show and affectation, but nonetheless he eats so zestfully he sometimes bites his own fingers. In a nutshell, maybe that is how to live. Eat of life with such brio that you're not afraid to bite your fingers.

EDWARD HOAGLAND

ANDRÉ ACIMAN

In Search of Proust

FROM THE NEW YORKER

IT WAS BY TRAIN that I had always imagined arriving in Illiers-Combray — not just any train but one of those drafty, pre–World War, rattling wagons which I like to think still leave Paris early every morning and, after hours of swaying through the countryside, squeak their way into a station that is as old and weather-beaten as all of yesteryear's provincial stops in France. The picture in my mind was always the same: the train would come to a wheezing halt and release a sudden loud chuff of steam; a door would slam open; someone would call out "Illiers-Combray"; and, finally, like the young Marcel Proust arriving for his Easter vacation just over a century ago, I would step down nervously into the small, turn-of-the-century town in Eure-et-Loir which he described so lovingly in À la Recherche du Temps Perdu.

Instead, when I finally made my way to Illiers-Combray, late last year, I arrived by car with Anne Borrel, the curator of the Proust Museum there, who had offered to pick me up at my Paris hotel that morning. In my pocket was a cheap and tattered Livre de Poche edition of Swann's Way, which I had brought in the hope that I'd find a moment to read some of my favorite passages on holy ground. That was to be my way of closing the loop, of coming home to a book I had first opened more than thirty years before.

I had bought it with my father, when I was fifteen, one summer evening in Paris. We were taking a long walk, and as we passed a small restaurant I told him that the overpowering smell of refried food reminded me of the tanneries along the coast road outside Alexandria, in Egypt, where we had once lived. He said he hadn't thought of it that way, but, yes, I was right, the restaurant did smell like a tannery. And as we began working our way back through strands of shared memories — the tanneries, the beaches, the ruined Roman temple west of Alexandria, our summer beach house — all this suddenly made him think of Proust. Had I read Proust? he asked. No, I hadn't. Well, perhaps I should. My father said this with a sense of urgency, so unlike him that he immediately tempered it, for fear I'd resist the suggestion simply because it was a parent's.

The next day, sitting in the sun on a metal chair in Lamartine Square, I read Proust for the first time. That evening, when my father asked how I had liked what I'd read, I feigned indifference, not really knowing whether I intended to spite a father who wanted me to love the author he loved most or to spite an author who had come uncomfortably close. For in the eighty-odd pages I had read that day I had rediscovered my entire childhood in Alexandria: the impassive cook, my bad-tempered aunts and skittish friends, the buzz of flies on sunny afternoons spent reading indoors when it was too hot outside, dinners in the garden with scant lights to keep mosquitoes away, the "ferruginous, interminable" peal of the garden bell announcing the occasional night guest who, like Charles Swann, came uninvited but whom everyone had nevertheless been expecting.

Every year, thousands of Proustotourists come to the former Illiers, which extended its name in honor of Proust's fictional town Combray, in 1971, on the centennial of his birth. The town knows it, proclaims it, milks it. Today, Illiers-Combray sells around two thousand madeleine pastries a month. The shell-shaped cakes are displayed in the windows of pastry shops like propitiatory offerings to an unseen god and are sold by the dozen — in case one wants to take some home to friends or relatives, the way pilgrims take back holy water from the Jordan or an olive twig from Gethsemane.

For the reader on a Proustian pilgrimage, tasting a madeleine is the supreme tribute to Proust. (As no pâtisserie fails to remind the tourists, it was on tasting a madeleine, now the most famous sponge cake in the history of world literature, that the adult narrator of Proust's novel was transported to his boyhood days in Combray.) It is also a gesture of communion through which readers hope, like Proust, to come home to something bigger, more solid, and ultimately, perhaps, truer than fiction itself. Anne Borrel often tells these Proust groupies that the cult of the madeleine is blasphemous, as are the claims made by one of the *pâtissiers* that members of the *famille* Proust used to purchase their madeleines on his premises. (In earlier drafts of the novel, Proust's madeleines may have been slices of melba toast, which evolved into toasted bread, only later to metamorphose into the sponge cakes.) But no one listens. Besides, going to Illiers-Combray and not tasting a madeleine would be like going to Jerusalem and not seeing the Wailing Wall or to Greenwich and not checking your watch. Luckily, I was able to resist temptation: during my visit, on a Sunday just a few days before Christmas, all the pastry shops were closed.

Before going to the Proust Museum, Anne Borrel and I had lunch at a tiny restaurant called Le Samovar. Plump and middle-aged, Borrel is the author of a cookbook and culinary history titled *Dining with Proust*. She told me that some of the tourists come from so far away and have waited so long to make the trip that as soon as they step into Proust's house they burst into tears. I pictured refugees getting off a ship and kneeling to kiss the beachhead.

I asked about Proust's suddenly increasing popularity.

"Proust," Borrel replied, "is a must." (She repeated these four words, like a verdict, several times during the day.) She reminded me that there were currently six French editions of *À la Recherche du Temps Perdu* in print. I told her that a fourth English-language edition was due to appear in 2001. And that wasn't all: trade books on Proust and coffee-table iconographies were everywhere; in Paris, I had seen at least half a dozen new books that bore Proust's name or drew on Proustian characters occupying precious space on the display tables of bookstores and department stores. Even Proust's notes, manuscripts, and publishing history had been deemed complicated enough to warrant a book of their own, called *Remembrance of Publishers Past*. Add to that T-shirts, watches, CDs, concerts, videos, scarves, posters, books on tape, newsletters, and a comic-strip version, entitled *Combray*, whose first printing, of 12,000 copies, sold out in three weeks. Not to mention the 1997–98 convention in Liège celebrating the seventy-fifth anniversary of Proust's death, with sessions on music and Proust, eating and Proust, a writing competition (on the subject of "Time Lost and Time Regained"), and a colloquium on asthma and allergies.

This kaleidoscope of Proustophernalia is matched by as many testimonials and tributes to Proust, in which he takes many forms.

There is Proust the élitist and high-society snob; Proust the son of a Jewish mother; Proust the loner; Proust the dandy; Proust the analytical aesthete; Proust the soulful lovelorn boy; Proust the tart, the dissembling coquette; the Belle Époque Proust; the professional whiner; the prankster; the subversive classicist; the eternal procrastinator; and the asthmatic, hypochondriac Proust.

But the figure who lies at the heart of today's Proust revival is the intimate Proust, the Proust who perfected the studied unveiling of spontaneous feelings. Proust invented a language, a style, a rhythm, and a vision that gave memory and introspection an aesthetic scope and magnitude no author had conferred on either before. He allowed intimacy itself to become an art form. This is not to say that the vertiginous spate of memoirs that have appeared recently, with their de-rigueur regimens of child, spouse, and substance abuse, owe their existence, their voice, or their sensibility to Proust — clearly, they owe far more to Freud. But it does help to explain why Proust is more popular today, in the age of the memoir, than he has been at any other time in the century.

Like every great memoirist who has had a dizzying social life and a profoundly lonely one, Proust wrote because writing was his way of both reaching for an ever elusive world and securing his distance from it. He was among the first writers in this century to disapprove of the critics' tendency to seek correspondences between an artist's work and his private life. The slow, solitary metamorphosis of what truly happened into what, after many years, finally emerges in prose is the hallmark of Proust's labor of love.

Proust is at once the most canonical and the most uncanonical author, the most solemnly classical and the most subversive, the author in whom farce and lyricism, arrogance and humility, beauty and revulsion are indissolubly fused, and whose ultimate contradiction reflects an irreducible fact about all of us: we are driven by something as simple and as obvious as the desire to be happy, and, if that fails, by the belief that we once have been.

My conversation with Anne Borrel was interrupted by the arrival of customers outside Le Samovar. "Take a look at those four," Borrel said, pointing to the two couples dawdling at the entrance. "I'll bet you anything they're *proustiens*." She referred to all tourists as *proustiens* — meaning not Proust scholars but individuals whom the French like to call *les amis de Proust*, Proustologues, Prousto-

laters, Proustocentrics, Proustomaniacs, Proustophiles, Prousto-
philiacs, Proustoholics . . . or *fidèles* (to use a term dear to Proust's
malevolent arch-snob, Mme. Verdurin).

One of the four opened the door of the restaurant and asked
in a thick Spanish accent whether lunch was still being served.
"Pintades" — Guinea hens — "are all that's left," snapped the
owner of Le Samovar. Borrel and I exchanged a complicitous
glance, because talk of fowl immediately brought to mind a discussion we'd had in the car about Proust's servant, Françoise, who in
Swann's Way butchers a chicken and then curses it for not dying
fast enough.

The four tourists were shown to a table. One asked the proprietor what time the Proust Museum would open that afternoon, and
he regretfully informed them that the museum was closed for the
holidays. They were crestfallen. "What a pity! And we've come all
the way from Argentina."

Anne Borrel had heard every word of the exchange. She reminded me of a teacher who, with her back turned to the class
while she's writing on the blackboard, knows exactly who's whispering what to whom. She leaned over and told one of the Argentines, "You may have come to the right place."

Overjoyed, the Argentine blurted out, "You mean Marcel Proust
used to eat here, in this restaurant?"

"No," Borrel answered, smiling indulgently. She told them that
an improvised tour of the house could be arranged after coffee,
and the Argentines went back to talking softly about Proust, staring
every once in a while at our table with the thrilled and wary gaze
of people who have been promised a miracle.

By the time our coffee was served, we had also acquired two
English and three French *proustiens,* and a warm, festive mood
permeated Le Samovar. It was like the gathering of pilgrims in
Chaucer's Tabard Inn. Introductions were unnecessary. We knew
why we were there, and we all had a tale to tell. By then, some of
us would have liked nothing more than a fireplace, a large cognac,
and a little prodding to induce us to recount how we had first
come to read Proust, to love Proust, how Proust had changed our
lives. I was, it dawned on me, among my own.

After dessert, Borrel put on her coat. *"On y va?"* she asked, rattling
a giant key chain that bore a bunch of old keys with long shafts

and large, hollowed oval heads. She led us down the Rue du Doc-
teur Proust, named after Proust's father, who by the turn of the
century had helped to halt the spread of cholera in Europe. The
sidewalks and streets were empty. Everyone seemed to be away
for the holidays. Franco-jazz Muzak emanated from loudspeakers,
mounted on various lampposts, that were apparently intended to
convey a festive Yule spirit, but otherwise Illiers-Combray was deserted and gray — a dull, cloying, humdrum, wintry, ashen town,
where the soul could easily choke. Small wonder that Marcel
developed asthma, or that he had the heebie-jeebies on returning
home after long evening walks with his parents, knowing that by
the time dinner was served life would hold no surprises — only the
inevitable walk up the creepy staircase and that frightful drama
called bedtime.

Borrel stopped at one of many nondescript doors along the
empty street. She stared at it for a moment, almost as though she
were trying to remember whether this was indeed the right address, then took out her keys, inserted one into the lock, and
suddenly gave it a vigorous turn, yanking the door open.

"C'est ici que tout commence," she said.

One by one, we filed into Proust's garden. Fortunately, no one
cried. Borrel pointed to a little bell at the top of the gate. I couldn't
contain myself. "Could this be the ferruginous bell?" I asked. It
was a question she'd heard before. She took a breath. "You mean
not the large and noisy rattle which deafened with its ferruginous,
interminable, frozen sound any member of the household who set
it off by coming in 'without ringing,' but the double peal, 'timid,
oval, gilded,' of the visitor's bell, whereupon everyone would ex-
claim, 'A visitor! Who on earth could it be?'" (She was quoting
from memory, and every time one of us asked a question after that
she would recite the answer.)

Next she led us into the restored, relatively humble middle-class
house — by no means the large villa I'd always imagined. The
kitchen, where I'd envisaged Françoise cooking the chicken she
had viciously butchered, was a sunless alcove. The dining room,
with a small round table and dark wood paneling, was a depressing
melee of browns. Then we came to Marcel's bedroom, with its tiny
Empire-style bed, the magic lantern that kept him company at
night when he dreaded sleep, and nearby the George Sand novel

bound in red. In another room was the sofa that Proust had given to his maid, Céleste Albaret, and which her daughter had donated to the museum — and which was perhaps the inspiration for the fictional sofa that Marcel inherited from his Tante Léonie, made love on, and eventually passed along to the owner of a brothel.

When Borrel indicated another room, on the second floor, I interrupted her to suggest that it must surely be the room where, under lock and key, Marcel discovered the secret pleasures of onanism. Borrel neither confirmed nor denied my allegation. She said only, "The little room that smelt of orris-root . . . [where] I explored, across the bounds of my own experience, an untrodden path which I thought was deadly." In this way, I was summarily put in my place — for presuming to show off and for implying that I could make obvious what Proust's oblique words had made explicit enough.

Back in the garden, I told her that the way she had opened the main door had reminded me of the moment in the novel when, after a long, moonlit family walk, Marcel's father pretends to be lost. Everyone in our group suddenly remembered the episode, and, excited, one of the Englishmen described it to his friend, explaining that it was only after making everyone else panic in the dark that Marcel's father had finally taken a key out of his pocket and quietly inserted it in what the others until then had failed to see was the back gate to their very own house. According to the Englishman, Marcel's admiring mother, stunned by her husband's ability to save the day, had exclaimed, *"Tu es fantastique!"*

"Tu es extraordinaire!" Borrel corrected him.

I had always liked that scene: the family wandering in the moonlight, the boy and his mother convinced that they're lost, the father teasing them. It reminded me of the way Proust's sentences roam and stray through a labyrinth of words and clauses, only to turn around — just when you are about to give up — and show you something you had always suspected but had never put into words. The sentences tell you that you haven't really drifted far at all, and that real answers may not always be obvious but aren't really hidden, either. Things, he reminds us, are never as scary as we thought they were, nor are we ever as stranded or as helpless as we feared.

Borrel left us for a moment to check on something inside the museum, and we spent some time discussing our favorite Proust passages. We all wondered which gate Swann's prototype would come through in the evenings, and where the aunts had been sitting when they refused to thank him for his gift but finally consented to say something so indirect that Swann failed to realize that they actually were thanking him.

"It all seems so small," said the Englishman, who was visibly disappointed by the house.

My thoughts drifted to a corner of the garden. The weather was growing colder, and yet I was thinking of Marcel's summer days, and of my own summer days as well, and of the garden where, deaf to the world, I had found myself doing what Proust described in his essay "On Reading":

> giving more attention and tenderness to characters in books than to people in real life, not always daring to admit how much I loved them . . . those people, for whom I had panted and sobbed, and whom, at the close of the book, I would never see again, and no longer know anything about. . . . I would have wanted so much for these books to continue, and if that were impossible, to have other information on all those characters, to learn now something about their lives, to devote mine to things that might not be entirely foreign to the love they had inspired in me and whose object I was suddenly missing . . . beings who tomorrow would be but names on a forgotten page, in a book having no connection with life.

The guided tour took more than two hours. It ended, as all guided tours do, in the gift shop. The guests were kindly reminded that, despite the impromptu nature of today's visit, they shouldn't forget to pay for their tickets. Everyone dutifully scrambled to buy Proust memorabilia. I toyed with the idea of buying a Proust watch on whose dial were inscribed the opening words of *À la Recherche du Temps Perdu: "Longtemps, je me suis couché de bonne heure."* But I knew I'd never wear it.

The visitors began talking of heading back to Paris. I was almost tempted to hitch a ride with one of them, but Borrel had promised to take me for a night walk through the streets of Illiers-Combray and then accompany me to the train station. The others stood idly about in the evening air, obviously reluctant to put Illiers-Combray behind them. They exchanged addresses and telephone numbers.

"Proust is a must," I heard the Argentine say, an infatuated giggle in his voice. When Borrel left the shop to lock the back door, I was suddenly alone.

As I looked out the window at the garden where the Proust family had dined on warm summer evenings, I was seized with a strange premonition of asthma. How could Marcel have ever loved such a place? Or had he never loved it? Had he loved only the act of returning to it on paper, because that was how he lived his life — first by wanting to live it, and later by remembering having wanted to, and ultimately by writing about the two? The part in between — the actual living — was what had been lost.

Proust's garden was little more than a place where he had once yearned to be elsewhere — never the primal scene or the ground zero. Illiers itself was simply a place where the young Proust dreamed of a better life to come. But, because the dream never came true, he had learned to love instead the place where the dream was born. That life did happen, and happened so intensely, to someone who seemed so reluctant to live it is part of the Proustian miracle.

This is the irony that greets all Proust pilgrims: they go in search of things that Proust remembered far better than he had ever really known them, and which he yearned to recover more than he had ever loved them. In the end, like the boy mentioned by Freud who liked to lose things because he enjoyed finding them, Proust realized that he couldn't write about anything unless he thought he had lost it first. Perhaps I, too, had come here in order to lose Combray, if only to rediscover it in the pages I knew I would read on the way home.

My train wasn't due for an hour and a half, and Anne Borrel invited me to have a cup of tea at her house before our walk. We closed the door to the museum and set off down dark and deserted alleys.

"Illiers gets so empty," she said, sighing.

"It must be lonely," I said.

"It has its pluses."

Her house was bigger than Proust's and had a far larger garden and orchard. This seemed odd to me — like finding that the gate-keeper owns a faster car and has better central heating than the owner of the palace.

As we headed back to the train station after our tea, I walked quickly. Borrel tried to stop long enough to show me the spot where the Prousts had returned from their Sunday promenades, but I didn't want to miss my connection to Paris. It seemed a shame that, after so many years, this longed-for moonlit walk, so near at hand, should be the very thing I'd forfeit. But the last thing I needed was to be sentenced to a sleepless night in Proust's boyhood town. I alluded to a possible next time. Borrel mentioned spring, when Proust's favorite flower, the hawthorn, would be in bloom. But I knew, and perhaps she knew too, that I had no plan to return.

On my way to Paris, I skimmed through the pages of "Combray," the first chapter of *In Search of Lost Time*. As I read about the steeples of Martinville or Tante Léonie, eternally perched in her bedroom, on the first floor, overlooking Rue Saint-Jacques, it occurred to me that I had rushed back to the book not to verify the existence of what I had just seen but to make certain that those places I remembered and loved as though my own childhood had been spent among them had not been altered by the reality of the dull, tile-roofed town shown to me by Anne Borrel.

I wanted to return to my first reading of Proust — the way, after seeing a film based on a novel, we struggle to resurrect our private portrait of its characters and their world, only to find that the images we've treasured for so long have vanished, like ancient frescoes exposed to daylight by a thoughtless archeologist. Would my original image of a stone villa with a spacious dining room and a wide staircase leading to the child's solitary bedroom be able to withstand the newly discovered little house with its squeaky wooden stairwell and drab, sunless rooms? And could this tawdry garden really be the glorious place where Marcel read away entire afternoons on a wicker chair under a chestnut tree, lost to the voices of those calling him inside and to the hourly chime of the church of Saint-Hilaire — whose real name, as I had found out that day, was not Saint-Hilaire but Saint-Jacques, which, moreover, was not really the name of the street watched over by Tante Léonie, who, it turned out, was herself more likely to have been an uncle.

Inside the sepia cover of *Swann's Way* I searched also for the sense of wonder I had brought to it that summer evening more than thirty years before, when I'd had the good fortune to be with a man who was the first person to mention Proust to me and who, because he was unable to give me so many things then, had only this to give me, and gave it tentatively, self-consciously, as though he were giving part of himself, as he told me about Proust — how Proust remembered things that everyone else seemed to forget, how he saw through people though they still managed to fool him, and how he did all those things in sentences that were ever so long — and steered me, as we rushed to buy the first volume before the stores closed, to a writer I have since loved above all others, not just because of who he was and what he wrote, or because of who I became the more I read him, but because on that late-summer evening I already knew I had just received, perhaps without my father's knowing it, his dearest, most enduring gift of love.

CHARLES BOWDEN

Torch Song

FROM HARPER'S MAGAZINE

I CAN'T TELL MUCH from her silhouette. She's sitting off to one side, her shoulders hunched, and toward the front is the box with the teddy bears. Or at least I think they're teddy bears. Almost twenty years have passed, and I've avoided thinking about it. There are some things that float pretty free of time, chronology, the book of history, and the lies of the experts. In the early eighties I went to a funeral as part of my entry into a world, a kind of border crossing.

It started as the gold light of afternoon poured through the high, slit windows of the newsroom. I had no background in the business and I'd lied to get the job. I was the fluff writer, the guy brought on to spin something out of nothing for the soft features and the easy pages about how people fucked up their marriages or made a quiche or found the strength to go on with their lives because of God, diet, or a new self-help book. Sometimes they wrote the book, sometimes they just believed the book. I interviewed Santa Claus, and he told me of the pain and awkwardness of having held a child on his fat lap in Florida as ants crawled up his legs and bit him. One afternoon the newsroom was empty, and the city desk looked out and beckoned me. I was told to go to a motel and see if I could find anything to say.

The rooms faced a courtyard on the old desert highway that came into town and were part of a strip of unhappy inns left to die after the interstate lanced Tucson's flank. When I was twelve this belt still flourished, and my first night in this city was spent in a neighboring motel with a small pool. I remember swimming until late at night, intoxicated with the idea of warm air, cool water, and palm trees. My sister was fourteen, and the son of the owners, a couple from the East with the whiff of Mafia about them, dated her; later, I read a newspaper story that cited him as a local purveyor of pornography. But the row of motels had since lost prosperous travelers to other venues and drifted into new gambits, most renting by the day, week, or month, as old cars full of unemployed people lurched into town and parked next to sad rooms where the adults scanned the classifieds for a hint of employment. The children always had dirty faces and anxious eyes. The motel I was sent to was a hot-sheet joint, with rooms by the hour or day, and featured water beds (WA WA BEDS, in the language of the sign), in-room pornographic movies, and a flock of men and women jousting through nooners.

The man at the desk had a weasel face and the small frame of the angry, smiling rats that inhabit the byways of America; the wife was a woman of some heft, with polyester pants and short-cropped hair. They seemed almost delighted to have a reporter appear, and after a few murmured words in the office, where I took in the posters for the featured films of cock-sucking, butt-fucking, and love, ushered me across the courtyard, with its unkempt grass, to the room. As we entered, she apologized and said she was still cleaning up. The linoleum floor looked cool, and the small chamber offered a tiny kitchenette and a small lavatory with shower, the old plastic curtain stained by years of hard water. The water bed, stripped of its sheets, bulged like a blue whale, and as the woman and I talked — he was quiet, she seemed nice, they didn't cause any fuss, the kid was a charmer — a dirty movie played soundlessly on the screen hanging off the wall and confronting the bed. I seem to remember a mirror of cheap streaked tiles on the ceiling.

I walked around aimlessly and popped open the door of the old refrigerator — shelves empty — and then the little door to the freezer, where two bottles of Budweiser, frozen solid, nestled as if someone with a powerful thirst had placed them to chill in a hurry and then been distracted. I heard the woman's voice in my ear explaining how the mother had gone to work — she danced at a strip joint, one of the new gentlemen's clubs that featured college-looking girls instead of aging women with bad habits — and so was gone when it happened. I nodded, purred soothing words, closed the freezer door, and strolled back by the water bed; the blue of its plastic had the gaiety of a flower in the tired room. I looked at a big splotch on the cinderblock wall, and she said, "I haven't had time to clean that off yet."

That's where the head had hit, the skull of the toddler just shy of two years, as the man most likely held him by the legs and swung him like a baseball bat. He probably killed the kid out of boredom or frustration with the demands of a small child, or because he'd been bopped around himself as a child, or God knows why. The man had taken off, then been caught by the cops, and was sitting in jail as they figured out what level of murder he'd scored. The dancer they'd found wandering in the desert, and they'd flung some kind of charges at her. As I stared at the block wall, the proprietress bubbled up in my ear again and said, with that small, cooing voice American women sometimes favor when indicating feeling, "We kind of made a collection and customers chipped in and we bought him an outfit for the burial." She told me they got the clothes at Kmart. I drove back to the paper, wrote an impressionistic piece pivoting on the frozen bottles and all the hopes and basic desires found in a beer chilling for a thirsty throat, and then phones started ringing at the city desk and I was hurled at the funeral.

So I sit through the service studying the mother's profile. She has fine hair, a kind of faint red. I once knew a woman with hair like that, and as I stare I can smell this other woman and feel my hands tracing a path through the slender strands. I can smell the soap, the scent of the other woman; the small smile and fine bones and clean, even teeth. In my memory the coffin is open, the boy's small face very pale and blank, and he is surrounded by donated teddy bears that came from a town that told itself these things are not supposed to happen, and if such things do happen they're not supposed to happen in our town.

Just before the service ends, I have a hunch that the cops are going to take the mother out the back so that the press cannot snap her image and I cannot scan her face. So I get up and leave the chapel of the cheap mortuary and go to the back, and, sure enough, suddenly the metal door opens and two cops burst through with the lap dancer handcuffed and sagging between their grip. The light is brilliant at 1:15 P.M. and merciless as it glares off the woman. Her face is small, with tiny bones, and her age is no longer possible to peg — somewhere between nineteen and one thousand. She is wearing tight pants on slender, girlish hips and a black leather vest over her blouse. The waist is small, the hair falls to her shoulders, the lips are very thin. A moan comes off her, a deep moan, and I sense that she is unaware of the sound she is making, just as she is unaware of what has happened to her. The only thing she knows is what I know. There is a toddler in a box with teddy bears, and the box sits in a room full of strangers from this town where she has bagged a job dancing for other strangers.

The cops look at me with anger, drag her slumping form away, and toss her into the back of a squad car. I stand still, make no notes. Then I go back to the newsroom and write up the funeral. That is when it begins. The toddler's death probably didn't have anything to do with child molestation, but for me this child became the entry point to rape and other categories of abuse. For the next three years I live in a world where the desire of people, almost always men, to touch and have their way with others makes them criminals. Gradually I began to lose the distinction between the desires of criminals and the desires of the rest of us. I am told I can't get off this kind of beat, because most reporters won't do it. This may be true, I don't really know, because those three years are the only ones I ever spent working for a newspaper and practically the only ones I ever spent working for anyone besides myself. I would quit the paper twice, break down more often than I can remember, and have to go away for a week or two and kill, through violent exercise, the things that roamed my mind. It was during this period that I began taking one-hundred- or two-hundred-mile walks in the desert far from trails. I would write up these flights from myself, and people began to talk about me as a nature writer. The rest of my time was spent with another nature, the one we call, by common consent, deviate or marginal or unnatural.

I can still see the woman coming through the metal door, slumping between the paws of the cops. I am standing northwest of her and about twenty feet away. It is 1:15 P.M., the glare of the sun makes her squint, her hips are bound in impossible pants, her face has never seen anything brighter than the dim lights of a strip joint, and her wrists, in the chrome gleam of cuffs, are tiny. I can remember this with photographic detail, only I can't remember what became of her or her lover. Just the boy, the splotch on the wall, the blue water bed, and the frozen Budweiser.

Until this moment, I've avoided remembering what became of me.

Night, the warm night of early fall, and they form up in the park, the women and their supporters, with candles and flashlights, banners and the will to take back the night. The green pocket of trees and grass hugs the road. They go a few blocks and swing down one of the city's main thoroughfares. Safety in numbers, group solidarity, sisterhood is powerful, protest, demands, anger, laughter, high spirits.

They find her later in a narrow slot between two buildings, more a gap in the strip of commercial facades than a planned path or walkway, the kind of slot that sees hard sun a few minutes a day and then returns to shadow. She is seven and dead. While the march to take back the night was passing through here, she apparently left her neighbor's yard nearby and came over to see the spectacle. The police and press keep back one detail: she has been eviscerated. That is part of what a newsroom feeds off, the secret facts that others do not know or cannot be told, the sense of being where the action is and where the knowing people gather. So we say to one another: opened up from stem to stern that night.

I come in the next morning ignorant of all this and am called into a meeting. The city editor, the managing editor, and the publisher are agitated. They have children; they want to do something, but they don't know what. I'm told to make a difference in the slaughter of our children. I nod and say, You'll have to give me time. The exchange is very short; this paper has no long meetings. I go back to my desk and remember another night long ago: the man crying. And when I remember, I don't want to take this assignment, but I do.

He speaks in a small voice as his hands cradle his face in the hospital waiting room, and he says, "My baby girl, my baby girl." His wife looks on stoically. The call came in the middle of the night, and when I arrive there is the cool of fluorescent lights, the sterile scent of linoleum floors, and the memory of her going down the corridor on a gurney with her face pulverized into raw flesh. She had gone to visit a friend near campus and stepped out of her car onto the quiet street.

That is when he took her. He forced her back into her car, and they drove out of town into the open ground. He raped her, pistol-whipped her, pumped two rounds into her, and then left her for dead. She saw a house light and crawled toward it. The people inside feared her pounding in the night and did not want to open up. Somehow an ambulance came, and now she is in surgery as I sit with her weeping father and stoical mother. At the time, I am related by marriage. But that does not help. I am a man, but that does not help. I am not a rapist, and that does not help at all. Nothing really helps — not words, not anger, not reflection. For days afterward, as the hospital reports come in, as the visits to the room present a bandaged and shaved head, as the unthinkable becomes normal for all of us, nothing really helps. We have stepped over a line into a place we refuse to acknowledge, a place of violence and danger, where the sexual impulses that course through our veins have created carnage.

I was in my late twenties then, and I remember my male friends all coming to me with visions of violence, scripts about what should be done to the rapist, what they would do to him, how these instances should be handled. I would nod and say very little.

I'm over at a house where friends live, the kind of male dormitory that has a dirty skillet festering on the stove, clothes tossed here and there, and empty beer bottles on the coffee table giving off stale breath. It is precisely 10:00 A.M., and one guy is just getting up from the mattress on the floor of his room. He is a Nam vet with a cluster of medals and has two interests after his war: hunting and women. A stack of skin magazines two feet high towers over the mattress, and a fine .270 with a polished walnut stock leans in the corner. He tells me they should take those guys out and cut their dicks off, and then he staggers down the hall with his hangover to take a piss. I feel that I am watching something happening on a screen but that I am not really here.

Eventually, a red-faced detective comes by to placate the victim's family and express his sense of urgency as we sit in the quiet kitchen. He explains all the things being done, but he convinces no one. How do you find a rapist when half the population is suspect? This is when I first hear the police read on rape: "Fifteen minutes for the guy, five years for the woman."

I had a vegetable garden then, and this was the only place where things made sense and fell into some kind of order. So I sit on the dirt amid the rows of bell peppers, tomatoes, eggplant, marigolds, and squash, sip red wine, and let my mind flow. I wonder if there is a monster lurking in all of us. I never cease, I realize, scanning faces when I prowl the city, and what I wonder is, Are you the one? I look over at the other cars when I am at a stoplight. This becomes an unconscious habit. Sometimes I think I have adopted the consciousness of a woman. Now I think like prey.

Later, a year or two later, a guy goes to a party near the campus, drinks and whoops it up, and leaves with a woman he meets there. He takes her out and rapes her and tries to kill her. Turns out he is the one, and they send him off to prison. By then, it hardly matters to me. I know he will be back and he will be older, and that that will be the only change. I bury the memories and go on pretty much as if nothing had ever happened. As does the woman who was raped, pistol-whipped, shot, and left for dead. You can know some things and the knowing seems to help you not at all.

"My baby girl, my baby girl." These memories resurface as I leave the editorial meeting with my instructions to figure out something for the paper to do about the slaughter of a seven-year-old girl during a march to take back the night. I sit at my gray desk and stare at the clock on the east wall. It is early in the morning, 7:00 or 8:00 A.M. I have no delusions that I will magically crack the case. But I decide to look into the world where such acts come from, though I do not consciously know what such a desire means in practical terms. I have no plan, just this sensation of powerlessness and corruption and violation and grief. I can feel my eyes welling with tears, and I know instantly that this feeling will do nothing for me or anyone else.

After that I follow my instincts, which is what the predators do also.

There are five things I know to be true. These rules come to me out of my explorations.

  1. No one can handle the children.
  2. Get out after two years.

3. Always walk a woman to her car, regardless of the hour of the day or the night.

4. Don't talk about it; no one wants to hear these things.

5. No one can handle the children.

The fourth lesson is the iron law. We lie about sex crimes because we lie about sex. We lie about sex because we fear what we feel within ourselves and recoil when others act out our feelings. American society has always been more candid about murder ("I felt like killing him," we can say out loud) than about the designs we have on each other's bodies. What destroys people who have to deal with sex crimes is very simple: you lose the ability to lie to yourself about your feelings, and if you are not careful you fail to lie appropriately to others. When we are in bed with each other we find it difficult to say what we want, and when we brush up against sex crimes we find it difficult to stomach what we see and even more difficult to acknowledge the tug of our fantasies. In the core of our being live impulses, and these impulses are not all bright and not all as comfortable as an old shoe.

Soon after I embark on this assignment, I am at the home of a friend, a very learned man who is elderly. When we sit and drink he is open to any topic — the machinations of the Federal Reserve, the mutilation of young girls in Africa, male menopause, or the guilt/innocence of Alger Hiss. I have just written a story for the newspaper on child molestation that runs four solid pages without one advertisement because no merchant wants products next to such a story. I vaguely remember the lead. I must do this from memory, because regardless of the passage of years, with their gentle soothing effect, I cannot look at the clips yet: "The polite term is child molestation. The father said he had done nothing but fondle his son. The boy had gonorrhea of the mouth. The polite term is child molestation."

As I sit with my friend and we ponder the intricacies of the world and swap lifetimes of reading, he suddenly turns to me and says, "I want you to know I didn't read your story. I don't read things like that."

I am not surprised. After the story hits the press, women at the newspaper come up to me for soft conversations and want to have lunch or drinks. They murmur that they are part of the sisterhood or secret society of the maimed. The men avoid me, and I can sense their displeasure with what I have written and the endless and relentless nature of the piece. I realize that if I had not written it, I would avoid reading it, too.

Another revelation comes from having drinks with a retired cop. We are kind of friends: cops and reporters are natural adversaries and yet, in some matters, have no one else to talk with (see rule number four). I ask him how the local police handled rape during his time.

He says, "Well, the first thing we'd do is take the suspect out of the house and into the carport, and then we'd beat the shit out of him with our saps. Then we'd take him downtown and book him for assault." He does not read the piece either.

Then there is the woman who is passionately into nonviolence and vegetarianism and speaks softly as if she embodied a state of grace. She comes to my door one night after a couple of my stories have run, and we make love on the cement floor. Afterward, she tells me that when she was a girl her father, who was rich and successful, would sit around with his male friends and they would take turns fucking her in the ass. I walk her to her car.

I am sitting on the north end of a back row facing the west wall. The room is institutional and full of therapists, counselors, and other merchants of grief who have gathered to share their experiences treating victims of sex crimes. I scan the crowd, mainly women without makeup wearing sensible shoes. I listen for hours as they outline play therapy, describe predators (with children, usually someone close and accepted by the family; with rape, often as not the mysterious stranger), call for a heightened public consciousness about the size of this plague. Their statistics vary but basically suggest that everyone is either a victim of a sexual crime or the perpetrator of a sexual crime or a therapist treating sexual crimes. They all agree that children do not lie and that more attention must be paid.

Late in the day a woman walks to the podium. I have been noticing her for hours, because she does not fit in with the group. Her lips are lacquered, her hair perfect, and she wears a tasteful lavender dress — one I sense she has bought just for this occasion — and high heels. She is the only woman wearing high heels. She speaks with a southern accent and tells the group that she is not a professional person. She is a mother, and a neighbor molested her daughter, her very young daughter. And she wants something done about it. In her case, she continues, nothing was done. The neighbor still lives a few doors down, and her daughter still lives in terror — they have had to seal her window with duct tape so "he can't look in."

The woman at the podium is on fire and very angry. Her words slap the audience in the face. She has no theory, she says, and no program. She simply wants her government, her police, and her city to pay attention to the problem. And she will not rest. She reads her words off sheets of yellow legal paper, and her articulation is harsh, as if she were drumming her fingers on a Formica kitchen table.

Afterward, I cut through the crowd and find her. I say I am a reporter and would like to talk more. She is flustered. She is not used to talking to audiences and not used to talking to the press. She gives me her number, and we agree to meet. I notice her eye makeup and the sensual nature of her lips.

When I turn, another woman comes up to me. I vaguely noticed her enter when the woman whose child was molested was speaking. She is about thirty and wears leather pants and a motorcycle jacket. Her eyes are very intelligent, and she tells me she is a therapist. Her smile is generous. We walk out and go to a nearby café, which is empty and half-lit in the late afternoon, and sit at a round table with a dark top. We both sip longnecks.

Her life has not been simple lately. She is distancing herself, she explains, from a bad relationship. She has been living with a man, and he is very successful. He came home a few days ago and they made love. He told her she was the sixth woman he had had that day but that he liked her the best. He never comes, she says; anything else, but he never comes. He withholds, don't you see? she asks.

When I go to her place she is in shorts and a shirt and is roller-skating in her driveway. She tells me she wanted me to see her that way, free and skating with delight. We lie on the floor. She says, "Squeeze my nipples hard, squeeze my titties as hard as you can." Later, we are in the bathroom, because she wants to watch us in the mirror. We go back to the bedroom and she rolls over on her stomach.

She says very softly, "Yes."

Somewhere in those hours my second marriage ends. I know

why. I, too, tend to say yes. The marriage ends because I do not want to live with her anymore, because she is a good and proper person and this now feels like a cage. I do not want to leave my work at the office. I do not want to leave my work at all. I have entered a world that is black, sordid, vicious. And actual. And I do not care what price I must pay to be in this world.

The therapist has a lot of patients who are fat women, and they fascinate her. She herself has not an extra ounce of fat; she is all curves and muscle, her calves look like sculpture, her stomach is flat, her features are cute. She is very limber. Once at a party, she casually picked up one of her legs while talking to a couple and touched her ear with her foot. She was not wearing panties when she performed this feat. She runs daily, has been part of a female rock and roll band, takes showers three or four times a day, and is proudly bisexual. She tells me one of her best tactics for keeping boyfriends is to seduce and fuck their girlfriends. She smiles relentlessly.

What fascinates her about the fat women is their behavior. Not the eating. She cannot even fathom the eating part, since she never gains weight and eats whatever she wishes. Her place is always cluttered with bowls of macadamia nuts for guests. No, it's their sexual lives she is interested in. Their sexual lives are very simple: they will do anything. That, she tells me, is why men like fat women. They will do anything; name your fantasy, try out your imagined humiliation.

She tells me how she became a therapist. She went to visit her own therapist once and he questioned her openness, and she wound up doing golden showers in his office. After that she fled to an analytic center on the West Coast and studied very hard. No, she says, she is not bitter about it. She learned he was right; she was not open enough.

I find her smile addictive. We sit in her kitchen and she makes a Greek salad. She becomes a blur cutting up the feta cheese and dicing olives. And then we go to the bedroom. She tells me I have green blood and smiles with the promise that she will make it red.

Here is how play therapy goes. You look through one-way glass at very small children on the floor. The child holds anatomically correct dolls, ones with actual sexual organs, and acts out what has happened in the past. It is something to see. The dolls look like

Raggedy Ann. And do pretty much exactly what adults do with each other. My guide in this place is a gray-haired woman who is very well-spoken and has the quiet calm of a Quaker lady. She used to work in a ward with terminally ill children. She tells me this work is harder. Ah, now the child is moving the two dolls.

We talk for twenty-two hours. Not all at once, no one can do that, but for very long stretches at a time. That is how the lady in the lavender dress with the hard words, the lady who stunned the seminar audience, begins. With talk.

We sit across from each other with the coffee table and a patch of rug between our chairs. She is cautious. This is her story and, like most people, she wishes to tell her story but only to the right person — the person who listens. I have no tape recorder, just a pen and a notebook, and we begin spiraling into the tale. It is night, her daughter is in the tub, she mentions pain and points. The mother hides her alarm, asks gentle questions, and it slowly comes out as the minutes crawl past. He is the older man, the pal of neighborhood kids. Always a smile, perfectly normal, you never would have guessed.

As she talks, her daughter, so very young and small, plays out in the yard, and from time to time I catch a glimpse of her as I look up from my notepad or glance away from the woman, her monologue flowing from her full lips. The child is in sunlight, gamboling about without a worry in the world. For a second, none of it ever happened. I see this apparition through the sliding glass doors, and then the woman's words pull me back to the night, the aftermath, the weeks and now months of coaxing the child back first from terror and then from a sense of betraying her special friend by telling — and, of course, she was warned not to tell, they always make sure to stress this warning.

When I am with the woman I enter, as she does, a kind of trance. When I am away the trance still holds to a degree, and I talk with no one about what I am doing. I make a point of filing other stories to disguise the hours I spend listening. I live in worlds within worlds, since the child's identity must not be revealed, and so for me things become generic and universal and yet at the same time, looking into one woman's face and taking down one woman's words, specific, exact, and full of color, scent, and feel.

I write the story in one long fury, and the print-out runs about twenty feet. I crawl along my floor, reading it and making changes. Sometimes my therapist roller skater drops by and finds me crawling on the floor with my felt pen, and she does not approve of this act. It is too involved, not suitable for things that should be done at a desk with a good lamp and a sound chair. I sense I am failing her by falling into myself, and our sex grows more heated and yet more empty. This goes on for weeks. I don't know what to do with the story, and then finally I turn it in and they print it.

Fifty subscribers cancel in less than an hour, I am told.

I prowl through the police blotter, savoring the rapes of the night: The woman who leaves the bar at 1:00 A.M. with the stranger. No, can't sell her. The woman who decides at 3:00 A.M. to take a walk in short shorts and a halter to the all-night market for a pack of cigarettes and then gets bagged. She's out, too. The girl who goes into the men's room with her boyfriend to give him head and then his friends follow and gangbang her. No sale. I course through the dull sheets of pain, hunting for the right one — the one I can sell, the one to which readers cannot say, "Well, that could never happen to me," the one they can't run away from so easily.

A woman rides the freights into town and then hooks up with two guys at a café, and they say if you need a place to crash come with us. She does. She decides she needs a shower, and they say go ahead. When she comes out of what she calls "the rain closet" they're on her. She later goes to the cops, describes herself as a motorcycle mechanic, and tells them of the rape. The paper takes one look at my story and says forget it. And, of course, they're right. Rape, like many things, is kind of a class matter. You have to not deserve it for the world to care even a little bit. This I learn.

Sometimes for a break I drop in on a small bookstore where a heavy woman with a British accent sells used volumes. A gray cat is always nestled inside, and the place has the feel of afternoon tea in someone's living room. Then she is attacked and held hostage in her home one night. The store closes; I don't know what happens to the cat. Eventually, she leaves town and settles in a somewhat distant city. Finally, I hear she kills herself.

I keep hunting, talking with fewer and fewer people. Except for those who live in this world or at least understand its dimensions. I'll be somewhere, maybe kicking back, feet up on the coffee table, glass of wine in hand, and someone will play, say, the Stones'

"Midnight Rambler," and my mood will sink and go black. Best not to visit people.

The days of the week cease to have meaning, as do the weeks of the month and the months of the year. My life went by clocks and dates and deadlines, but the order implied in paychecks, withholding taxes, dinner at six, and Sunday-morning brunch vanished with my consent. I did not lose control of my life; I gave up the pretense of normal life, and followed crime and appetite. I learned things on the run and without intention. Knowledge came like stab wounds, and pleasure came with the surprise of a downpour from a blue sky in the desert. I remember sitting with some women who had been raped after I wrote a profile of the rapist. Turns out all the guy's co-workers, mainly women, found him to be a polite, nice person.

One woman looked at me and said flatly, "He wasn't that way when I was with him."

Stab wounds.

I have become furious, but mainly with myself. Certain protocols in writing about such matters anger me. I decide never to write the phrase "child molestation" or "sexual assault" except in a context of deliberate mockery. I am angry at the pain I witness and listen to each day as I make my appointed rounds, and I am angry at the hypocrisy of it all. We want to believe that the intersection between sex and crime happens only in an alien country, one that does not touch our lives or feelings or lusts of the midnight hours.

A woman is at the door and she has three balls on a string she wishes to insert in my ass, and then she will pull the string at the moment of orgasm.

A woman is at the door and she says she has cuffs.

A woman is at the door late at night and we make love, and as she leaves she says she can't see me again because she is getting married in the morning.

Two women are at the door . . .

We like to call things that disturb us a jungle, to wall them off from our sense of order and self. But we all inhabit that forest, a dense thicket of desire and dread, both burning bright. We want to categorize: victims or studs, seduced or seducers. And we can hardly look at people who we agree are criminals and admit we feel some of their passions and fantasies within ourselves. My life in those days erased boundaries and paid no attention to whether I was a predator or a victim or a newspaper savior with a byline. I was attractive to women because what I knew made me somehow safe. Ruined people were telling me things they never told anyone else, and the women dealing with ruined people were sharing secrets as well, and some of those secrets were fantasies they wished to act out. There is a way to go so deep into the secrets and hungers of your culture that you live without concern for the mores and with a keen sense of your own needs. I have seen this state most often in the old, who finally realize that the rules of conduct are optional and read what they wish, say what they think, and live in sin without a qualm. I didn't feel guilt. Then or now. I didn't feel love. I didn't seek a cure. Getting in bed with women was a pleasure but not the center of my life. The center of my life was crime. And sex was also an attempt to redeem or exorcise what I saw. As the crimes piled up and corroded my energy and will, I ceased to find even cold comfort in women, and everything in my life became perfunctory except for the crimes. I have hard memories of my life then but not bad memories. But of the work, I still have nightmares. I still drive by commonplace haunts and see weeping women, bodies, a terrified child, an eviscerated girl. There are accepted ways of dealing with such experiences: the secular renunciation of a clinical visit to all the Betty Ford centers out there, the religious rebirth of being born again. I did neither. I simply continued plowing my way into that night.

She sits up in bed and asks, "Aren't my breasts beautiful? Aren't they the best you've ever seen?"

I nuzzle her hair. Time has passed, the story long gone, the woman in the lavender dress with the hard words and the maimed child is now the woman here.

She tells me her husband has been suspicious of me.

I ask her what she told him.

"Don't worry." She smiles. "I told him you were a queer."

Then she slides over, gets up, and rolls a joint.

Rule Number One: No One Can Handle the Children.

I'll tell you something that although not a trade secret is not

generally said to others outside the work. The rapes are bad but
not that bad. The mind is protected from what adults do to adults.
There is a squeamishness about the rapes, an embarrassment
among the men who investigate them, and an anger among the
women who treat the casualties. But the rapes can be handled to
a degree. Of course, it's not as easy as homicide; people stay in
homicide forever and never lose pleasure in their work. Sex crimes
generally cycle people out in two years. And it is the kids who
do it. No one can handle the kids. But then the highway patrol
always dreads the car wreck with kids. It goes against nature as we
know it.

Once I was helping a guy move — him, his wife, their two young
daughters — and a box I was carrying out broke open and small
paperbacks spilled to the ground in the bright sunshine. I gathered
them up and then idly flipped through one, and then another and
another. They were all cheap things from no-name presses about
men — daddies, uncles, whoever — fucking kids. I was stunned
and did not know what to do. I felt oddly violated, like it was wrong
for me to have to know this. So I put them back in the box and
put the box in the truck and said nothing and did nothing.

That is part of what I feel as I enter the gray police station and
go to the offices where the sex-crimes unit works. They've got a
treasure trove of child pornography seized from perps, and in my
memory the stack rises six or seven feet. They leave me at a table
with it, and what they want is for me to look at it and come out
with an article recommending that people who possess such materials go to prison.

The collection mainly features boys, seven, eight, nine from the
looks of them, and they are sucking off men, taking it in the ass,
being perfect pals about everything. I am struck not by what I feel
but by how little I feel. It is like handling the treasured and sacred
icons of a dead religion. I have careful constitutional qualms filed
in my mind — basically, that to think something is not a crime.
Fucking kids and taking pictures — that is already against the law.
So I stand firmly on the Constitution of the United States and look
at photographs I do not believe should exist made by and for
people I do not believe should exist. I look for hours and still feel
nothing. I am in a place beyond the power of empathy.

A few months later I get a thick packet of fifty or sixty typed

pages. The writer is facing a long prison sentence for having had
sex with Scouts, as I recall. He writes with courtesy, clarity, and an
almost obsessive sense of detail. Essentially, nothing ever happened
except that he tried to comfort and love his charges. I doubt him
on his details but come to sense that he means his general thesis
about love. He loves children, totally, and locks on them with the
same feeling I have for adult women.

That is what I take away from the photos the police want out-
lawed and the autobiography of the man they eventually send away
to be raped and possibly murdered by fellow convicts for being a
child molester. A crime is being committed by people who see
themselves as the perfect friend. Other things are being committed by people who see themselves as lovers. And, of course, a lot
of things are being done by people who have no romantic delusions about their desires but are full of hate, who drag women off
into the bushes or a corner because they hate them and are going
to get even by causing pain, humiliation, and, at times, death.
Cycles of abuse, the role of pornography, the denigration of
women by Hollywood and glossy magazines — there is no single,
simple explanation for sex crimes. But in the case of the men who
use children for sex there is often this fixation, this sense of love,
which always leads them to betray the very idea of love itself by
using children for their own selfish ends.

During this period of my life my musical taste changes and
slowly, without my awareness, starts sliding backward through the
decades. One day I decide to look up a style of music I've been
listening to in a big Merriam-Webster dictionary. Torch song: from
the phrase "to carry a torch for" (to be in love); first appeared
1930; a popular sentimental song of unrequited love.

The walls are block, humming fluorescent lights replace windows,
and we sit in rows forming a semicircle as the woman teaching the
class speaks. She is very nicely done up in a sedate professional
suit, tasteful hair, low-key makeup; she has a serious and clear
voice. The prisoners mark time as I go through rape therapy in
the joint. I am not here because of a story. I've come to find
something beneath the stories or deep within myself. The boundaries between normal, accepted sexual appetite and crime are blurring for me. People get an erotic charge out of playing with con-

sent — holding each other down, tying each other up — indulging in ritualized dominance. Rape is an eerie parody of accepted life, an experience using the same wardrobe but scratching the word "consent" from the script. I am obeying the law and the rules of consent, but I am losing a sense of distance between my obedient self and those who break the law. When I listen to women tell of the horrors they've experienced, the acts they recount are usually familiar to me, and what they recount as true terror, the sense of powerlessness, strikes chords within me also. I can't abide being in the joint even for this class. I can't take the bars, guards, walls.

The men, struggling to earn good time, feign attention. They answer questions appropriately and wear masks of serious thought. I don't believe them for an instant, and I think that this class is a farce and that nothing will deter my colleagues from their appointed rounds when they leave this place. The woman herself, from a good family and with sound religious values, has been attacked — "I am part of the sisterhood," she once told me shyly — and she has brought me here so that I will see hope and share her hope. So I sit with the current crop of convicted rapists — "There are no first-time offenders," a cop once snarled at me, "just sons of bitches that finally get caught" — and feel no hope. Of course, prison is rape culture — "just need a bunk and a punk," one local heroin dealer offered in explaining his lack of concern about doing time.

The session finally ends, and we bleed out the door of the room into the prison corridor. I am ambling along in a throng of convicts, the woman walking just ahead in her prim suit with her skirt snug on her hips. The guy next to me is singing some kind of blues about what he's gonna do to that bad bitch. I've blotted out the actual song. I can remember the corridor (we are strolling east), see her up ahead, hear him singing next to me, his lips barely moving as he floats his protest against the class and her fucking control and all that shit, but not the lyrics themselves. They're gone, erased by my mind, I suspect in self-defense. Afterward, she and I go to a truck stop and eat apple pie, and I can still see the whiteness of her teeth as she smiles and speaks brightly about her work.

Later, I taste child-molestation therapy, a regimen where men

who have fucked their own children sit in a circle and talk while
their wives run the show. It's either show up at such sessions or
the joint — so attendance is rather good. Afterward, I go off with
the boys and we have beers. In recounting his lapse from accepted
behavior, each and every one of them describes the act itself as
fondling. Apparently, there are hordes of diligently caressed children out there. I nurse my beer and say little, pretending to try to
understand. But I understand nothing at all. I have seen the end
result of fondling, and it does not look at all like fondling to me.
I cannot put myself in their place. I cannot see children as sexual
objects, it does not seem to be in me. I fixate, I realize, on women.
And my fixation is sanctioned, as long as I toe the line. Such
thoughts lead to a place without clear light. We all share a biology
and deep drives, and what we have created — civilization, courtesy,
decency — is a mesh that comes from these drives and also contains and tames them. Whatever feels good is not necessarily good.
But what I learn is that whatever is bad is not necessarily alien to
me. Or to you.

She loves pornography. It's around midnight, and she is standing
in the motel room clutching a bottle of champagne against her
black garter belt and peering intently into the screen of the television as fornicating couples, powered by the handyman of American fantasy, the telephone man, frolic. This is one of the seedy
motels that cultivate hourly rates, water beds, and hard-core cin-
ema, a place much like the room where my life in this world began
with the splotch on the wall left by the toddler's head. She is a
counselor, one of the many I now deal with, and she likes sex and
is fascinated by pornography. This is not unusual; another woman,
a professional woman I deal with, has several hundred pornographic tapes. But the interests of the woman in the black garter
belt are kept off the table at her work and left to the night hours
and random bouts with me. Days are for the maimed — in her
case, children with cigarette burns and sore orifices. Some nights
are like this.

   I glance at her naked ass, see the serene concentration of her
face as she tracks the movie, and I am empty. She and I share the
same country, and there is a big hole in us, so we come here. We
live in a place past the moral strictures of sin and lust; we run on

empty. For us, sex has been drained of its usual charge, delight is beyond our reach. This is a fact. As the months roll past, I feel this slippage within me. I will have lunch or dinner or a drink or coffee with someone and wind up in a place like this. Romance is not a consideration. There is seldom anyone to talk with, and when there is someone, a person like the woman in the black garter belt watching the porn movie, a person stumbling across the same terrain, there is nothing to say, since we both know. So we come here. A proper distance from our appetites has been denied us, so we seek moments of obliteration. I have never regretted those moments or fully understood them. I just knew then, and know now, that they come with the territory.

But the slippage bothers me. I seem to drift, and the drift is downward. Not into sin and the pit but into that emptiness. I am losing all desire and mechanically go through the motions of life. Food also does not tempt me. I flee into the wild country with my backpack, flee again and again for days and days, but increasingly this tactic does not work. Once I am lying by a water hole in July and it is 104 degrees at 1:00 A.M. (I get up with my flashlight and check my thermometer.) I am crawling with crabs. When I go back I buy twelve bottles of the recommended cure and for a day have coffee or drinks with a succession of women, handing each a bottle. I take this in stride, as do they. One woman is briefly anxious because she fears I have called her only to deliver the medicine, but this feeling passes when I assure her that this is not true, that I really wanted to see her. I think we then go to bed. It turns out that this mini-epidemic has come from the therapist who showers three or four times a day. She also is quite calm about it and prefers to talk about her new favorite movie, something entitled *Little Oral Annie*. She tells me she resents the smirks of the male clerks when she rents it at the video store, and I politely sympathize.

The moments of my impotence increase. I am not alarmed by this fact but clinically engaged. I sense that I am walling off everything, all appetites, and have room for nothing but this torrent of pain and squalor that pours through me from the daily and weekly harvest of rapes and killings and molestations. I remember once reading a statement allegedly made by Sophocles in his old age, when sexual desire had left his loins; he said he was glad to be free of the mad master. So I am becoming classic and

care not at all. I repeatedly try to leave the work, but the city desk
always wins because a part of me feels bound to the crimes. So I
protest, and then return. I tell myself it is a duty, but what I feel is
the desire to run out my string, to see how much I can stomach
and learn. And yet then, and now, I cannot really say what this
knowing entails. I can just feel its burden as I lie with caring women
in countless cheap motels, the movies rolling on the screen.

The end begins in the bright light of afternoon on a quiet street
lined with safe houses. One moment an eight-year-old girl is riding
her bicycle on the sidewalk near her home; the next moment the
bicycle is lying on the ground and the girl is gone with no one the
wiser.

This one is my torch song. The rudiments are simple. The
alleged perpetrator is a man in his twenties from a very good home
in another city, a man whose life has been a torment of drugs,
molestation of himself by others and of others by himself, a man
who has slipped from his station in life into dissipation and wound
up roaming the skid rows of our nation. None of this concerns
me, and I leave ruin in my wake. I fly to that distant city, talk my
way through a stout door, and gut his mother like a fish. When I
leave she is a wreck, and later that night her husband goes to the
hospital for perturbations of his heart. I get into files — legal,
psychiatric — that I should not have had access to, and I print
them fulsomely. The child favored a certain doll, and I buy one
and prowl the city with it on the truck seat beside me, a touchstone.
I am standing in the back yard as the mother of the missing girl
makes a plea to whoever took her daughter to bring her home safe
and sound. The woman's face is grief made flesh, and I note its
every tic and sag. It turns out that the alleged perpetrator stayed
for a time with a couple in a trailer court. I visit; the man is facing
child-molestation charges himself, the woman is a hooker with a
coke habit. "Do I have to tell you that?" she whines. I remember
leaving them, driving to a saloon, setting my small computer on
the bar, and begging a phone for the modem. I sip my drink and
write in one quick take. The story flits through the wires and
descends into the next edition. The following night a local PTA
meeting takes a recess, walks over to the trailer, and then it goes
up in flames.

My temper is short, my blood cold. A young mother who works in the newsroom comes over to my desk and asks me what I think the chances are of the girl being alive. I snap, "Fucked, strangled, and rotting out there." And keep typing. The sheriff leaps into the public wound and starts leading marches of citizens holding candles and decrying violence and the rape of children. It is much like the time so long ago when things began for me with a seven-year-old eviscerated while people marched to take back the night. I pay no notice to these marches; they are for others. The reporters on the story all speculate about the girl — even when the arrest comes and still the girl is missing. I do not. I know. Bones bleach out there. It is months and months before her remains turn up, but this hardly matters to me. I know. This is my country.

It ends several times, but at last it finally ends. The city desk asks my help to find a woman whose son, a famous local rapist, has just escaped. I leave, chat up some neighbors, and within an hour I am in a state office, a bullpen of women toiling over desks and processing forms. She has done everything she can — changed her name, told no one of her son, gone on and tried to fashion a life. I approach her desk and tell her my errand. She pleads with me, Don't do this to me. She leans forward and whispers that no one typing away at the other desks, none of them knows anything about this. Leave me in peace, she says. I look into her careworn eyes and I say yes. I tell her I will now leave and she will never read a word of my visit in the newspaper. Nor will I tell anyone of her identity.

When I enter the newsroom, the editor comes over and asks, "Did you find her?"

I say, "Yes."

"When can I have the story?"

"I'm never writing the story."

He looks at me, says nothing, then turns and walks away.

That is when one part of me is finished. I know I must quit. I cannot take the money and decide what goes into the newspaper. I do not believe in myself as censor and gatekeeper. And yet I know I will never write this story, because I have hit some kind of limit in pain. The phone rings. It is a woman's voice. She says, "Thanks to you she has had to go to the hospital. I hope you are happy."

I tell her I am not writing the story. I tell her I told the mother I would not write the story. She does not believe me. This does not matter to me. My hands are cold, and I know from past experience this means I can take no more. I am righteously empty.

The other ending is more important, because it does not involve the work, the little credos and dos and don'ts of journalism. It involves myself. It happens the night the arrests come down for the missing eight-year-old snatched off her bicycle on that safe side street. Around three in the morning, I wrap the story and reach into my desk drawer, where I stashed a fifth of Jack Daniel's bought earlier in the day. I do not drink hard liquor, and I bought the bottle without questioning myself and without conscious intent. So I finish the story, open the drawer, take the bottle, and go home. I sit in my back yard in the dark of the night, those absolutely lonely hours before dawn. I drink, the bite of the whiskey snapping against my tongue, and drink in the blackness.

After a while I feel a wetness and realize that I am weeping, weeping silently and unconsciously, weeping for reasons I do not understand. I know this is a sign that I am breaking down, this weeping without a moan or a sound. I feel the tears trickle, and step outside myself and watch myself clinically in a whiskey-soaked out-of-body experience. That is the other ending.

I quit the paper, never again set foot in a newsroom, and go into the mountains off and on for months and write a book about them. That helps but not enough. I sit down and in twenty-one days write another book about the land, the people, and the city. That helps, but although I barely touch on the world of sex and crimes in this book, it broods beneath the sentences about Indians and antelope and bats and city streets. Nothing really helps.

That is what I am trying to say. Theories don't help, therapies don't help, knowing doesn't help. The experts say they have therapies that are cutting recidivism, and maybe they do, but I doubt it. I live with what I am and what I saw and what I felt — a residue that will linger to the end of my days in the cells of my body. I have never been in an adult bookstore. Two years ago I was at a bachelor party in a lap-dancing place and lasted fifteen minutes before I hailed a cab and fled. This is not a virtue or a position. I have no desire to outlaw pornography, strip joints, blue movies, or much of anything my fellow citizens find entertaining. Nor have I led an orderly life since my time in sex crimes. I write for men's magazines and pass over without comment their leering tone and arch expressions about the flesh. I am not a reformer. So what am I?

A man who has visited a country where impulses we all feel become horrible things. A man who can bury such knowledge but not disown it, and a man who can no longer so glibly talk of perverts or rapists or cretins or scum. A man who knows there is a line within each of us that we cannot accurately define, that shifts with the hour and the mood but is still real. And if we cross that line we betray ourselves and everyone else and become outcasts from our own souls. A man who can be an animal but can no longer be a voyeur. A man weeping silently in the back yard with a bottle of whiskey who knows he must leave and go to another country and yet never forget what he has seen and felt. Just keep under control. And try not to lie too much.

Just before I quit, I am in a bar in a distant city with a district attorney. He shouts to the barkeep, "Hey, give this guy a drink. One of our perverts whacked a kid in his town."

The bartender pours and says, "Way to go."

And I drink without a word. Nobody wants to hear these things.

FRANKLIN BURROUGHS

Compression Wood

FROM THE AMERICAN SCHOLAR

I TEACH ENGLISH in Maine, and I come from Conway, South
Carolina. When I was young, an old lady introduced me to the
facts of life. "Up north," she said, "all they want to know is 'What
do you do?' Down south, all they care about is 'Where do you come
from?'"

In my childhood, that was welcome news. The northern question would obviously be harder to answer than the southern one,
since it required self-justification. So I figured I might as well stay
put. I wouldn't have to *do;* I could simply *be,* as though I were an
aristocrat along the lines of John of Gaunt or Guy of Warwick:
Franklin of Conway.

Before I was a great deal older, I discovered more facts of life,
and one of them was that most of the people I knew, North and
South, were de facto copperheads or carpetbaggers — Confeder-
ate Yankees or Yankee Confederates. Whichever question they
asked you first, the other one was sure to follow.

If you think about it, it could hardly be otherwise, whether you
are answering to a stranger or just talking, as usual, to yourself.
Your boss or your conscience accosts you and demands one thing:
"What have you *done* for me lately?" You can't very well answer that
you have come from where you came from. But there are plenty
of other times when you are doing whatever it is that the boss or
your conscience has gotten you into and you are suddenly overcome by the sheer speciousness of it. There has been some ludicrous or lamentable misapprehension. You are not so much an
impostor as a case of mistaken identity. Who are all these people

and who are you? Why are you all in such solemn earnest, like so many emperors assiduously complimenting each other on their new and identical and nonexistent wardrobes?

It probably doesn't make much difference whether you stay home or light out for the territories. Even Thoreau, who strove to shrink the gap between vocation and location to the disappearing point, often felt, as he said, "a certain doubleness, by which I stand as remote from myself as from another," and that enabled him to see Concord as though it were a distant land, from which he was writing home, to a kinsman. Something about writing, or even about the committed kind of reading that is a vicarious form of writing, takes you well away from your life and makes you homesick for it.

This essay is about a poem, Gerard Manley Hopkins's "Pied Beauty," because writing or talking about poems is one of the things that English professors profess to do. We have been doing it, in ever-increasing numbers, for almost the whole of this century. The more something is written or talked about, the less real and distinct it becomes. If you attend to the doings of English professors these days at all — if you so much as know the difference between a deconstructionist and a dirt dauber — then you know that this is a fact. You know that we are now unsure whether a poem is really a poem or just an overprivileged text, which in turn turns out to be not a text but a mere pretext for the next metatextual meditation.

I am uncomfortable with this state of affairs, but will avail myself of the license it grants and talk about "Pied Beauty" in an utterly idiosyncratic way, which is from the perspective of where I come from and how that consorts with what I do.

I was in fact driving north through Pennsylvania, headed from Conway back up toward Maine, and so just about exactly halfway between where I come from and what I do, when Hopkins's poem came into my mind. Hopkins isn't anybody I regularly teach or ever write about, but I had loved his poems when I first read him as an undergraduate, and that had led me to memorize a few. An enthusiasm of that kind is like a wonderful correspondence that you carry on for a while — it runs in your head and affects how you see and describe to yourself the things around you. As is usual in such cases, the enthusiasm waned, the correspondence dried up, not because of any particular reason, but just because of the way the same old same old takes over your life and you don't have any time for such things, and perhaps do not like to face the contrast between your imaginary and your actual existence.

It was a small and pleasant surprise, then, to find myself back in touch with Hopkins, and able at least partially and approximately to reassemble "Pied Beauty" out of my memory. But right now I need to leave him again and tell about this trip south and how, near the end of it, as I drove north through Pennsylvania, the poet and the poem came to mind.

This was three or four years ago, in March, which is the best season for such a junket. When you drive south from New England at that season, you also drive ahead, into springtime — the weeks hurtle past as though your life were in fast-forward. When you return north, you go backward, the season rewinding itself, unfrocking the trees, silencing the birds, returning the daffodils to the cold storage of the bulb. It's like crossing the international date line, and then crossing it back. You've gained time, and then you've lost almost all of it again, and the only evidence that the whole trip wasn't just a hallucination is the odometer.

There are other changes besides the seasonal one that accompany the journey south. When you stop for gas in the Virginia tidewater, you hear that something has happened to the language. Tongues seem to have lost their agility. Vowels and consonants thicken and soften; cadences and sentences ooze and eddy and ebb, and you can stand there, half listening to the attendant and half thinking of the silt-laden, leisurely rivers and streams and swamps that wind through this flat country and in fact created it, and wonder if they also had a kind of subliminal shaping effect on what had come across the Atlantic as English.

Along with this change in the language, there is also another one for me, one that has less to do with going from North to South than with going from what I do to where I come from.

Teaching English means a day-to-day linguistic environment of lectures, seminars, conferences, committee meetings, office hours, recommendations. Professionally speaking, this world of words is the only string in my fiddle, the only capital I've got to invest, and the only return the investment brings. But knowing that makes the words seem more like walls than like windows, because their circuit seems so closed. They beget each other endlessly, weave a web that unravels even as it is being woven from the yarn of yesterday's web.

South Carolina, God knows, is also a world of words. But because I neither commit professional activities nor associate with those who do when I am there, the words still seem to speak to me, as the old lady did, about the facts of life. Around a college, if a man is said to be outstanding in his field, it probably indicates that he knows and writes a great deal about a relatively specialized topic. Around Conway, if a man is said to be out standing in his field, it quite possibly indicates that he is shooting doves. It isn't that the one kind of activity is superior to the other. It's just that it's a relief to be reminded occasionally that words, like people, came from somewhere to start with and had a pedestrian solidity there. Packed off to college, they gain an upward mobility into abstraction and, with it, a wider reference. Intellectual gain can be imaginative loss. *This man was outstanding in his field* sounds like an epitaph — a flat assertion and end of story. *This man was out standing in his field* sounds like the beginning of a story: because the man is in space, he is in time, and time will require him to do and to die, and so a certain suspense is involved.

Anyway, I went to South Carolina three or four springs ago, when timber salvage from Hurricane Hugo was still going on. And one of the places it was going on was about fifty miles south of Conway, in the Santee Refuge, where it was being performed with scrupulous care by the lowest bidder. He was in fact charging the state nothing at all except the right to a certain percentage of the timber he salvaged and an electrical hookup for his secondhand, Eisenhower-administration Airstream trailer, where he would live until he had finished the job. This was my peripatetic friend McIver, somebody I grew up with and was not destined to outgrow. I went down to the Refuge to join him for a couple of days of what was business as usual for him, and the finest kind of truancy for me.

McIver had set up his portable sawmill on a sandy ridge, under some young live oaks. We'd spent the morning sawing the last few logs he had there, and now were stacking and sorting lumber. It was all longleaf pine — bold-grained, handsome, heavy wood. The wood, our clothes, and the sawdust underfoot were all so redolent

of turpentine that it evoked studios and painting classes, and got
you thinking about the proximity of the most sophisticated arts to
the most elementary ones. What we lifted, lugged, and stacked
were timbers: six-by-sixes, four-by-fours, two-by-fours — structural
stuff. There were also planks, of assorted standard widths and
lengths and various grades. The timbers we piled according to
their dimensions; the planks we piled according to their grade.

And, McIver being McIver, what we lifted, lugged, and stacked
also included slats and stakes, wood you might use to build a
chicken coop or prop up your tomatoes. He can't bear throwing
anything away. He'd had a partner once, and the partner quit,
being unable to see the economic logic of sawing slats that might
bring five dollars a bundle, provided you could find the time to
bundle them and the gardeners to buy them. But economics for
McIver has always been a branch of applied philosophy, and philosophy a sort of folk art, like making patchwork quilts, where you
stitch together something that will serve your purpose and express
your sense of proportion and design out of whatever odds and
ends and bits and pieces come to hand. Partners, of either the
business or the connubial variety, have always found upon closer
examination that this philosophy is chiefly admirable from a distance, and now my hardheaded old friend lives and works alone.

With regard to trees and lumber and a good many other things,
his credo is simple. "I waste nothing," McIver says, "except my
time."

You pile lumber as though it were fragile. Each pile is level.
There is a half-inch gap between each pair of planks in each tier
of lumber, and the tiers are separated from each other by stringers
— narrow battens that McIver saws from slabwood. The stringers
are roughly half an inch wide and exactly half an inch thick, a little
longer than the tier is wide, and placed across it at three-foot
intervals. As the pile mounts, the weight coming to bear on the
lower levels also mounts. As long as that weight is evenly distributed, there is no harm in this, and even some good — it reduces
the tendency of the planks to bow or bend as they dry. But if one
stringer is even slightly thicker or thinner than the others, it will
stress the board it rests on and the board that rests on it as the
weight piles up. So we stack meticulously and methodically — the
right plank properly placed on the right pile — as though we were
file clerks or librarians reshelving books.

Spaced along the sandy road, the stacks of new-cut wood are pleasing. They are overhung by the gnarled oaks with their streamers of moss; the leafy shadows and soft humid light flit and flicker over them. They draw the eye and hold it. If you block from your sight and thinking the saw, the sawdust, and the slabwood — all the evidence of ordinary human agency and ordinary economic activity — the whole scene, a random imposition of strict, rectilinear order on the disorder of nature, exerts a minor spiritual magnetism, as though you'd come upon some rudimentary, homemade Stonehenge.

Such money as McIver makes will come from the smallest of the piles of planks — top-quality, cabinet-grade lumber. Longleaf is a slow-growing pine, almost as dense and hard as oak. From the standpoint of commercial forestry, it is a tree that wastes time. Economics pretty well dictates that you reseed a plot with slash or loblolly, fast-growing trees, once you've cut the longleaf. But no other pine produces its quality of lumber. The slow years get stored in the grain; they become strength inseparable from beauty. The wood is prized for flooring, paneling, furniture.

We hoist a plank, examine one side. Smooth, straight-grained, no knots. We flip it and examine the other side. It looks fine to me, but McIver sighs. He wants to put it on the small pile, the money pile; but instead it goes in with the lowest grade of all — the next step down would be the sawdust pile.

"What was wrong with that one?" I ask him. "SAT scores too low?"

"Nope," he says. "Compression wood. See?" I see, but only because I am shown.

Compression wood comes from a leaning tree. The force of gravity would cause the trunk to bend and sag, and eventually to break, if the tree did not automatically respond by a more rapid, denser production of cellular wood along the underside of the trunk — something like the tensing of a muscle to resist whatever pushes or pulls against it. Once the counterpressure is removed, a tensed muscle can relax. But a plank isn't like that. It can't forget the torques and tensions that shaped it as part of a living and misaligned organism. Freed from the log, it will contort itself, warp, rack, or bulge, no matter how long you cure it or how much you clamp, nail, steam, or spike it. Under stress, it may snap with explosive suddenness.

McIver and I grew up within a few hundred yards of each other, went through school and then to college together. We get along because we are in the habit of it, and understand our roles. Mine combines the wise guy, the Fancy Dan, and the straight man. "Look," I say to him from my end of the plank. "What we are talking about here is neurosis, pure and simple. This plank ain't a *bad* plank. It just suffers from posttraumatic stress syndrome. Has anybody ever tried a little elementary psychothcrapy on compression wood?"

McIver gives me a look. He's missing a little finger; he has, as consequence of a misstep taken in Southeast Asia, slivers of shrapnel in one leg and a custom-fitted, stainless-steel patch in his skull. "No need for them to try it on compression wood," he says. "They've tried it elsewhere. And I am here to tell you, *it don't work.*"

When he's in his customary mode of working alone, McIver has a transistor radio with headphones. He listens exclusively to the local NPR station, except when it plays jazz, which he dislikes. When it schedules jazz, he schedules chain sawing, which makes listening impossible in any case. If there's no chain sawing to be done, he may shift over briefly to a Top 40, evangelical, or talk station — fluff, salvation, or the vox populi, against which to hone his disdain. But mostly he likes the NPR news of local and global affairs. It requires him to adjust his homemade philosophic patchwork so that it can incorporate a mosaic of rumors, wars, trends — epidemics of revolution, multinational finance, resurgent tribalism, ecological catastrophe, congressional reform, the colonization of cyberspace, and the long-term outlook for the catfish industry — all of this to be seriously mulled over while he aligns the log on the carriage, walks the little high-pitched band saw down through the log, and lays off the planks he will stack later, to Mozart, Haydn, Debussy.

He knows where he stands and why he stands there. You could blindfold him and put him down anywhere in North America, remove the blindfold, and tell him only what month it was. If the place had trees, he would find them and study them. It might take a day or two. Then he would tell you where he was — latitude, longitude, elevation. He might be wrong, but he would not be hesitant beforehand or apologetic afterward. He would prefer his way of being wrong to your way of being right. His way involves independent observation and deduction, the laws of Humboldt, a close reading of habitat through a coherent idea of geography. Yours involves numbered highways and road signs, mere slogans and hearsay. You might as well stay home and read a map.

The barrage of world news and news closer to home confirms his faith in what he calls primary resources — wood, crops, animals, ores: things that come out of the earth and water to provide us food, fuel, and shelter. In the course of one conversation, McIver lays down a law: "People who don't work with primary resources don't understand reality. And not understanding reality is a functional definition of insanity." That leads him inevitably to conclude that the trouble with the world today is that the inmates are running the asylum. You need to be grounded and rooted in geography; you need to understand that money measures time in one way and a longleaf pine measures it in another. The pine can make money, but the money can't afford to return the favor. If McIver were Robinson Crusoe, alone on his desert island, his way of thinking and living would require surprisingly few adjustments. He achieves by logic and implacable opinion what Crusoe achieved by shipwreck: isolation, and the consequent opportunity to reinvent civilization, starting with the simplest necessities and working up and out from them.

When he isn't on a job and living in the Airstream trailer, he lives in Conway, on an otherwise respectable street. The house hasn't been painted in a long time, nor has the shrubbery been trimmed, the grass mowed, or the mildew or the rot in any way inconvenienced in its operations. A row of small sweet gums has sprouted in a gutter; every year, the whole structure has faded a little further back into nature, and now, except for its size, it resembles an abandoned duck blind. Inside, the only sign of neatness is in the front corner of the living room, where there are a small table and chair beside a window, and some bookshelves made of pine he cut himself. In those things, you can recognize the tidy, thrifty worker. On the table is a complicated mechanism for sharpening the band-saw blades. He comes here every week or two, bringing an accumulation of blades, and sits down and sharpens. It is as precise as any task a jeweler does. He dons glasses and a scholarly air. Every tooth must be aligned just so, raked alter-

nately to one side and the other. When he is done, the facets of
the teeth gleam delicately and sliver paper or skin as elegantly as
a razor.

The rest of the room and the rest of the house are bad to look
at. Possessions have become jetsam. They are thrown on chairs,
jammed in closets, abandoned on the floor. You let appearances
slide, and it is harmless; then you let them slide further, let them
go altogether, and discover that there was more reality in them
than you thought. They take away whatever energy and self-respect
you had invested in them, and they keep it. There is grit in the
rug; a scum of dust, as thick as the springtime pollen, covers
everything. Even a man in his worst, most worn-out working
clothes would wipe off any surface before he sat on it. McIver
doesn't have a vacuum cleaner, which doesn't matter because the
electricity has been cut off for months. "And anyway," he says,
looking at the clutter, "I don't need a vacuum cleaner. I need a
backhoe."

When he was a boy, he was neat, his room as spruce and spare
as a barracks. It was the same in college and in the marines. After
that he was a smoke jumper in the United States Forest Service,
and smoke jumpers, whatever else they are, are fanatically orderly
about their personal effects, packing and repacking their para-
chutes, maintaining their gear as though their lives depended on
it, because their lives depend on it. He smoke-jumped for more
years than anybody in the history of the organization; in a book
I can't sufficiently praise, *Young Men and Fire,* Norman McLean
refers to him in passing simply as "Rod McIver, dean of the Montana smoke jumpers." When he finally landed wrong and ruined
his knee and couldn't jump anymore, the Forest Service told him
that if he'd accept a desk job for five years, he would qualify for a
pension that would pretty much take care of him for the rest of
his life. He declined, took his severance pay, came home, and used
the money to buy his portable mill.

Somewhere along the way, he lost his aptitude for domestic life
and developed a great harshness toward that side of himself which
still craved it. That was what his house said, and in bleak moments
he comes close to saying it himself. Indispensable small tools, hardware, and spare parts that might get buried and lost in the rub-
bish of his house, he keeps in his disconnected refrigerator. He
steps carefully over a pile of magazines, opens the refrigerator

door, and takes out a packet of sheet-metal screws. You half expect to see him sit down at the kitchen table, toss them lightly in WD-40, and eat them.

"Some people think of a house as a home," McIver says. "I prefer to think of it as an equipment shed. Where I sometimes store myself." And he says one thing more to me before I go back to Maine. "Drop by and see Mama before you go. It always pleases her. She says you're my last link to civilization."

I would have done so in any case. When we were growing up, I knew her house as well as my own; I came and went in it as freely and breathed in it almost more freely. I stop by on the last morning, on my way out of town.

She is retired from teaching now, old and crippled by arthritis. We sit in her small parlor, a room that has scarcely changed from my childhood: the same furniture, the same Audubon print of the wild turkey over the hearth, the coal grate on the hearth, and beside it a scuttle and a basket. The scuttle is filled with coal, the basket is mounded with longleaf pinecones. These are spent cones, their teeth splayed open; you can pick them up by the bushel in the Santee Refuge. In both size and shape, they roughly approximate footballs. In the basket, they are woody, dark, and handsome, with the understated decorative look of dried flowers. She prizes them for that, but also because they are an excellent kindling. Like much in her household, they combine simplicity, a provident thriftiness, and a natural elegance that I wish I could have absorbed by osmosis, simply from all the hours and days and years spent there.

We talk for a while, and then it is time to go. With difficulty, she sees me to the door, and we stand there a minute longer. She asks about the drive back up to Maine. How long does it take? Are the roads safe? Is my car reliable? And that leads her to fret some, and not for the first time, about her son's truck. He bought it right after he was discharged from the marines. Now, like his house, it appears to be held together by force of habit rather than by any surviving principle of structural integrity. The door on the passenger side is wired shut, but a passenger could conceivably escape, if he had to, through the floor, which yawns open like a bomb bay between his feet. The odometer conked out somewhere in the Great Plains, five or six years ago, at 297,411 miles. It's getting hard to find spare parts now. Even the most comprehensive junkyards aren't likely to have a supply of '69 Ford F 250 pickups on hand, and McIver doesn't like parking the truck too close to a junkyard anyway, for fear that when he gets back to it, he may find that another customer, by a perfectly innocent and natural confusion, has removed some one of its remaining operative systems.

"You know," Mrs. McIver says, "I do worry about that old truck. I'm afraid that one of these days it's going to break right down and leave him by the road. I wish he'd take it now while it's still running and just trade it in."

I say that I guess that's right, but that he has had the truck for so long that it seems like part of his personality now.

"Well, yes," says Mrs. McIver. "And sometimes I wish he'd just trade *that* in too."

Then I drove back north, trading longleaf pine for white pine, dahoon and yaupon for bayberry and viburnum, sweet gum for sugar maple, cypress for hemlock, and always losing species as I drove, moving through arboreal environments of progressively diminishing complexity until I was back in Maine, which has wound up being home. That coincided with another process of simplification, as experience became memory, and memory concentrated on some details and lost others. By the time I was up into Pennsylvania, the days spent with McIver had reduced themselves to a single image, something I could pick up and turn over and squint at from several angles — the plank of compression wood, as a metaphor or an epitome, or maybe just a souvenir.

Most obviously, the plank could be taken to stand for my old friend himself. Something that could not forget the history that had shaped it and had necessitated and justified its idiosyncrasies. Something that so perfectly incorporated the stresses and misalignments and imperatives of the circumstance from which it had been abstracted that it would never accept as real or rational any other circumstance to which fate consigned it. Something that did not fit in; that was, to the vexation of all concerned, a manifestly high-quality article of rare integrity, ingrained recalcitrance, and small market value.

But even as a metaphor, compression wood does not keep still; in the environment of the mind, few things do. I considered the difference between McIver's world and my own, the difference between days spent handling wood and days spent handling paper. Both the wood and the paper came from trees, but only the wood reminded you of that fact. At the end of a day of sawing, you had a product — the trim, carefully organized stacks of lumber. This is what we have done since we became human — taken things out of nature and shaped them into a secondary environment for ourselves. McIver has always seemed to me to appreciate better than most what is lost and what is gained in the process. He might run his fingers over a fine plank. When the wood is first exposed to air, it is moist and smooth and alive. "The best finish you can put on good lumber will never make it look quite as pretty as it does when it's first cut," McIver says, "but that's what it should try to do. Otherwise, it's vandalism."

All I ever have to show for my work is paper: a paycheck at the end of the month, a grade sheet at the end of term, and, at erratic intervals, something printed somewhere. Not much sense of product there — nothing to stand back from, and wipe the sawdust of it off your hands, and admire.

Writing is in fact a mystery, an invention that grew out of the most mysterious and revolutionary human invention of all, which was language — the environment we inhabit and that inhabits us. Of all the secondary environments we have created, language seems the most like a natural system, something that grows, evolves, embraces, metamorphoses, and hybridizes according to laws that we can partially deduce but didn't devise and can't control. But when you are using it all the time, talking to yourself even when you are trying to listen to somebody else, language doesn't seem mysterious or revolutionary at all. It seems like self-generated static.

So it was a great satisfaction, as I drove back north, to try to picture McIver's world again, to replay the days on the sandy ridge. You'd watch the small saw travel through the log. You'd rotate the log a quarter turn with a cant hook, level it, and watch the saw go through again. You'd do this twice more. The lumpy, imperfect carcass of the log — tree trunks are far less straight and cylindrical than we imagine them to be — gives birth to solid geometry. It is not as though the tree were being dismembered. It is as though its innate idea, its inmost formal principles, were being elucidated.

There is something Greek about it, something out of Plato by way of Euclid and Pythagoras. Even after you'd spent a day lifting and lugging, an individual board could stop you short with its beauty — the wavering, flamelike fluency of the grain arrested by the severe, abstract symmetry of the plank.

Geometry and *geography* share the same root. Geometry came into being because we needed to measure the earth, so that we could comprehend and claim our place on it. Speaking of the arts that created civilization, Yeats said very simply what seems to me very simply true: "Measurement began our might." From it came the pyramids, the Roman roads, the sciences of cartography, architecture, astronomy, mechanics, and so forth. And also, more obliquely, the measures of music and poetry, the power of aural, visual, and intellectual form over what Yeats called the "mere complexity" of experience. *Ratio* and *rationality* also come from a single root, suggesting that reason itself has to do with measured proportions and connects back, via geometry, to geography — the ground that is under our feet.

The plank that McIver unhappily examined and sentenced to the junk pile — that plank looks like the fly in the ointment. It conformed to standard dimensions but would not conform to standardized purposes. Like the other lumber, it seemed an expression of something innately Euclidean in a tree. But it also expressed something stubbornly local, peculiar to the particular life of that particular tree.

However much I might think of McIver by analogy to the plank of compression wood, he himself could afford to think of it only as he thinks of most things, unsentimentally and literally. The plank was of minimal utility; it might do for sheathing on a pigsty. But as I drove back north, back toward my own work, I found myself thinking of the plank in almost exactly the opposite way. In its lack of extrinsic or practical value, it resembled a work of art. Whatever value it had could only be intrinsic, generated by a rationale peculiar to itself, the outcome of a single organism's negotiation between the fixed reality in which it was rooted and the unpossessable light that it required. To make the process of my thinking much more conclusive and schematic than it actually was, I thought of the plank as a specimen of the kind of writing that gets called literature, of the tree as the writer who produced

it, and of the forest as the writer's milieu, the place where he or
she lived, drew nourishment, and contrived to grow up out of.

Where you're from is never simply a matter of geography. It
involves intersections of history, economics, family, and so forth,
as well as the coordinates of latitude and longitude. Self-location,
with or without maps, is ultimately as complicated and incomplete
a process as self-knowledge. Something in us won't keep still.
Geography gave us geometry; geometry gave us ratios and rationality, and rationality can remove us from the face of the earth,
enabling us to live entirely in the secondary environments it creates. We can especially begin to live exclusively in the world of
words, without even considering that that is what has happened.
We sign checks and contracts, buy, sell, gossip, read the sports
page, and think no more about language than we do about the
boards in the floor under our feet. When it is taken for granted
that way, language gets predictable, and because we live inside its
walls, we begin to get the uneasy sense of being confined in a
bland, elastic prison. In it, we seem to have words only for thoughts
that have already been thought, and for emotions and perceptions
that don't quite feel like our own.

I think that literature is made because some people find this
state of affairs unwholesome and undertake to do something about
it. The works that seem to have mattered and lasted seldom grow
out of or reflect a life that is tranquilly organic and rooted; they
are more likely to involve some sensation of displacement — of being out of place, or cut off from place, or imprisoned by place. The
place that causes the discomfort isn't the actual geography. It is
the atmosphere of assumptions that lies over it and seems to in-
sulate us from it. What is assumed that way gradually becomes invisible.

It was these thoughts, which really began as just another kind of
timber salvage, that eventually brought Hopkins to mind. I was not
at that time thinking about his life — when you learn about a poet
poems-first, the life can seem a shadowy sort of business that takes
place backstage, a footnote to the poetry. As an advantaged and
splendidly educated young Englishman, he started out as something of an aesthete, with a good deal of the snobbery and prig-
gishness that are likely to accompany that stance. Maybe his con-

version to Catholicism and his entry into the Jesuit order, while outwardly an attempt to conquer or at least to mortify that part of his nature, were in reality expressions of it. He does not appear to have ever truly escaped from himself and into his vocation. He no doubt struggled to love and serve his poor and mostly Irish parishioners and students in Liverpool and Dublin, but *caritas,* because it never wholly overcame his sense of genteel birth, his very English fastidiousness, winds up making those qualities in him seem especially unlovely, small, and sour.

"Pied Beauty" hardly brings such a constricted, self-enclosed life to mind. One line from it came to me partway through Pennsylvania as I was mulling over the piece of compression wood: "All things counter, original, spare, strange." Those four adjectives that clash and echo against each other seemed to formulate what I had been fumbling toward, as I recalled the almost worthless plank of longleaf pine and the sawyer who sawed it.

Remembering the rest of the poem was harder. Like somebody struggling with a difficult crossword puzzle, I very imperfectly and provisionally filled in around that one line, and knew that I was missing some parts and misplacing others. It is good to have something like that to occupy your mind when you are driving, and I would not have looked up "Pied Beauty" if I'd had it on the seat beside me. But by the time I got home, I was ready to give in. I got the book down from the shelf, and there it was in its abrupt, contorted perfection, and here it is:

> Glory be to God for dappled things —
>   For skies of couple-colour as a brinded cow;
>   For rose-moles all in stipple upon trout that swim;
> Fresh-firecoal chestnut-falls; finches' wings;
>   Landscape plotted and pieced — fold, fallow, and plough;
>   And áll trádes, their gear and tackle and trim.
>
> All things counter, original, spare, strange;
>   Whatever is fickle, freckled (who knows how?)
>   With swift, slow; sweet, sour; adazzle, dim;
> He fathers-forth whose beauty is past change:
>   Praise Him.

A poem is not the same poem from reading to reading, because the reader is not the same reader. What I could see now was a development I would not have seen when I was an undergraduate and knew almost nothing about what things I could and couldn't, would and wouldn't, leave behind me in Conway.

The poem starts with *God* and *things* — two thoroughly nondescript nouns from opposite ends of the metaphysical spectrum. The next three lines are all dappled things, images out of nature — skies, cow, trout, chestnuts, finches' wings. They are seen kaleidoscopically — disconnected and conflated and piecemeal all at once. This is hardly the expected, stable, and stabilizing view of Nature as an evidence of faith.

The sixth line now seems to me the true pivot of the poem, and it is a surprise. It isn't about natural things at all, but about the gear and tackle and trim of all trades, the creations of men, not of God. It appears to grow out of the line just before, when Hopkins is looking at the landscape. The landscape is pied and beautiful because of human intervention. It is *plotted* — divided into small plots, fields with different crops, hedgerows, and so forth; it looks *pieced* together, like a quilt. *Fold, fallow,* and *plough* add detail: a fold is an enclosure for keeping livestock; fallow is ground left out of cultivation; and plough, as it is used here, refers to tillage land, land that is ploughed and planted as opposed, for example, to pastures or orchards. But the word also suggests the actual implement — the plough that does the ploughing — and that takes us to the line about the trades and their tools, almost as though those trades had grown up out of the earth itself.

Those trades show up in other poems by Hopkins. They are the manual trades of rural England — ploughing, blacksmithing, scything. One of the ways Hopkins freed himself from the Victorian nature poem was by watching and listening to the uneducated practitioners of these trades. The opportunity to do so may have been one of the few rewards of his difficult and unhappy choice of life. His poetry borrowed these people's tools and it borrowed their vocabulary, too — for example, the odd dialect word *brinded* in the second line. And perhaps it borrowed something larger and more basic. The people who used the tools fit McIver's definition of sanity — they were working with primary resources. They were at the point where human purpose and natural process encounter each other with some violence. The tools of the trade are sharp, sturdy, hot, and heavy; you can't handle them absentmindedly. I feel something analogous to that violence, that muscular strain and strife, in Hopkins's language, its brusque dismissal of traditional mellifluousness. This quality is what saves his poetry from conventional piety or conventional melancholy, and makes his poems in praise of God sudden and powerful, like momentary, ecstatic inversions of despair.

So the first half of the poem is all natural images until the sixth line, where we find the tools that convert natural creations into human ones. The second half of the poem has no images. It's virtually all adjectives. We leave the world of vivid perceptions and enter a world where language seems to generate itself. *Fickle* begets *freckled* by a recombination of consonants. *Swift, slow; sweet, sour; adazzle, dim* are produced by logical opposition and alliteration. Observation has led to generalization; the things of this world have led us out of this world, into language. That is the development in the poem that I was able to see this time, its unintended plot. And that is, almost inevitably, the plot of much of what is loosely called nature writing, hard though nature writers try to avoid it.

And it was also pretty much the plot of my trip to South Carolina and back. In one way, its final point was the familiar one about how words always manage to lose most of the cargo they are sent to fetch and how your thought winds up chasing its own tail, while language once again builds up its wall around you.

But the world outside poems and essays — the world they come from and yearn toward — exists in its literal and unliterary processes, its power, and its indifference to whatever language may make or unmake of it. I can pick up the telephone on my desk and dial McIver's number. He has a phone; he now pays the bills. Even more remarkably, he also has an answering machine. It is necessary to his business. The voice that comes over the line isn't the least bit cordial: "You have reached the residence of Rod McIver. I am either unable or unwilling to answer the phone at present. Leave your message and a number where you can be reached." The machine was the cheapest one on the market, and he paid a little extra to get a free-replacement-at-absolutely-no-charge guarantee for it. He renews the guarantee each time they have to replace the machine, and fears only that someday they'll give him one that will outlast its warranty. But thus far that hasn't happened, and he deals with his calls every week or so, when he comes in to sharpen his blades.

And so I know that he has traded — *jettisoned* would be more like it, he'd say — his truck, without discernible effect on his personality. He is through with the salvage job at the Santee Refuge now and is doing small contract jobs out in the county around Conway and in the neighboring counties. As an independent businessman, he is still going nowhere, at thirty-two feet per second per second. "I hope to hit the grave so hard I bounce," he says, quite cheerfully.

McIver's work can be agreeable in the early spring and late fall, and it's really best of all during bright winter weather. But you don't even want to think about what it's like from the middle of May until early October. The insects alone are enough to make you swear off fresh air forever. The heat builds up and bears down. It thrums inside your skull, like a bad fever. You get light-headed. The trunks of the pines across the clearing wobble and ripple in your sight, as though they, or your eyes, were actually melting.

The only thing for it is method, method. Every hour, McIver checks the coolant level in the saw. Then he pulls out his pocket watch and takes his pulse. If it's over 140, he stops, shuts off the saw, and clambers up onto the bed of the truck and lies down, a piece of cheesecloth over his face to keep off the bugs. He takes his pulse every three minutes. As soon as it drops out of the red zone, he clambers back down and prepares to restart the saw.

In the buzzing, dizzying glare, he moves slowly, ponderously, like a diver in his diving suit, sleepwalking through an atmosphere almost opaque with heat. The world can look strange then, as if it were in the process of growing unreal, sublimating itself into a mirage. You have to breathe carefully, and keep calm, and focus only on the task immediately in front of you, and not think about any future beyond the end of one more day, the completion of one more load of lumber. You cannot ask yourself what you are doing here, or why you are doing it, because those questions lack answers that would fit anybody's definition of sanity. You can only keep doing it, doggedly, deliberately, scrupulously, as though in obedience to something, or in honor of it.

At such times, I want to say to him that he is my last link to the point of origin, where originality must return to measure itself. But he is sun-stunned, a little addlebrained, and he fumbles at this Fancy Dannery for a minute, trying to get his mind around it.

"Origin?" he asks. "Originality?" You can almost see the sluggish engine resisting the starter, churning heavily against its inertia. Finally it fires, coughs, catches, runs roughly at first, and then smooths out. The gears mesh and engage, and now the invincible aphorist is back in business. "The wages of originality is failure. Or maybe it's the other way around. I don't know. I don't care. Either way," McIver says to me, "I aim to get paid in full."

MICHAEL W. COX

Visitor

FROM NEW LETTERS

MY FATHER kept a boy in the basement. He'd tell me not to go
down there, but I'd go anyway, sometimes, and talk to the boy.
He'd smoke a cigarette, usually, while he talked to me. He'd tell
me things.

We had two basements, really, one indoor, one out. The boy
stayed in the outdoor one, for part of one whole summer. Really,
it was a fine basement, the outdoor one. It had been a kind of
playhouse for me and my brothers, but by the time the boy had
arrived we had forgotten about it, to play instead in a gigantic field
of horseweed down below our house, beyond the railroad tracks
and before the river. Outside the basement door, in a small alcove,
my father kept our trash cans; and at night, you'd hear him out
there, beneath the window, taking out the bags of garbage. He
would take the bag of trash from our kitchen, through the indoor
basement and out its side door, and walk the few steps to the trash
can. From there you could look into the dark outdoor basement,
the door having long since been removed from its hinges — the
house came that way when we moved in, the outdoor basement
being doorless, I mean. Inside, the front half of the floor was dirt
and, often, especially with the rain that seeped in through the
bricks, mud. We boys had laid down planks across the dirt, so we
could walk to the back half without getting our shoes wet, where
one of the previous owners of the house had built a wooden floor
elevated about six inches off the ground. There was a kind of half
wall in there, too, and a ceiling above the wall, the whole structure
being like an indoor tree house — my brother had taken the

stepladder from our bunk bed and put it down there in the basement, so we could climb up to the ceiling and sit between it and the bottom side of the front porch above our heads. Inside the half-room in that basement, I would guess the clearance was about six or seven feet — we were all of us small, but to imagine my father in there, with that boy, he might've had to duck his head down inside that room. There was an old couch in there, I remember, and a blanket for the couch. The boy must've slept on that at night, when he'd come from being out somewhere in the daytime; he'd walk up the railroad tracks — I could hear him, would crawl to my window to watch, unseen, through the screen — up the short hillside path into our yard, in the dark so as not to be seen by neighbors, and on up to the basement, then my father, a while later, taking out the trash and then going on inside for a few minutes, my mother on the other side of the wall from my bedroom, listening to the television set in the summer night, losing track of the time in some mindless plot. And all the while I was supposed to be sleeping, but I'd tick off the minutes my father was inside there — one one-thousand, two one-thousand — keeping time. He never took too long, though more than once I think I heard him, from my bed, go downstairs in the night to get a glass of milk — I'd hear him whisper to mom first, who'd be dead asleep anyway, and then the walking of my father's feet down the stairs in the creaking night and, fifteen seconds later, the basement door clicking open beneath the window of my room, then clicking shut a few minutes later, etc. One morning as I was eating my cereal across from him, he asked me what I was looking at.

"Nothing," I said. "I'm not looking at anything."

He went back to his paper.

"Don't go in the basement," he said from behind it.

"How come?"

"Saw a possum there, when I was taking out the trash."

"Possum?" I said.

"Might be living in that basement," he said. "Might be rabid."

"Might be," I said. And that was that.

But I stepped inside there one day, in broad daylight but dim inside, because I wanted to see how the boy might be living in there. Summer nights were warm, always, never dipping below sixty, so a blanket and dry clothes would be enough. As I walked in along the planks I could smell his cigarette and knew I was not alone — I hadn't expected him in there in the daytime, and most days, I expect, he wasn't there at all — he might be working somewhere, I thought, or maybe be down at the river swimming, I thought, or maybe he'd stop inside the stores down on Main Street and shoplift him a little something — I didn't know, I could only imagine, and he said hello to me. I stopped, let my eyes adjust and then I could see him — him, who I'd seen for the most part only the top of as he'd walk beneath my window, a baseball cap on always, which was off now and lying on the couch beside him. His legs were crossed, I could see as my eyes got better at it, and he was wearing dark pants and a jacket and I could see his cigarette brighten when he put it up to his face, his mouth, lips. Hey youngun, he called, but quietly. Come on over, he said, have a seat — he patted the couch beside himself, mashing his cap, then realizing that and grabbing it by the bill and popping it out.

Who are you? I asked but without fear in my voice, I'm pretty sure, and he told me his name was Jody, and then he told me, if I wanted to be his buddy, I could go back inside the house and make him a sandwich and bring it on back out here, to his couch. I did exactly what he asked, made him a potted meat sandwich on white bread and even, when he asked, went back inside the house for mustard, so he could spice up the sandwich, he said. I knew right away I would get him real food and not do anything so rank as substitute dog food for potted meat (though some would argue, I knew even then, as to the relative difference between the two), or pee in a glass and tell him that it was lemonade — yes, I had done these things to marginal acquaintances, it's true, and I am not exactly proud of it, and when I think of these things these days I kind of laugh to myself while grimacing at the same time, hoping no such thing was ever done to me, hoping that they are wrong, whoever they may be, when they say what goes around etc. But you just can't know sometimes: you cannot file a taste away in your mind and retrieve it, precisely, twenty years later and say my god, that boy fed me dog food, or piss water, or some such thing.

And Jody was grateful and liked my sandwich very much, and then he sent me back inside, promptly, to fix him another and another, telling me that my daddy liked to keep him hungry. You eat good inside there? he asked, and I nodded as he devoured his fourth and, that day, final sandwich, three trips having been made inside by then (odd trip being the mustard). Well that's good, he said, to eat good, though I must say you are a skinny boy and he was right, I was, it's true, and have remained thin to this day, more or less, a couple of periods of drunkenness having led to weight gain, but get sober and it comes right off, pizza boxes and empty bags of chips aside, in the trash, wherever your trash can might be located. And he and I, Jody, I mean, became fast friends, I bringing him sandwiches each day at the same "bat time," as he called it, same bat place (I knew the show he referred to but did not know that the reference was humorous — it all seemed sincerely serious to me, just like my sandwich bringing — he was careful to make sure I brought my mother's plates back inside, not wanting, as he put it, to tip off the old lady).

I was reading a novel that summer about an alien boy who dropped into our dimension from another — he fell through a portal right into a family's life and, though he did not come to our dimension knowing English, learned it right away, the vocabulary, the grammar, all by listening, processing, and then, one day, by practicing. He was a good boy but frightened, and he wanted, very badly, to find the portal and get back home. I wished my father's boy might be just such an alien, but he wasn't. When he'd strike a match I'd look at him nonetheless, searching for signs: pointed ears, high forehead, hairlessness. He had none of that, and in fact he told me he'd only come from down the road apiece, just a few counties away.

He was a funny boy even so, and by that I mean strange. He laughed at odd times, and not a nice laugh either. He was older than me significantly — had I been a little younger, I'd've thought him a man. But he wasn't a man, just a teenager. He asked me one day what my mother was like, and I asked him what did he mean. Is she pretty, he asked, and I said that yes, I thought she was. Does your father think she's pretty, he asked, and I thought and then I said that yes, I thought that he too thought her pretty. Well that's a pretty picture then, don't you think, he asked, and stuck his tickling fingers against my stomach right then, to get me to laugh.

He wore a jacket, that much I remember. There was a blanket in there, as I have said, and a couch. It is painful sometimes for me, when I think back, to picture him in there in the night, alone, nothing but his cigarettes for company. It is possible he did not have many thoughts, and so was not bothered by the lack of things in there in the night, or possibly he had many thoughts and so he could entertain himself for hours on end. Maybe he'd read books and would remember them, or see, in his mind, TV shows he'd already seen, maybe, or maybe he'd remember his home life and the way his parents and he got along. I cannot know, cannot remember not being, as it were, omniscient. Certainly I could create a life for him, if I wished. At the heart of an enigma is nothing but what you put there yourself. He would tell me tales about the road, for he was, he claimed, a kind of hobo. Did he ride the rails, I'd ask, motioning to the railroad tracks just down the hill, and he told me no, of course not, that hopping trains was dangerous. He would tell me of hitchhiking, and of how you could tell who might be friendly, as a driver, and who might not be. It was always men driving alone, he said, who were the friendly ones, and he made his voice kind of crackle then, he'd start laughing, I mean, like it was a private joke with him, and he'd not tell me, precisely, what he meant. I'm a mystery to you, he'd say, and he liked that, I could tell, because he nodded and would take a big pull off his cigarette, blow that smoke into the air, nod again and take another big pull. He taught me how to smoke, that's the one thing he taught me, not being any kind of abuser so much as the object of one or two along the way, or, probably, many. Your father's a funny man, he'd say, and I could not bring myself to ask Jody to tell me what he meant.

At night sometimes I'd see Jody leave. He would walk beneath my window, where I learned to watch for him or for my father or for them both. He would walk beneath my window, quietly, along the side of the house, his baseball cap turning toward the kitchen window and, as he passed the back porch, the back door. He'd traipse along the short hillside down to the tracks, then head off for downtown. Maybe my father had given him money. Maybe he'd go out to hit the town, paint it red. He came back one night singing something loud and Irish, an eyes-smiling sort of song, sang all the way up the tracks and on up into the yard. Across the lawns I saw a neighbor's light come on, old Mrs. Welch's drapes opening just as he disappeared inside the outdoor basement, her kerchiefed head with rabbit ears twisting in her window — but she wouldn't be able to see him, not with her light turned on — you had to look outside with your lights off, I knew this, having looked outside so many nights and having seen so much. And there was a fight then between my parents, in their bedroom, my father leaving that room with a flashlight, muttering and going down the stairs, my mother hissing to him from the top of the staircase, and then, beneath my window, finally, the basement door opening, and, outside my room, my mother's feet sweeping into my bedroom, quietly, so as not to wake me, or so she thought (I was lying in my bed by then, barely breathing). She stood in the window where I had so often stood looking down, and she may or may not have seen him step inside that basement. Then the sound, in the night, of two men murmuring, voices, a slap — my mother putting an ear close to the window.

At night sometimes I'd see him leave. I told you that. And that night, very late, pretty near dawn — I could see the morning star already out my window, on the violet horizon — he slunk away from the basement for what would be the last time, not bothering to check the kitchen window as he passed, and headed away from town, once he got to the tracks, instead of downtown for the beer gardens. My father insisted to my mother that she had been hearing things — there had been no singing, he insisted — and that all there was involved in all this was a rabid possum. But I saw her the next day talking to Mrs. Welch by her back door, Mrs. Welch pointing over to our basement. Later, I asked my father over breakfast what happened to Jody. Behind his paper he told me he'd never heard that name before, that he had no idea who I meant. The paper did not move; he studied sports figures the rest of the morning; I know because I waited, and when I left the room, I heard the paper fall to the table.

Except for asking my father about him that one time, I kept my knowledge of Jody to myself. My brothers may have come upon him, for all I knew. Sometimes I played with my brothers down in the field of horseweed, as I have said, but often I preferred to be alone and to go exploring. There was what we called back then an old drunk hole down by the railroad tracks below the house, maybe a hundred feet away — a place where drunks could go and sleep off their cheap wine. At the height of summer once, when the honeysuckle vines rioted across the drunkards' hiding place, covering up nearly everything — the trees there, the broken fence — I journeyed inside the place to study the plant life. I was digging moss up to take back home and plant in the yard, when beside me, from beneath the vines, a sleeping drunk arose and reached for me. I got a good look at the man — old, gray, red-faced — and ran home and told my father (my mother was away just then). He asked me what the man looked like, and I asked him what did he mean. How old was he, my father asked, and I could tell he was thinking of going down there himself, to investigate.

When I was very small, once — once is all I remember of this — my father had me go for a drive with him. He stopped at a store along the road, finally, where a little boy played outside. Two men watched the boy play, one perhaps being the boy's father. He told me, my father, to stay inside the car but that I should act friendly very soon, to look happy when he talked to the men on the porch and pointed my way, where I would be smiling inside the car. And here is what I could hear him telling them: that I was a lonely little boy who had no boys his age living nearby, and that we drove the countryside looking for playmates for me — a lame story now, perhaps, but back then, out in the country, it would fly.

We drove the boy up a dirt road far out in the woods, me and my father. He had packed a lunch for us, sandwiches, soda, candy, wrapped in a paper bag that he grabbed quickly, when the road finally stopped, and he told me to wait for them. From the back seat of the car I watched them, hand in hand, disappear into the dark woods. I waited for what seemed like a long, long time. When they returned, my father was practically dragging the boy, who was crying. My father kept telling him, as he loaded him into the front seat, that it was I who had hurt him — me — that I had come along in the dark woods like an Indian and surprised the boy. He stood up in the seat in front of me and began throwing feeble punches my way, and my father shoved him down into the seat and yelled at him to stop crying. He tossed the bag into the back seat beside me; it was empty, crumpled. We drove the boy back to the country store and then sped away.

He took me to carnivals, too, and would buy me a fistful of tickets and make me ride the rides while he wandered the grounds. He'd meet me at the gates when the tickets were gone. He'd rehearse me on the ride back home, in the car, telling me that he had watched me on every ride, standing alongside the other parents, that he had even ridden the ferris wheel with me. You can see everything from up there, he'd say. What did we see, I asked. The people, he'd say. Popcorn concessions. Candy apples, cotton candy. I see, I said. It's important, he said, that you be able to see it. I can, I said. So how was the tilt-a-whirl, he'd say as we whirled into our driveway. It was fun, I said. And where was I, he asked. Right down in front watching, I said, by the man who worked the gears. That's right, he said. Now tell your mom — and I ran inside the house, eager to tell his stories.

That summer the boy was staying in the basement, I used to wonder what might have happened if my father had gone in there one night and found him gone. Maybe this is why Jody eventually left that plush abode, because he was not available for one of my father's late night whims. My father would take out the trash, say — he would bag it up in the kitchen, walk across the tiles and into the doorway of the inner basement, his hands clutching the bag, tightening on it. He'd be driven now, moving faster, out the door of the basement to that little alcove where he'd take the lid off that trash can. Upstairs his kids'd be asleep, he'd think, his wife watching TV — a commercial'd be on, the music drifting out the window to where he'd be standing before the gaping hole of the trash can. He'd let the bag drop, loudly, into the can, announcing to the neighbors that all he was doing was taking out the garbage. And then he'd look around, out there in the night, and walk quietly across the planks into the basement. Hey, he'd call out to the small room there in back. But there'd be nothing there but darkness.

JOAN DIDION

Last Words

FROM THE NEW YORKER

In the late summer of that year we lived in a house in a village that looked across the river and the plain to the mountains. In the bed of the river there were pebbles and boulders, dry and white in the sun, and the water was clear and swiftly moving and blue in the channels. Troops went by the house and down the road and the dust they raised powdered the leaves of the trees. The trunks of the trees too were dusty and the leaves fell early that year and we saw the troops marching along the road and the dust rising and leaves, stirred by the breeze, falling and the soldiers marching and afterward the road bare and white except for the leaves.

So goes the famous first paragraph of Ernest Hemingway's *A Farewell to Arms*, which I was moved to reread by the recent announcement that what was said to be Hemingway's last novel would be published posthumously next year. That paragraph, which was published in 1929, bears examination: four deceptively simple sentences, one hundred and twenty-six words, the arrangement of which remains as mysterious and thrilling to me now as it did when I first read them, at twelve or thirteen, and imagined that if I studied them closely enough and practiced hard enough I might one day arrange one hundred and twenty-six such words myself. Only one of the words has three syllables. Twenty-two have two. The other hundred and three have one. Twenty-four of the words are "the," fifteen are "and." There are four commas. The liturgical cadence of the paragraph derives in part from the placement of the commas (their presence in the second and fourth sentences, their absence in the first and third), but also from that repetition of "the" and of "and," creating a rhythm so pronounced that the omission of "the" before the word "leaves" in the fourth sentence ("and we saw the troops marching along the road and the dust rising and leaves, stirred by the breeze, falling") casts exactly what it was meant to cast, a chill, a premonition, a foreshadowing of the story to come, the awareness that the author has already shifted his attention from late summer to a darker season. The power of the paragraph, offering as it does the illusion but not the fact of specificity, derives precisely from this kind of deliberate omission, from the tension of withheld information. In the late summer of *what* year? *What* river, *what* mountains, *what* troops?

We all know the "life" of the man who wrote that paragraph. The rather reckless attractions of the domestic details became fixed in the national memory stream: *Ernest and Hadley have no money, so they ski at Cortina all winter. Pauline comes to stay. Ernest and Hadley are at odds with each other over Pauline, so they all take refuge at Juan-les-Pins. Pauline catches cold, and recuperates at the Waldorf-Astoria.* We have seen the snapshots: the celebrated author fencing with the bulls at Pamplona, fishing for marlin off Havana, boxing at Bimini, crossing the Ebro with the Spanish loyalists, kneeling beside "his" lion or "his" buffalo or "his" oryx on the Serengeti Plain. We have observed the celebrated author's survivors, read his letters, deplored or found lessons in his excesses, in his striking of attitudes, in the humiliations of his claim to personal machismo, in the degradations both derived from and revealed by his apparent tolerance for his own celebrity.

"This is to tell you about a young man named Ernest Hemingway, who lives in Paris (an American), writes for the *transatlantic review* and has a brilliant future," F. Scott Fitzgerald wrote to Maxwell Perkins in 1924. "I'd look him up right away. He's the real thing." By the time "the real thing" had seen his brilliant future both realized and ruined, he had entered the valley of extreme emotional fragility, of depressions so grave that by February of 1961, after the first of what would be two courses of shock treatment, he found himself unable to complete even the single sentence he had agreed to contribute to a ceremonial volume for President John F. Kennedy. Early on the Sunday morning of July 2, 1961, the celebrated author got out of his bed in Ketchum, Idaho, went downstairs, took a double-barreled Boss shotgun from a storage room in the cellar, and emptied both barrels into the center of his forehead. "I went downstairs," his fourth wife, Mary Welsh Hemingway, reported in her 1976 memoir, *How It Was,* "saw a crumpled heap of bathrobe and blood, the shotgun lying in the disintegrated flesh, in the front vestibule of the sitting room."

The didactic momentum of the biography was such that we sometimes forgot that this was a writer who had in his time made the English language new, changed the rhythms of the way both his own and the next few generations would speak and write and think. The very grammar of a Hemingway sentence dictated, or was dictated by, a certain way of looking at the world, a way of looking but not joining, a way of moving through but not attaching, a kind of romantic individualism distinctly adapted to its time and source. If we bought into those sentences, we would see the troops marching along the road, but we would not necessarily march with them. We would report, but not join. We would make, as Nick Adams made in the Nick Adams stories and as Frederic Henry made in *A Farewell to Arms,* a separate peace: "In the fall the war was always there, but we did not go to it any more."

So pervasive was the effect of this Hemingway diction that it became the voice not only of his admirers but even of those whose approach to the world was in no way grounded in romantic individualism. I recall being surprised, when I was teaching George Orwell in a class at Berkeley in 1975, by how much of Hemingway could be heard in his sentences. "The hills opposite us were grey and wrinkled like the skins of elephants," Orwell had written in *Homage to Catalonia* in 1938. "The hills across the valley of the Ebro were long and white," Hemingway had written in "Hills Like White Elephants" in 1927. "A mass of Latin words falls upon the facts like soft snow, blurring the outlines and covering up all the details," Orwell had written in *Politics and the English Language* in 1946. "I was always embarrassed by the words sacred, glorious, and sacrifice and the expression in vain," Hemingway had written in *A Farewell to Arms* in 1929. "There were many words that you could not stand to hear and finally only the names of places had dignity."

This was a man to whom words mattered. He worked at them, he understood them, he got inside them. When he was twenty-four years old and reading submissions to Ford Madox Ford's *transat-*

lantic review he would sometimes try rewriting them, just for practice. His wish to be survived by only the words he determined fit
for publication would have seemed clear enough. "I remember
Ford telling me that a man should always write a letter thinking of
how it would read to posterity," he wrote to Arthur Mizener in
1950. "This made such a bad impression on me that I burned
every letter in the flat including Ford's." In a letter dated May 20,
1958, addressed "To my Executors" and placed in his library safe
at La Finca Vigia, he wrote, "It is my wish that none of the letters
written by me during my lifetime shall be published. Accordingly,
I hereby request and direct you not to publish or consent to the
publication by others of any such letters."

His widow and executor, Mary Welsh Hemingway, describing the
burden of this restriction as one that "caused me continuous
trouble, and disappointment to others," eventually chose to violate
it, publishing excerpts from certain letters in *How It Was* and
granting permission to Carlos Baker to publish some six hundred
others in his *Ernest Hemingway: Selected Letters, 1917–1961.* "There
can be no question about the wisdom and rightness of the decision," Baker wrote, for the letters "will not only instruct and entertain the general reader but also provide serious students of literature with the documents necessary to the continuing investigation
of the life and achievements of one of the giants of twentieth-cen-
tury American fiction."

The peculiarity of being a writer is that the entire enterprise involves the mortal humiliation of seeing one's own words in print.
The risk of publication is the grave fact of the life, and, even
among writers less inclined than Hemingway to construe words as
the manifest expression of personal honor, the notion that words
one has not risked publishing should be open to "continuing
investigation" by "serious students of literature" could not be cal-
culated to kindle enthusiasm. "Nobody likes to be tailed," Hemingway himself had in 1952 advised one such investigator, Charles
A. Fenton of Yale, who on the evidence of the letters was torment-
ing Hemingway by sending him successive drafts of what would be
The Apprenticeship of Ernest Hemingway: The Early Years. "You do not
like to be tailed, investigated, queried about, by any amateur
detective no matter how scholarly or how straight. You ought to

be able to see that, Fenton." A month later Hemingway tried again. "I think you ought to drop the entire project," he wrote to Fenton, adding, "It is impossible to arrive at any truth without the co-operation of the person involved. That co-operation involves very nearly as much effort as for a man to write his autobiography." A few months later, he was still trying:

> In the first page or pages of your Mss. I found so many errors of fact that I could spend the rest of this winter re-writing and giving you all the true gen and I would not be able to write anything of my own at all. . . . Another thing: You have located unsigned pieces by me through pay vouchers. But you do not know which pieces were changed or re-written by the copy desk and which were not. I know nothing worse for a writer than for his early writing which has been re-written and altered to be published without permission as his own.
>
> Actually I know few things worse than for another writer to collect a fellow writer's journalism which his fellow writer has elected not to preserve because it is worthless and publish it.
>
> Mr. Fenton I feel very strongly about this. I have written you so before and I write you now again. Writing that I do not wish to publish, you have no right to publish. I would no more do a thing like that to you than I would cheat a man at cards or rifle his desk or wastebasket or read his personal letters.

It might seem safe to assume that a writer who commits suicide has been less than entirely engaged by the work he leaves unfinished, yet there appears to have been not much question about what would happen to the unfinished Hemingway manuscripts. These included not only "the Paris stuff" (as he called it), or *A Moveable Feast* (as Scribner's called it), which Hemingway had in fact shown to Scribner's in 1959 and then withdrawn for revision, but also the novels later published under the titles *Islands in the Stream* and *The Garden of Eden,* several Nick Adams stories, what Mrs. Hemingway called the "original treatment" of the bullfighting pieces published by *Life* before Hemingway's death (this became *The Dangerous Summer*), and what she described as "his semifictional account of our African safari," three selections from which she had published in *Sports Illustrated* in 1971 and 1972.

What followed was the systematic creation of a marketable product, a discrete body of work different in kind from, and in fact tending to obscure, the body of work published by Hemingway in his lifetime. So successful was the process of branding this product that in October, according to the House & Home section of the *New York Times,* Thomasville Furniture Industries introduced an "Ernest Hemingway Collection" at the International Home Furnishings Market in High Point, North Carolina, offering "96 pieces of living, dining and bedroom furniture and accessories" in four themes, "Kenya," "Key West," "Havana," and "Ketchum." "We don't have many heroes today," Marla A. Metzner, the president of Fashion Licensing of America, told the *Times.* "We're going back to the great icons of the century, as heroic brands." Ms. Metzner, according to the *Times,* not only "created the Ernest Hemingway brand with Hemingway's three sons, Jack, Gregory and Patrick," but "also represents F. Scott Fitzgerald's grandchildren, who have asked for a Fitzgerald brand."

That this would be the logical outcome of posthumous marketing cannot have been entirely clear to Mary Welsh Hemingway. During Hemingway's lifetime, she appears to have remained cool to the marketing impulses of A. E. Hotchner, whose thirteen-year correspondence with Hemingway gives the sense that he regarded the failing author not as the overextended and desperate figure the letters suggest but as an infinite resource, a mine to be worked, an element to be packaged into his various entertainment and publishing "projects." The widow tried to stop the publication of Hotchner's *Papa Hemingway,* and, although the correspondence makes clear that Hemingway himself had both trusted and relied heavily on its author, presented him in her own memoir mainly as a kind of personal assistant, a fetcher of manuscripts, an arranger of apartments, a Zelig apparition in crowd scenes. "When the *Ile de France* docked in the Hudson River at noon, March 27, we were elated to find Charlie Sweeny, my favorite general, awaiting us, together with Lillian Ross, Al Horowitz, Hotchner and some others."

In this memoir, which is memorable mainly for the revelation of its author's rather trying mixture of quite striking competence and strategic incompetence (she arrives in Paris on the day it is liberated and scores a room at the Ritz, but seems bewildered by the domestic problem of how to improve the lighting of the dining room at La Finca Vigia), Mary Welsh Hemingway shared her conviction, at which she appears to have arrived in the face of consid-

erable contrary evidence, that her husband had "clearly" expected
her to publish "some, if not all, of his work." The guidelines she
set for herself in this task were instructive: "Except for punctuation
and the obviously overlooked 'ands' and 'buts' we would present
his prose and poetry to readers as he wrote it, letting the gaps lie
where they were."

Well, there you are. You care about the punctuation or you don't,
and Hemingway did. You care about the "ands" and the "buts" or
you don't, and Hemingway did. You think something is in shape
to be published or you don't, and Hemingway didn't. "This is it;
there are no more books," Charles Scribner III told the *New York
Times* by way of announcing the "Hemingway novel" to be published in July of 1999, to celebrate the centennial year of his birth.
This piece of work, for which the title *True at First Light* was chosen
from the text ("In Africa a thing is true at first light and a lie by
noon and you have no more respect for it than for the lovely,
perfect weed-fringed lake you see across the sun-baked salt plain"),
is said to be the novel on which Hemingway was trying intermit-
tently to work between 1954, when he and Mary Welsh Hemingway
returned from the safari in Kenya which provides its narrative, and
his suicide in 1961.

This "African novel" seems to have presented at first only the
resistance that characterizes the early stage of any novel. In September of 1954, Hemingway wrote to Bernard Berenson from
Cuba about the adverse effect of air conditioning on this thing he
was doing: "You get the writing done but it's as false as though it
were done in the reverse of a greenhouse. Probably I will throw it
all away, but maybe when the mornings are alive again I can use
the skeleton of what I have written and fill it in with the smells and
the early noises of the birds and all the lovely things of this finca
which are in the cold months very much like Africa." In September
of 1955, he wrote again to Berenson, this time on a new typewriter,
explaining that he could not use his old one "because it has page
594 of the [African] book in it, covered over with the dust cover,
and it is unlucky to take the pages out." In November of 1955, he
reported to Harvey Breit, of the *New York Times,* "Am on page 689
and wish me luck kid." In January of 1956, he wrote to his attorney,
Alfred Rice, that he had reached page 810.

There then falls, in the *Selected Letters,* a certain silence on the matter of this African novel. Eight hundred and ten pages or no, there comes a point at which every writer knows when a book is not working, and every writer also knows when the reserves of will and energy and memory and concentration required to make the thing work simply may not be available. "You just have to *go on* when it is worst and most helpless — there is only one thing to do with a novel and that is go straight on through to the end of the damn thing," Hemingway had written to F. Scott Fitzgerald in 1929, when Fitzgerald was blocked on the novel that would be published in 1934 as *Tender Is the Night.*

In 1929, Hemingway was thirty. His concentration, or his ability to "*go on* when it is worst and most helpless," was still such that he had continued rewriting *A Farewell to Arms* while trying to deal, in the aftermath of his father's suicide in December of 1928, with the concerns of his mother, his sixteen-year-old sister, and his thirteen-year-old brother. "Realize of course that thing for me to do is not worry but get to work — finish my book properly so I can help them out with the proceeds," he had written to Maxwell Perkins within days of his father's funeral, and six weeks later he delivered the finished manuscript. He had seen one marriage destroyed, but not yet three. He was not yet living with the residue of the two 1954 plane crashes that had ruptured his liver, his spleen, and one of his kidneys, collapsed his lower intestine, crushed a vertebra, left first-degree burns on his face and head, and caused concussion and losses of vision and hearing. "Alfred this was a very rough year even before we smashed up in the air-craft," he wrote to Alfred Rice, who had apparently questioned his tax deductions for the African safari:

> But I have a diamond mine if people will let me alone and let me dig the stones out of the blue mud and then cut and polish them. If I can do it I will make more money for the Government than any Texas oilman that gets his depreciation. But I have been beat-up worse than you can be and still be around and I should be working steadily on getting better and then write and not think nor worry about anything else.

"The literal details of writing," Norman Mailer once told an interviewer, "involve one's own physiology or metabolism. You

begin from a standing start and have to accelerate yourself to the
point of cerebration where the words are coming — well, and in
order. All writing is generated by a certain minimum of ego: you
must assume a position of authority in saying that the way I'm
writing it is the only way it happened. Writer's block, for example,
is simply a failure of ego." In August of 1956, Hemingway advised
Charles Scribner, Jr., that he had "found it impossible to resume
work on the Africa book without some disciplinary writing," and
so was writing short stories.

In November of 1958, he mentioned to one of his children that
he wanted to "finish book" during a winter stay in Ketchum, but
the "book" at issue was now "the Paris stuff." In April of 1960, he
told Scribner to scratch this still untitled Paris book from the fall
list: "Plenty of people will probably think that we have no book
and that it is like all the outlines that Scott had and borrowed
money on that he never could have finished but you know that if
I did not want the chance to make it even better it could be
published exactly as you saw it with a few corrections of Mary's
typing." Ten months later, and five months before his death, in a
letter written to his editor at Scribner's between the two courses
of shock treatment administered to him at the Mayo Clinic in
Rochester, Minnesota, the writer tried, alarmingly, to explain what
he was doing:

> Have material arranged as chapters — they come to 18 — and am
> working on the last one — No *19* — also working on title. This is
> very difficult. (Have my usual long list — something wrong with all of
> them but am working toward it — Paris has been used so often it
> blights anything.) In pages typed they run 7, 14, 5, 6, $9\frac{1}{2}$, 6, 11, 9, 8,
> 9, $4\frac{1}{2}$, $3\frac{1}{2}$, 8, $10\frac{1}{2}$, $14\frac{1}{2}$, $38\frac{1}{2}$, 10, 3, 3: 177 pages + $5\frac{1}{2}$ pages +
> $1\frac{1}{4}$ pages.

I recall listening, some years ago at a dinner party in Berkeley, to
a professor of English present *The Last Tycoon* as irrefutable proof
that F. Scott Fitzgerald was a bad writer. The assurance with which
this judgment was offered so stunned me that I had let it slip into
the *donnée* of the evening before I managed to object. *The Last
Tycoon*, I said, was an unfinished book, one we had no way of
judging because we had no way of knowing how Fitzgerald might

have finished it. But of course we did, another guest said, and others joined in: We had Fitzgerald's "notes," we had Fitzgerald's "outline," the thing was "entirely laid out." Only one of us at the table that evening, in other words, saw a substantive difference between writing a book and making notes for it, or "outlining it," or "laying it out."

The most chilling scene ever filmed must be, for a writer, that moment in *The Shining* when Shelley Duvall looks at the manuscript on which her husband has been working and sees, typed over and over again on each of the hundreds of pages, only the single line: "All work and no play makes Jack a dull boy." The manuscript for what became *True at First Light* was, as Hemingway left it, some eight hundred and fifty pages long. The manuscript as edited for publication is half that. This editing was done by Hemingway's son Patrick, who has said that he limited his editing to condensing (which inevitably works to alter what the author may have intended, as anyone who has been condensed knows), changing only some of the place names, which may or may not have seemed a logical response to the work of the man who wrote "There were many words that you could not stand to hear and finally only the names of places had dignity."

This question of what should be done with what a writer leaves unfinished goes back, and is conventionally answered by citing works we might have lost had the dying wishes of their authors been honored. Virgil's *Aeneid* is mentioned. Franz Kafka's *The Trial* and *The Castle* are mentioned. In 1951, clearly shadowed by mortality, Hemingway judged that certain parts of a long four-part novel on which he had been working for a number of years were sufficiently "finished" to be published after his death, and specified his terms, which did not include the intrusion of any editorial hand and specifically excluded the publication of the unfinished first section. "The last two parts need no cutting at all," he wrote to Charles Scribner in 1951. "The third part needs quite a lot but it is very careful scalpel work and would need no cutting if I were dead. . . . The reason that I wrote you that you could always publish the last three parts separately is because I know you can in case through accidental death or any sort of death I should not be able to get the first part in proper shape to publish."

Hemingway himself, the following year, published the fourth part of this manuscript separately, as *The Old Man and the Sea*. The "first part" of the manuscript, the part not yet "in proper shape to publish," was, after his death, nonetheless published, as part of *Islands in the Stream*. In the case of the "African novel," or *True at First Light*, eight hundred and fifty pages reduced by half by someone other than their author can go nowhere the author intended them to go, but they can provide the occasion for a chat-show hook, a faux controversy over whether the part of the manuscript in which the writer on safari takes a Wakamba bride does or does not reflect a "real" event. The increasing inability of many readers to construe fiction as anything other than roman à clef, or the raw material of biography, is both indulged and encouraged. The *New York Times*, in its announcement of the publication of the manuscript, quoted Patrick Hemingway to this spurious point: "'Did Ernest Hemingway have such an experience?' he said from his home in Bozeman, Mont. 'I can tell you from all I know — and I don't know everything — he did not.'"

This is a denial of the idea of fiction, just as the publication of unfinished work is a denial of the idea that the role of the writer in his or her work is to make it. Those excerpts from *True at First Light* already published can be read only as something not yet made, notes, scenes in the process of being set down, words set down but not yet written. There are arresting glimpses here and there, fragments shored against what the writer must have seen as his ruin, and a sympathetic reader might well believe it possible that had the writer lived (which is to say had the writer found the will and energy and memory and concentration) he might have shaped the material, written it into being, made it work as the story the glimpses suggest, that of a man returning to a place he loved and finding himself at three in the morning confronting the knowledge that he is no longer the person who loved it and will never now be the person he had meant to be. But of course such a possibility would have been in the end closed to this particular writer, for he had already written that story, in 1936, and called it "The Snows of Kilimanjaro." "Now he would never write the things that he had saved to write until he knew enough to write them well," the writer in "The Snows of Kilimanjaro" thought as he lay dying of gangrene in Africa. And then, this afterthought, the saddest story: "Well, he would not have to fail at trying to write them either."

ANNIE DILLARD

For the Time Being

FROM NOTRE DAME MAGAZINE

IN 135 C.E., Romans killed Rabbi Akiva for teaching Torah. They killed him by flaying his skin and stripping his bones with curry-combs. He was eighty-five years old. A Roman currycomb in those days was an iron scraper; its blunt teeth combed mud and burrs from horsehair. To flay someone — an unusual torture — the wielder had to bear down. Perhaps the skin and muscles of an old scholar are comparatively loose.

"All depends on the preponderance of good deeds," Rabbi Akiva said. The weight of good deeds bears down on the balance scales. Paul Tillich also held this view. If the man who stripped Rabbi Akiva's bones with a currycomb bore down with a weight of, say 200 psi, how many pounds of good deeds tip the balance to the good?

"Are we only talking to ourselves in an empty universe?" a twen-tieth-century novelist asked. "The silence is often so emphatic. And we have prayed so much already."

Akiva Ben Joseph was born in the Judean lowlands in 50 C.E. He was illiterate and despised scholarship; he worked herding sheep. Then he fell in love with a rich man's daughter. She agreed to marry him only when he vowed to devote his life to studying Torah. So he did. He learned to read along with their son.

Rabbi Akiva systematized, codified, explained, analyzed, and amplified the traditional religious laws and practices in his pains-taking Mishnah and Midrash. Because of Akiva, Mishnah and Midrash joined scripture itself in Judaism's canon. His interpreta-tions separated Judaism from both Christian and Greek influence.

His contemporaries prized him for his tireless interpretation of each holy detail of Torah. They cherished him for his optimism, his modesty, his universalism (which included tolerance of, and intermarriage with, Samaritans), and his devotion to *Eretz Yisrael,* the land of Israel. He taught that "Thou shalt love thy neighbor as thyself" is the key idea in Torah.

Nelly Sachs wrote, "Who is like you, O Lord, among the silent, remaining silent through the suffering of His children?"

Emperor Hadrian of Rome had condemned Rabbi Akiva to his henchman and executioner Rufus. Rufus was present in the prison cell as the currycombs separated the man's skin and muscles from his bones. Some of Rabbi Akiva's disciples were there, too, likely on the street, watching and listening at the cell window.

Rabbi Akiva had taught his disciples to say, "Whatever the all-merciful does he does for the good" — the sentiment Voltaire ridiculed. During Akiva's innovative execution he was reciting the Shema, because this was the time of day for reciting the Shema. It was then his disciples remonstrated with him, saying, "Our master, to such an extent?"

Spooked that the dwindling rabbi continued to say prayers, Rufus asked him, conversationally, if he was a sorcerer. Rabbi Akiva replied that he was happy to die for God. He said he worshiped the Lord with all his heart, and with all his mind, and now he could add, "with all my soul."

When Rabbi Akiva died, Moses was watching from heaven. Moses saw the torture and martyrdom, and complained to God about it. Why did God let the Romans flay an eighty-five-year-old Torah scholar? Moses' question — the tough one about God's allowing human, moral evil — is reasonable only if we believe that a good God either causes or at any rate allows everything that happens, and that it's all for the best. (This is the doctrine Voltaire, and many another thinker before and since, questioned — or in Voltaire's case mocked.)

God told Moses, "*Shtok,* keep quiet. *Kakh ala bemakhshava lefanai,* this is how I see things." In another version of the same story, God replied to Moses, "Silence! This is how it is in the highest thought."

Rabbi Akiva taught a curious solution to the ever-galling problem that many good people and their children suffer enormously, while many louses and their children prosper and thrive in the pink of health. God punishes the good, he proposed, in this short life, for their few sins, and rewards them eternally in the world to come. Similarly, God rewards the evil-doers in this short life for their few good deeds, and punishes them eternally in the world to come. I do not know how that sat with people. It is, like every ingenious, God-fearing explanation of natural calamity, harsh all around.

Is it not late? A late time to be living? Are not our generations the important ones? For we have changed the world. Are not our heightened times the important ones? For we have nuclear bombs. Are we not especially significant because our century is? — our century and its unique Holocaust, its refugee populations, its serial totalitarian exterminations, our century and its antibiotics, silicon chips, men on the moon, and spliced genes? No, we are not and it is not. These times of ours are ordinary times, a slice of life like any other. Who can bear to hear this, or who will consider it? Though perhaps we are the last generation — now there is a comfort. Take the bomb threat away and what are we? We are ordinary beads on a never-ending string. Our time is a routine twist of an improbable yarn.

We have no chance of being here when the sun burns out. There must be something heroic about our time, something that lifts it above all those other times. Plague? Funny weather? Dire things are happening. People have made great strides at obliterating other people, but that has been the human effort all along, and our cohort has only enlarged the means, as have people in every century. Why are we watching the news, reading the news, keeping up with the news? Only to enforce our fancy — probably a necessary lie — that these are crucial times, and we are in on them. Newly revealed, and we are in the know: crazy people, bunches of them. New diseases, shifts in power, floods! Can the news from dynastic Egypt have been any different?

In the beginning, according to Rabbi Isaac Luria, God contracted himself — *zimzum*. The divine essence withdrew into itself to make room for a finite world. Evil became possible: those genetic defects that dog cellular life, those clashing forces which erupt in natural catastrophes, and those sins human minds invent and human hands perform.

Luria's Kabbalist creation story, however baroque, accounts boldly for both moral evil and natural calamity. The creator meant his light to emanate, ultimately, to man. Grace would flow downward through ten holy vessels, like water cascading. Cataclysm — some say creation itself — disrupted this orderly progression. The holy light burst the vessels. The vessels splintered and scattered. Sparks of holiness fell to the depths, and the opaque shards of the broken vessels (*gelippot*) imprisoned them. This is our bleak world. We see only the demonic shells of things. It is literally sensible to deny that God exists. In fact, God is hidden, exiled, in the sparks of divine light the shells entrap. So evil can exist, can continue to live: the spark of goodness within things, the Gnostic-like spark that even the most evil tendency encloses, lends evil its being.

"The sparks scatter everywhere," Martin Buber said. "They cling to material things as in sealed-up wells, they crouch in substances as in caves that have been bricked up, they inhale darkness and breathe out fear; they flutter about in the movements of the world, searching where they can lodge to be free."

The Jews in sixteenth-century Palestine were in exile — "a most cruel exile," Gershom Scholem called it. They had lived in Muslim Spain a thousand years — far longer than any Europeans have lived in the Americas. In 1492, Christians expelled Muslims and Jews. About ten thousand Spanish Jews moved to Palestine. In Safad they formed the core of the community of the devout. Here unmolested, they contemplated their exile, which they understood as symbolizing the world's exile from God. Even the divine is estranged from itself; its essence scatters in sparks. The *Shekinah* — the Divine Presence — is in exile from *Elohim,* the being of God, just as the Jews were in exile in Palestine.

Only redemption — restoration, *tikkun* — can return the sparks of light to their source in the primeval soul; only redemption can restore God's exiled presence to his being in eternity. Only redemption can reunite an exiled soul with its root. The holy person, however, can hasten redemption and help mend heaven and earth.

*

The presenting face of any religion is its mass of popular superstitions. It seems to take all the keenest thinkers of every religion in every generation to fend off this clamoring pack. In New Mexico in 1978, the face of Jesus arose in a tortilla. "I was just rolling out my husband's burrito . . ." the witness began her account. An auto-parts store in Progresso, Texas, attracted crowds when an oil stain on its floor resembled the Virgin Mary. Another virgin appeared in 1998 in Colma, California, in hardened sap on a pine trunk. At a Nashville coffee shop named Bongo Java, a cinnamon bun came out of the oven looking like Mother Teresa — the nun bun, papers called it. In 1996 in Leicester, England, the name of Allah appeared in a halved eggplant. Several cities — Kandy, Sri Lanka, is one — claim to own a tooth from the jaw of Buddha. A taxonomist who saw one of these said it belonged to a crocodile.

When he leads trips to Israel, Abbot Philip Lawrence of the monastery of Christ in the Desert in Abiquiu, New Mexico, gives only one charge to his flock. "When they show the stone with the footprint of Christ in it," he says, "don't laugh." There is an enormous footprint of Buddha, too, in Luang Prabang, Vietnam.

"Suddenly there is a point where religion becomes laughable," Thomas Merton wrote. "Then you decide that you are nevertheless religious." Suddenly!

One of the queerest spots on earth — I hope — is in Bethlehem. This is the patch of planet where, according to tradition, a cave once stabled animals, and where Mary gave birth to a son whose later preaching — scholars of every stripe agree, with varying enthusiasm — caused the occupying Romans to crucify him. Generations of Christians have churched over the traditional Bethlehem spot to the highest degree. Centuries of additions have made the architecture peculiar, but no one can see the church anyway, because many monasteries clamp onto it in clusters like barnacles. The Greek Orthodox Church owns the grotto site now, in the form of the Church of the Nativity.

There, in the Church of the Nativity, I took worn stone stairways to descend to levels of dark rooms, chapels, and dungeonlike corridors where hushed people passed. The floors were black stone or cracked marble. Dense brocades hung down old stone walls. Oil lamps hung in layers. Each polished silver or brass lamp seemed to absorb more light than its orange flame emitted, so the more lamps shone, the darker the space.

Packed into a tiny, domed upper chamber, Norwegians sang, as every other group did in turn, a Christmas carol. The stone dome bounced the sound around. The people sounded like seraphs singing inside a bell, sore amazed.

Descending once more I passed several monks, narrow men, fine-faced and black, who wore tall black hats and long black robes. Ethiopians, they use the oldest Christian rite. At a lower level, in a small room, I peered over half a stone wall and saw Europeans below; they whispered in a language I could not identify.

Distant music sounded deep, as if from within my ribs. The music was, in fact, people from all over the world in the upper chamber singing harmonies in their various tongues. The music threaded the vaults.

Now I climbed down innumerable dark stone stairs to the main part, the deepest basement: the Grotto of the Nativity. The grotto was down yet another smoky stairway at the back of a stone cave far beneath street level. This was the place. It smelled of wet sand. It was a narrow cave about ten feet wide; cracked marble paved it. Bunched tapers, bending grotesque in the heat, lighted a corner of the floor. People had to kneel, one by one, under arches of brocade hangings, and stretch into a crouch down among dozens of gaudy hanging lamps, to see it.

A fourteen-pointed silver star, two feet in diameter, covered a raised bit of marble floor at the cave wall. This silver star was the X that marked the spot: here, just here, the infant got born. Two thousand years of Christianity began here, where God emptied himself into man. Actually, many Christian scholars think "Jesus of Nazareth" was likely born in Nazareth. Early writers hooked his birth to Bethlehem to fit a prophecy. Here, now, the burning oils smelled heavy. It must have struck many people that we were competing with these lamps for oxygen.

In the center of the silver star was a circular hole. That was the bull's-eye, God's quondam target.

Crouching people leaned forward to wipe their fingers across the hole's flat bottom. When it was my turn, I knelt, bent under a fringed satin drape, reached across half the silver star, and touched its hole. I could feel some sort of soft wax in it. The hole was a quarter inch deep and six inches across, like a wide petri dish. A newborn's head would be too small for it; a newborn's body would be too big. I have never read any theologian who claims that God is particularly interested in religion, anyway.

Any patch of ground anywhere smacks more of God's presence on earth, to me, than did this marble grotto. The ugliness of the blunt and bumpy silver star impressed me. The bathetic pomp of the heavy, tasseled brocades, the marble, the censers hanging from chains, the embroidered antependium, the aspergillum, the crosiers, the ornate lamps — some humans' idea of elegance — bespoke grand comedy, too, that God put up with it. And why should he not? Things here on earth get a whole lot worse than bad taste.

"Every day," said Rabbi Nachman of Bratslav, "the glory is ready to emerge from its debasement."

It is "fatal," Teilhard said of the old belief that we suffer at the hands of God omnipotent. It is fatal to reason. It does not work. The omnipotence of God makes no sense if it requires the all-causingness of God. Good people quit God altogether at this point, and throw out the baby with the bath, perhaps because they last looked into God in their childhoods, and have not changed their views of divinity since. It is not the tooth fairy. In fact, even Aquinas dissolved the fatal problem of natural, physical evil by tinkering with God's omnipotence. As Baron von Hugel noted, Aquinas said that "the Divine Omnipotence must not be taken as the power to effect any imaginable thing, but only the power to effect what is within the nature of things."

Similarly, Teilhard called the explanation that God hides himself deliberately to test our love "hateful"; it is "mental gymnastics." Here: "The doctors of the church explain that the Lord deliberately hides himself from us in order to test our love. One would have to be irretrievably committed to mental gymnastics . . . not to feel the hatefulness of this solution."

Many times in Christian churches I have heard the pastor say to God, "All your actions show your wisdom and love." Each time I reach in vain for the courage to rise and shout, "That's a lie!" — just to put things on a solid footing.

"He has cast down the mighty from their thrones, and has lifted up the lowly.

"He has filled the hungry with good things, and the rich he has sent away empty." Again, Paul writes to the Christians in Rome, "In all things God works for the good of those who love him."

When was that? I missed it. In China, in Israel, in the Yemen, in the Ecuadorean Andes and the Amazon basin, in Greenland, Iceland, and Baffin Island, in Europe, on the shore of the Beaufort Sea inside the Arctic Circle, and in Costa Rica, in the Marquesan Islands and the Tuamotus, and in the United States, I have seen the rich sit secure on their thrones and send the hungry away empty. If God's escape clause is that he gives only spiritual things, then we might hope that the poor and suffering are rich in spiritual gifts, as some certainly are, but as some of the comfortable are too. In a soup kitchen, I see suffering. *Deus Otiosus* — do-nothing God, who, if he has power, abuses it.

Of course God wrote no scriptures, neither chapter nor verse. It is foolish to blame or quit him for his admirer's claims superstitious or otherwise. "God is not on trial," I read somewhere. "We are not jurors but suppliants."

Maybe "all your actions show your wisdom and love" means that the precious few things we know that God did, and does, are in fact unambiguous in wisdom and love, and all other events derive not from God but only from blind chance, just as they seem to.

The Baal Shem Tov, by his own account, ascended to heaven many times. During these ascents, his friends said, he stood bent for many hours while his soul rose. He himself related in a letter on his return from two such vertical expeditions that he could not, much as he tried, deflect either moral evils or natural calamities. He could, however, report how God explained his actions. At that time Polish Christians were already killing Jews. On Rosh Hashanah (September 15, 1746) during an ascent to heaven, the Baal Shem Tov complained about the killings to God. He knew that some Jews apostasized, and they died along with the devout. Why — why any of it? God's answer: "So that no son of Israel would convert." (It would not even save their lives.) Later, an epidemic was scourging Poland. Again on Rosh Hashanah the Baal Shem Tov's soul climbed to heaven. Why the epidemic? The epidemic, God gave him to understand, came because he himself, the Baal Shem Tov, had prayed, "Let us fall into the hands of the Lord but let us not fall into the hands of man." Now God, into whose

plaguey hands they had fallen, asked him on the spot, "Why do
you want to cancel?" — to cancel, that is, your earlier prayer. Now
you want the Christian Poles instead of the epidemic? The best
bargain the Baal Shem Tov could strike was to keep the epidemic
from his town.

In other words, the Baal Shem Tov, who was not a theologian,
believed that God caused evil events — both moral evil (the Jew-
killing Poles) and natural evil (the epidemic) — to teach or punish. The Baal Shem Tov learned much about God, but theodicy
was not his bailiwick, and he did not shed the old "fatal" explanation that we suffer at the hands of God omnipotent.

In 1976 an earthquake in Tangshan killed 750,000 people.
Before it quaked, many survivors reported, the earth shone with
an incandescent light.

"Your fathers did eat manna and are dead," Jesus told people —
one of his cruelest remarks. Trafficking directly with the divine, as
the manna-eating wilderness generation did, and as Jesus did,
confers no immunity to death or hazard. You can live as a particle
crashing about and colliding in a welter of materials with God, or
you can live as a particle crashing about and colliding in a welter
of materials without God. But you cannot live outside the welter
of colliding materials.

Are we ready to think of all humanity as a living tree, carrying on
splendidly without us? We easily regard a bee hive or an ant colony
as a single organism, and even a school of fish, a flock of dunlin,
a herd of elk. And we easily and correctly regard an aggregate of
individuals, a sponge or coral or lichen or slime mold, as one
creature — but us? When we people differ, and know our consciousness, and love? Even lovers, even twins, are strangers who will
love and die alone. And we like it this way, at least in the West; we
prefer to endure any agony of isolation rather than merge and
extinguish our selves in an abstract "humanity" whose fate we
should hold dearer than our own. Who could say, I'm in agony
because my child died, but that's all right, mankind as a whole has
abundant children? The religious idea sooner or later challenges
the notion of the individual. The Buddha taught each disciple to
vanquish his fancy that he possessed an individual self. Huston

Smith suggests that our individuality resembles a snowflake's: the
seas evaporate water, clouds build and loose water in snowflakes,
which dissolve and go to sea. This simile galls. What have I to do
with the ocean, I with my unique and novel hexagons and spikes?
Is my very mind a wave in the ocean, a wave the wind flattens, a
flaw the wind draws like a finger?

We know we must yield, if only intellectually. Okay, we're a lousy
snowflake. Okay, we're a tree. These dead loved ones we mourn
were only those brown lower branches a tree shades and kills as it
grows; the tree itself is thriving. But what kind of tree are we
growing here, that could be worth such waste and pain? For each
of us loses all we love, everyone we love. We grieve and leave. What
marvels shall these future whizzes, damn their eyes, accomplish?

"How can evil exist in a world created by God, the Beneficent
One? It can exist, because entrapped deep inside the force of evil
there is a spark of goodness. This spark is the source of life of the
evil tendency. . . . Now, it is the specific mission of the Jew to free
the entrapped holy sparks from the grip of the forces of evil by
means of Torah study and prayer. Once the holy sparks are released, evil, having lost its life-giving core, will cease to exist." So
wrote Rabbi Yehuda Aryeh Leib Alter of Ger, in nineteenth-cen-
tury Poland. It was the Baal Shem Tov who taught this vital idea.

God is spirit, spirit expressed infinitely in the universe, who does
not give as the world gives. His home is absence, and there he finds
us. In the coils of absence we meet him by seeking him. God lifts
our souls to their roots in his silence. Natural materials clash and
replicate, shaping our fates. We lose the people we love, we lose
our vigor, and we lose our lives. Perhaps, and at best, God knows
nothing of these temporal accidents, but knows souls only. This
God does not direct the universe, he underlies it. Or he "prolongs
himself" into it, in Teilhard's terms. Or in dear nutcase Joel Gold-
smith's terms, God is the universe's consciousness. The consciousness of divinity is divinity itself. The more we wake to holiness, the
more of it we give birth to, the more we introduce, expand, and
multiply it on earth, the more God is "on the field."

God is — for the most part — out of the physical loop of the fallen
world he created, let us say. Or God is the loop, or pervades the
loop, or the loop runs in God like a hole in his side he never

fingers. Certainly God is not a member of the loop like the rest of us, passing the bucket to splash the fire, kicking the bucket, passing the buck. After all, the semipotent God has one hand tied behind his back. (I cannot prove that with the other hand he wipes and stirs our souls from time to time; he spins like a fireball through our skulls, and knocks open our eyes so we see flaming skies and fall to the ground and say "Abba!")

A man who struggles long to pray and study Torah will be able to discover the sparks of divine light in all of creation, in each solitary bush and grain and woman and man. And when he cleaves strenuously to God for many years he will be able to release the sparks, to unwrap and lift these particular shreds of holiness, and return them to God. This is the human task: to direct and channel the sparks' return. This is *tikkun,* restoration.

Yours is a holy work on earth right now, they say, whatever that work is, if you tie your love and desire to God. You do not deny or flee the world, but redeem it, all of it — just as it is.

Who is dead? The Newtonian God, some call that tasking and antiquated figure who haunts children and repels strays, who sits on the throne of judgment frowning and figuring, and who with the strength of his arm dishes out human fates, in the form of cancer or cash, to 5.9 billion people — to teach, dazzle, rebuke, or try us, one by one, and to punish or reward us, day by day, for our thoughts, words, and deeds.

"The great Neolithic proprietor," Teilhard called him, the God of the old cosmos, who was not yet known as the soul of the world but as its mage. History, then, was a fix.

People once held a "Deuteronomic" idea of God, says Rabbi Lawrence Kushner. God intervened in human affairs "without human agency." He was a Lego lord.

The first theological task, Paul Tillich said fifty years ago, by which time it was already commonplace, is to remove absurdities in interpretation.

It is an old idea, that God is not omnipotent. Seven centuries have passed since Aquinas wrote that God has power to effect only what is in the nature of things. Leibnitz also implied it; working within the "possible world" limits God's doings. Now the notion of

God the Semipotent has trickled down to the theologian in the
street. Teilhard in his day called the belief that we suffer at the
hands of an omnipotent God "fatal," remember, and indicated
only one escape: to recognize that if God allows us both to suffer
and to sin it is "because he cannot here and now cure us and
show himself to us" — because we ourselves have not yet evolved
enough. Paul Tillich said in the 1940s that "omnipotence" symbol-
izes Being's power to overcome finitude and anxiety in the long
run, while never being able to eliminate them.

God is no more blinding people with glaucoma, or testing them
with diabetes, or purifying them with spinal pain, or choreograph-
ing the seeding of tumor cells through lymph, or fiddling with
chromosomes than he is jimmying floodwaters or pitching tornadoes at towns. God is no more cogitating which among us he plans
to be born as bird-headed dwarfs or elephant men — or to kill by
AIDS or kidney failure, heart disease, childhood leukemia, or
sudden infant death syndrome — than he is pitching lightning
bolts at pedestrians, triggering rock slides, or setting fires. The very
least likely things for which God might be responsible are what
insurers call "acts of God."

Then what, if anything, does he do? If God does not cause
everything that happens, does God cause anything that happens?
Is God completely out of the loop?

Sometimes God moves loudly, as if spinning to another place
like ball lightning. God is, oddly, personal; this God knows. Sometimes en route, dazzlingly or dimly, he shows an edge of himself
to souls who seek him, and the people who bear those souls,
marveling, know it, and see the skies carousing around them, and
watch cells stream and multiply in green leaves. He does not give
as the world gives; he leads invisibly over many years, or he wallops
for thirty seconds at a time. He may touch a mind, too, making a
loud sound, or a mind may feel the rim of his mind as he nears.
Such experiences are gifts to beginners. "Later on," a Hasid master
said, "you don't see these things anymore." (Having seen, people
of varying cultures turn — for reasons unknown, and by a mechanism unimaginable — to aiding and serving the poor and afflicted.)

Mostly God is out of the physical loop. Or the loop is a spinning hole in his side. Simone Weil takes a notion from Rabbi Isaac Luria to acknowledge that God's hands are tied. To create, God did not extend himself but withdrew himself; he humbled and obliterated himself, and left outside himself the domain of necessity, in which he does not intervene. Even in the domain of souls, he intervenes only "under certain conditions."

Does God stick a finger in, if only now and then? Does God budge, nudge, hear, twitch, help? Is heaven pliable? Or is praying eudaemonistically — praying for things and events, for rain and healing — delusional? Physicians agree that prayer for healing can work what they routinely call miracles, but of course the mechanism could be self-hypnosis. Paul Tillich devoted only two paragraphs in his three-volume systematic theology to prayer. Those two startling paragraphs suggest, without describing, another mechanism. To entreat and to intercede is to transform situations powerfully. God participates in bad conditions here by including them in his being and ultimately overcoming them. True prayer surrenders to God; that willing surrender itself changes the situation a jot or two by adding power which God can use. Since God works in and through existing conditions, I take this to mean that when the situation is close, when your friend might die or might live, then your prayer's surrender can add enough power — mechanism unknown — to tilt the balance. Though it won't still earthquakes or halt troops, it might quiet cancer or quell pneumonia. For Tillich, God's activity is by no means interference, but instead divine creativity — the ongoing creation of life with all its greatness and danger. I don't know. I don't know beans about God.

Nature works out its complexities. God suffers the world's necessities along with us, and suffers our turning away, and joins us in exile. Christians might add that Christ hangs, as it were, on the cross forever, always incarnate, and always nailed.

"Spiritual path" is the hilarious popular term for those night-blind mesas and flayed hills in which people grope, for decades on end, with the goal of knowing the absolute. They discover others spread under the stars and encamped here and there by watchfires, in groups or alone, in the open landscape; they stop for a sleep, or for several years, and move along without knowing toward what or why. They leave whatever they find, picking up each stone, carrying it awhile, and dropping it gratefully and without regret, for it is not the absolute, though they cannot say what it is.

Their life's fine, impossible goal justifies the term "spiritual." Nothing, however, can justify the term "path" for their bewildered and empty stumbling, this blackened vagabondage — except one thing: they don't quit. They stick with it. Year after year they put one foot in front of the other, though they fare nowhere. Year after year they find themselves still feeling with their fingers for lumps in the dark.

The planet turns under their steps like a water wheel rolling; constellations shift without anyone's gaining ground. They are presenting themselves to the unseen gaze of emptiness. Why do they want to do this? They hope to learn how to be useful.

Their feet catch in nets; they untangle them when they notice, and keep moving. They hope to learn where they came from. "The soul teaches incessantly," said Rabbi Pinhas, "but it never repeats." Decade after decade they see no progress. But they do notice, if they look, that they have left doubt behind. Decades ago they left behind doubt about this or that doctrine, abandoning the issues as unimportant. Now, I mean, they have left behind the early doubt that this feckless prospecting in the dark for the unseen is a reasonable way to pass one's life.

"Plunge into matter," Teilhard said — and at another time, "Plunge into God." And he said this fine thing: "By means of all created things, without exception, the divine assails us, penetrates us, and molds us. We imagine it as distant and inaccessible, whereas in fact we live steeped in its burning layers."

Only by living completely in the world can one learn to believe. One must abandon every attempt to make something of oneself — even to make of oneself a righteous person. Dietrich Bonhoeffer wrote this in a letter from prison a year before the Nazis hanged him for resisting Nazism and plotting to assassinate Hitler.

"I can and must throw myself into the thick of human endeavor, and with no stopping for breath," said Teilhard, who by no means stopped for breath. But what distinguishes oneself "completely in the world" (Bonhoeffer) or throwing oneself "into the thick of human endeavor" (Teilhard), as these two prayerful men did, from any other life lived in the thick of things? A secular broker's life, a shoe salesman's life, a mechanic's, a writer's, a farmer's? Where else is there? The world and human endeavor catch and hold everyone alive but a handful of hobos, nuns, and monks. Were these two men especially dense, that they spent years learning what every kid already knows, that life here is all there is? Authorities in Rome or the Gestapo forbade them each to teach (as secular Rome had forbidden Rabbi Akiva to teach). One of them in his density went to prison and died on a scaffold. The other in his density kept his vows despite Rome's stubborn ignorance and righteous cruelty and despite the importunings of a woman he loved. No.

We live in all we seek. The hidden shows up in too-plain sight. It lives captive on the face of the obvious — the people, events, and things of the day — to which we as sophisticated children have long since become oblivious. What a hideout: holiness lies spread and borne over the surface of time and stuff like color.

What to do? There is only matter, Teilhard said; there is only spirit, the kabbalists and gnostics said. These are essentially identical views. Each impels an individual soul to undertake to divinize, transform, and complete the world, to — as these thinkers say quite as if there were both matter and spirit — "subject a little more matter to spirit," to "lift up the fallen and to free the imprisoned," to "establish in this our place a dwelling place of the Divine Presence," to "work for the redemption of the world," to "extract spiritual power without letting any of it be lost," to "help the holy spiritual substance to accomplish itself in that section of Creation in which we are living," to "mend the shattered unity of the divine worlds," to "force the gates of the spirit," and cry, "'Let me come by.'"

Our lives come free; they're on the house to all comers, like the shopkeeper's wine. God decants the universe of time in a stream, and our best hope is to, by our own awareness, step into the stream and serve, empty as flumes, to keep it moving.

The birds were mating all over Galilee. I saw swifts mate in midair. At Kibbutz Lavi, in the wide-open hills above the Sea of Galilee, 300 feet above me under the sky, the two swifts flew together in swoops, falling and catching. These alpine swifts were large, white below. How do birds mate in midair? They start high. Their beating wings tilt them awkwardly sometimes and part those tiny places where they join; often one of the pair stops flying and they lose altitude. They separate, rest in a tree for a minute, and fly again. Alone they rise fast, tensely, until you see only motes that chase, meet — you, there, here, out of all this air! — and spiral down; breaks your heart. At dusk, I learned later, they climb so high that at night they actually sleep in the air.

Rabbi Menachem Nahum of Chernobyl: "All being itself is derived from God and the presence of the Creator is in each created thing." This double notion is pan-entheism — a word to which I add a hyphen to emphasize its difference from pantheism. Pan-entheism, according to David Tracy, theologian at the University of Chicago, is the private view of most Christian intellectuals today. Not only is God immanent in everything, as plain old pantheists hold, however loosely, but more profoundly everything is simultaneously in God, within God the transcendent. There is a divine, not just bushes.

I saw doves mate on sand. It was early morning. The male dove trod the female on a hilltop path. Beyond them in blue haze lay the Sea of Galilee, and to the north Mount Meron and the town of Safad traversing the mountain Jebel Kan'an. Other doves were calling from nearby snags. To writer Florida Scott Maxwell, doves say, "Too true, dear love, too true." But to poet Margaret Gibson, doves in Mexico say, "No hope, no hope." An observant Jew recites a grateful prayer at seeing landscape — mountains, hills, seas, rivers, and deserts, which are, one would have thought, pretty much unavoidable sights. "Blessed art Thou, O Lord, our God, King of the Universe, THE MAKER OF ALL CREATION." One utters this blessing also when he meets the sea again — at seeing the Mediterranean Sea, say, after an interval of thirty days.

All the religions of Abraham deny that the world, the colorful array that surrounds and grips us, is illusion, even though from time to time anyone may see the vivid veil part. But no one can deny that God per se is wholly invisible, or deny that his voice is very still, very small, or explain why.

That night there was a full moon. I saw it rise over a caperbush, a still grove of terebinths, and a myrtle. According to the Talmud, when a person is afraid to walk at night, a burning torch is worth two companions, and a full moon is worth three. Blessed are Thou, O Lord our God, creator of the universe, who brings on evening; whose power and might fills the world; who did a miracle for me in this place; WHO HAS KEPT US IN LIFE AND BROUGHT US TO THIS TIME.

BRIAN DOYLE

The Meteorites

FROM THE AMERICAN SCHOLAR

THE SUMMER I was eighteen, hardly more than a child myself, I found myself ministering to a mob of boys, age four to six, who ran like deer, cried like infants, fought like cats, and cursed like stevedores. My first day as their camp counselor was utter chaos, in part because the boys were all wearing their names pinned to their chests on fluttering paper, and the papers flew off in the brisk early summer wind, and the pins stuck the boys, and they stuck each other with the pins, etc. But things settled down over the next few days, and we became easy with each other, as easy as a coltish and dreamy teenage boy can be with a gaggle of boys mere months, in some cases, from toddlerhood.

There was David, who hardly spoke, and Daniel, who spoke for him and who wept when he soiled himself once, too frightened to tell me his pressing need. David told me about it, quietly, touching me on the shoulder, whispering *Counselor, Danny needs you.* Daniel, five years old, was the first child I ever wiped clean, and I believe now that when we stood together in a sweltering dirty toilet on a July morning many years ago, Daniel sobbing convulsively as I washed him with a moist cloth, that we were engaged in a gentle sacrament: Daniel learning that he must confess to be cleansed, me understanding dimly that my silence with this weeping child was the first wise word I had ever spoken.

There was Anthony, a tough even then; and there were his running mates, brothers who guarded their real names and went by Tom and Tim; and there was Lucius, a long lock of a boy, closed for repairs all that summer, unwilling to be touched, first to lash

out. There was Miguel, age four physically, age fourteen emotionally, who fell in love with the ethereally lovely teenage girl who ran
the arts-and-crafts room. Miguel came to me one rainy morning
and asked *Counselor, can you give me away?* I conducted negotiations,
traded him, and saw him only occasionally the rest of the summer,
usually trailing in the scented wake of his love, sucked along in her
sweet eddy like a lifeboat trailing an exquisitely beautiful ocean
liner. Although once, late in the afternoon, just as the buses were
pulling away in pairs from the parking lot, I saw Miguel, alone,
sitting in a front passenger seat, buckled in, hunched, sobbing;
and for a moment, for all his eerie bravura, he was a baby again,
frightened and bereft. I was not man enough myself then to go to
him, and I drove away and left him in tears.

A sin: not my first, not my last.

There were Seth and Saul and Milton, who arrived together
every morning in a large car driven by a silent man in a uniform,
the boys spilling out of the car with gym bags intertwined like forest
vines, the three of them inseparably tangled, yet apparently incapable of affection. They argued all day long in their shrill birdy
voices, argued about balls and lanyards and swim trunks, about
towels and mothers and thermos jugs, about sneakers and small
gluey houses made of ice-cream sticks, argued all the way back to
the elm tree where they waited late in the day for their driver, who
never once opened his mouth, but drove up silently in the humming car, parked, emerged slowly from the front seat (unfolding
himself in stages like an enormous jackknife), ushered the boys
into the back seat (their thin sharp voices hammering away at each
other like the jabs of featherweights), closed the back door (the
camp air suddenly relieved of the shivered fragments of their tiny
angers), plopped back into the front seat (the fat dark leather
cushions exhaling sharply with a pneumatic hiss), and drove away
(the long dark car dervishing the leaves of summer in its wake).

These then were the Meteorites, ten strong before we traded
Miguel, nine strong on good days, that is to say the days when
David's mother let him come to camp. She worried that he was
autistic, which he was not, just quiet to the point of monastic
silence, except when it came to jelly orgies, during which he
howled as madly as his fellows as the jelly was cornered, slain, and

gobbled raw. None of the Meteorites ate anything but jelly, sopping, dripping, quivering plates of it, attacked swiftly with white plastic spoons, the spoons clicking metronomically against their teeth, the vast cacophonous lunchroom filled to bursting with small sweating children shrieking and gulping down jelly as fast as they could get the shrieks out and the jelly in. In my first days in the jelly maelstrom, I raged at the boys as loudly as they howled at me; but by the end of the summer, I had learned to sit quietly and watch the waves of sound crash on the gooey tables, slide halfway up the long windows, and slowly recede.

Although I was by title a camp counselor, there was no camp proper at the camp, which was actually a vast estate owned by the town and rented out in the summer to an organization that offered the summer day-camp experience to children from three counties for six different fee scales, the lowest just manageable for poor families and the highest enough to buy a car. The estate house itself was enormous, labyrinthine, falling apart, very nearly a castle in its huge architectural inexplicability. Its unkempt grounds sprawled for many acres of fields, forests, and glades. Beneath the honeycombed house ran a small-gauge railroad that the childless owner had built for his nieces and nephews; it consisted of three cars, each as big as a sofa, and an ingeniously laid track that slipped in and out of the house and hill like a sinuous animal. The cars and track were, of course, expressly forbidden to campers and counselors alike, and so, in the way of all things forbidden, they were mesmerizingly alluring and were filled every evening with counselors in various states of undress and inebriation.

But the counselors in the railroad cars at night were only a fraction of the counselors as a whole, for most of us drove off in the afternoon in the camp's buses, carting home our charges and returning them sticky and tired to their parents. The buses peeled away two by two, and when they were gone, the camp stood nearly silent in the long afternoon light, bereft of the bustling populace of the day except, here and there in the forest fringes or sunning by the pool, a few counselors in entangled pairs. Once that summer I persuaded a friend to take my bus route, and I stayed at camp until dark. I clambered up the stairs inside the house as far as I could go, and then climbed out onto a roof and sat for hours, high above the tops of the oaks and maples, watching. I remember

the long bars of slanting light, the sighing and snapping of the
metal roof as it cooled from the roaring heat of the day, the soaring
of a brown hawk over the farthest softball field, the burbling of
three pigeons on a nearby roofline, the wriggles of marijuana
smoke from the archery yard, the faint sounds of voices far below
me, under the house, in the tunnels. When dusk came, I climbed
down, leaving the roof to the pigeons. I could pick out the shapes
of counselors against the hunched trees, some running, some
walking arm in arm, the only lights in the thick grainy twilight the
blazing ends of their cigarettes and joints, moving through the
dark like meteorites. I found a friend and hitched a ride home.

The Meteorites and I were for the most part interested in the same
things — games, balls, hawks, bones, food, trees, hats, buses, songs
with snickered words about body functions, the girl who graced
Miguel's dreams, and archery. They were absolutely *obsessed* with
archery, although they could hardly handle even the tiniest bows,
and even those bows mostly snapped emptily and whizzed over
their ducking heads when they tried to draw back the strings, the
arrows falling heavily to the ground without even a semblance of
flight. When Meteorites ran away from the herd, which they did
about once per week per boy, they could without fail be found in
the archery alley, a broad grassy sward lined with stone walls and
sheltered by sycamores whose fingers waved high above us and sent
down shifting flitches of sunlight.

My great fear as counselor was that runaway boys would head
either to the pool or through the woods to the highway, but they
never did, not once. To the bows they went like arrows, and I would
find them there a little later, watching the patient archery girl show
them, for the hundredth time, how to grip the bow, how to notch
the arrow to the string (the arrow shaking badly), how to pull the
curve of the bow back to their sighting eye (their soprano grunts
like the hoarse chuffing of pigeons as they hauled on the little
bows with all the power they could muster), and how to loose the
arrow with a flick of the fingers (a rain of bows in the air, a shower
of arrows falling limply to the earth). At that point I would emerge
from the sycamores and reclaim my lost Meteorite.

I don't remember that I ever scolded a runaway, for the archery
girl was beautiful as well as gentle, and the archery lane a tranquil

island. Years later, when I read books about the Middle Ages in England and France, filled with castles and falconry and archery and knights and such, my mind reflexively set the action in that quiet green alley where bows flew and arrows lay facedown in the grass. For all the violence of the sharp arrows that did, on rare occasions, actually puncture the hay-stuffed targets, the archery lane was a wonderfully peaceful place, and my mind wanders back there even now, from the chaos and hubbub of my middle years.

The days of the Meteorites were circumscribed by geography. We were to be in certain places at certain times — the basketball court in the early morning (dew on the court, a toad or two), the arts-and-crafts room midmorning (Miguel's eyes riveted to the face of his beloved), the gym before lunch (the rubbery slam of dodge-balls against walls, the clatter of glasses flying to the floor when a small boy was hit full in the face), the softball field after lunch (languid, hot, song of cicadas), the pool (shimmering and cool and perfect) and archery lane in midafternoon, the basketball court again late in the day. I was nominally the basketball teacher, and so conducted ragged drills and motley scrimmages not only for the Meteorites, some of whom were barely bigger than the ball, but also for young Comets, Planets, and Asteroids (known to the rest of the camp as Hemorrhoids). I also coached the older boys, who came to the court in increasingly insolent waves, ending with my last class of the day, the Seniors, sneeringly fourteen and fifteen years old, some as tall and strong as their teacher, and one — only one, always one — determined to defeat his teacher in pitched combat.

That one was Andy, Randy Andy, sniggering scourge of the Senior Girls, artfully tousled black hair and pukka-shell necklace, quick fists and a switchblade carried for show. Andy stole a bus, stole money, groped girls, smoked dope, came to camp drunk, started a brushfire near the softball field, cursed the camp direc-tor, urinated on walls, crucified toads to trees, beat a smaller boy bloody, and, hours after he struck out near the end of a counselors-Seniors softball game, carefully smashed all sixteen of the camp's bats to splinters — sizes 24 (Pee Wee Reese model) through 42 (Richie Allen model).

I have sometimes imagined the dark poetry of that act, the camp silent after hours, Andy emerging from his hiding place in the estate house, strolling down through the gathering dusk to the softball fields, dragging out the dusty canvas bat bag from the equipment shed, selecting the Pee Wee Reese model (you want to start small before working up to Dick Allen), taking a couple of practice cuts, selecting a young oak to absorb the blow in its belly, and then the sick *crump* of bat barrel against tree bone and the sudden green welt lashed oozing into the oak, and then a second swing and crack and shatter as the bat explodes. Andy drops the shaggy handle, shakes his hands to shuck the sting, and reaches for a 26: a Luis Aparicio. And through the thin woods the sound of vengeance echoes for almost an hour, until darkness.

Andy and I hated each other from the first minute we met, as he slouched against a tree and muttered a joke under his breath while I explained a basketball drill to the restless Seniors. I was only a few years older than he was, and nervous, so I got in his face, and from that instant — a windy late afternoon in July, our faces an inch apart, his blackheads marching from one temple to another, my finger poking too hard into the little bowl of skin at the base of his throat — we were relentless enemies. It is a mark of my own chalky insecurity and mulish youth that I hounded Andy every chance I got, reporting his crimes to the director, ragging him from the sidelines of softball games, and once, by incredible luck, catching his fist in midblow (he was about to punch another boy for the second time) and so mortifying him before a girl, the ultimate humiliation for him and for me too, then. And now.

So every day at three o'clock, when the Seniors slouched up to my court and ran my drills and then circled watchfully as Andy and I stripped off our shirts to play one-on-one, there was the entrancing shock of possible blood in the air, and once there *was* blood in the air, mine. Andy waited patiently for the right long rebound and the right angle of me chasing it headlong, and as I lunged for the ball, he lashed his elbow into my mouth as hard as he could. But I won, and his hate rose another notch. I remember the garlic taste of my rage in my throat, and the tight circle of boys around us, staring, the only sounds the sharp shuffle of sneakers on pavement and the relentless hammer of the ball.

Flirting with the female lifeguards was a nearly universal and daily habit among the hundreds of male creatures at the camp. It was

a rare male counselor who did not detour his charges past the pool
on their way to anywhere else. Not even the camp director, an
ebullient and brilliant con man named Buck, was immune. He
arranged his office in such a way that his gaze naturally strolled
out the open French doors of the house veranda and down a short
flight of stone steps to the pool. He spun on his huge chair, his
eyes on the bikinis in the middle distance, recruiting students *there
is no camp on the entire North Shore that can offer the recreational and
educational amenities we can*, charming parents *I understand that Marc
has been named Camper of the Week three weeks running an unprecedented
honor I may say and speaking of honor we would be honored to see you
and Mr. Harrow at the annual Inner Circle dinner for special friends and
benefactors*, chasing delinquent fees *I don't think you understand, Mrs.
Kaplan, if we do not receive remuneration of your outstanding bill we will
have to cancel Glen's pool privileges which will come as a terrible blow to
the boy*, evading creditors *my accountant tells me that the check was
delivered yesterday via registered mail*, arguing with his wife *you told the
Kaufmans their twins could come free!?*, flirting with his wife *what say
we knock off early and knock one off*, checking his toupee in the mirror
goddamned rugs, writing camp advertisements *more than one hundred
acres of fields and fun staffed by one hundred board-certified educators*,
badgering food and gasoline and sports equipment and T-shirt
vendors *yes, sixteen bats, various weights*, and placating angry parents
*I can assure you Mrs. Steinberg that David's counselor was with him from
the minute the accident occurred until his arrival at the oral surgeon's
office, and that this young fellow, a Cornell University engineering major
I might add, had foresightedly brought both of David's teeth with him in
the ambulance*. At every possible opportunity, Buck sauntered down
to the pool, ostensibly to check on the insurance, the floats, the
filter, the schedule, but really to savor the lithe bodies of his female
employees. Because the camp sat high on a windy hill not far from
the ocean, it was cold in the morning, even in July and August,
and the lifeguards wore their sweatsuits until noon or so. After a
few weeks I noticed that Buck conducted all his business in the
morning so that he could be at the pool in the afternoon, when
the sweatsuits were off.

    The geometric light of high summer, the smell of chlorine, the
shouts of children in the shallow end, the cannonball geysers of
older boys hurtling into the middle by the bobbined rope, the
streaming hair of Senior girls emerging blinking from the deep

end, I remember it all now, my mind back in the itchy young cat-body I had then. I am bouncing down the stone steps toward the pool, peeling off my wet shirt, one eye on the shambling parade of Meteorites behind me *watch the steps gentlemen the steps,* the other eye staring at the shadow between the breasts of a girl in a bright yellow bikini fifty feet away. I take the last four steps in a casual easy bound and then lean easily into the pool, shorts and socks and sneakers and all, and as I go under I can hear the high-pitched voices of my boys rising in wild amazement: *Counselor went in with his sneakers on . . . !*

Of course I fell in love that summer, led there by the Meteorites. For weeks they watched me stare helplessly at one of the lifeguards, a shy lovely girl, and then one day they somehow conspired among themselves to bring her to me. They led her by the hand up the rickety stone steps of the castle, up the balustrade, down a sagging wooden hall lined with sagging metal lockers, to our locker room, lined with sagging benches. I was slumped in the corner, adjusting the bandanna I wore all that summer, waiting impatiently for the boys to change into their bathing trunks, their thin white slippery bodies like the startling white roots of plants just pulled from the ground. In walked Nancy, in her bathing suit. She was flanked by David and Daniel, who led her toward me by the hand, and then stepped back, Daniel giggling, David not.

I was very startled. There are few moments in life when you are idly dreaming about a book, a place, a meal, a girl, and you look up and there is your dream before you. Her hair was drying at the ends but still wet and tight to her head; one foot rested on the other as she leaned against a locker. Daniel was dancing about like an elf, quite proud of himself, but David was staring at me, waiting for something: a look I would not see again for twenty years, until one of my own children, at the same age, regarded me as soberly, with such powerful expectation.

Please sit down, here, sit here, move over Lucius, I say.

Lucius glares.

I'm so seeprised to see you here, I say.

The boys giggle at my tangled tongue.

The boys told me you liked me very much, she says.

My God.

And I like you, she says. *Very much.*

My God.

I, I've liked you for a long time, I say.

And with that we rose, as if rising simultaneously was what we had in mind, as if we had agreed on something. We collected the boys (Tim was hiding behind the locker naked), and we paraded the Meteorites down the rickety stairs and toward the pool. Somewhere on the stairs we held hands, and so began that summer love, doomed and perfect, having much to do with the taste of sunburned skin, car radios, bitter words on lawns, letters on looseleaf paper, bright yellow notes on the driver's seat of my bus at dusk, her college boyfriend, her coy best friend, her mother's sharp eyes, the door of her room half-open, her shirt half-off, her face half-turned away.

The Meteorites are in their mid-twenties now, college graduates mostly, I would guess, and at work, married, in prison, who knows? I have thought about them every summer — summer brings me the Meteorites, ten strong always, Miguel still one of us — but I have never made the slightest effort to see them again. They would not remember me, and in their rangy men's bodies, long-boned, tending to first fat, I would not recognize the four- and five- and six-year-olds they were. Yet I think of them more every year. I have small children of my own now, and I am surrounded again by hubbub and jelly; and it is summer as I write, with the smell of hot afternoon on my shirt.

But there is more than memory here, more than nostalgia, more than a man's occasional yearning to be the quick boy he was. I learned about love, how to love, that summer — and not from the girl who came from the water, although I loved her and she me, for a time. No, I loved David because he loved Daniel; because David came to me that August morning and touched me on the shoulder and whispered *Counselor, Danny needs you;* because after I cleaned Daniel, in that filthy bathroom, David was waiting, his glasses askew, and when Daniel and I emerged into the clean sunshine, the boys embraced each other, their thin fluttering hands like birds on the bones of their shoulders.

Counselor, Danny needs you, spoken by a small boy on a high hill, and the four words fell from his mouth and were scattered by the four winds, years ago: but they have been a storm in me.

IAN FRAZIER

A Lovely Sort of Lower Purpose

FROM OUTSIDE

As KIDS, my friends and I spent a lot of time out in the woods. "The woods" was our part-time address, destination, purpose, and excuse. If I went to a friend's house and found him not at home, his mother might say, "Oh, he's out in the woods," with a tone of airy acceptance. It's similar to the tone people sometimes use nowadays to tell me that someone I'm looking for is on the golf course or at the hairdresser's or at the gym, or even "away from his desk." The combination of vagueness and specificity in the answer gives a sense of somewhere romantically incommunicado. I once attended an awards dinner at which Frank Sinatra was supposed to appear, and when he didn't, the master of ceremonies explained that Frank had called to say he was "filming on location." Ten-year-olds suffer from a scarcity of fancy-sounding excuses to do whatever they feel like for a while. For us, saying we were "out in the woods" worked just fine.

We sometimes told ourselves that what we were doing in the woods was exploring. Exploring was a more prominent idea back then than it is today. History, for example, seemed to be mostly about explorers, and the semirural part of Ohio where we lived still had a faint recollection of being part of the frontier. At the town's two high schools, the sports teams were the Explorers and the Pioneers. Our explorations, though, seemed to have less system than the historic kind: something usually came up along the way. Say we began to cross one of the little creeks plentiful in the second-growth forests we frequented and found that all the creek's moisture had somehow become a shell of milk-white ice about

eight inches above the now-dry bed. No other kind of ice is as
satisfying to break. The search for the true meridian would be
postponed while we spent the afternoon breaking the ice, stomping it underfoot by the furlong, and throwing its bigger pieces
like Frisbees to shatter in excellent, war-movie-type fragmentation
among the higher branches of the trees.

Stuff like that — throwing rocks at a fresh mudflat to make
craters, shooting frogs with slingshots, making forts, picking black-
berries, digging in what we were briefly persuaded was an Indian
burial mound — occupied much of our time in the woods. Our
purpose there was a higher sort of un-purpose, a free-form aim-
lessness that would be beyond me now. Once as we tramped for
miles along Tinker's Creek my friend Kent told me the entire plot
of two Bob Hope movies, *The Paleface* and *Son of Paleface*, which he
had just seen on a double bill. The joke-filled monotony of his
synopsis went well with the soggy afternoon, the muddy water, the
endless tangled brush. (Afterward, when I saw the movies themselves, I found a lot to prefer in Kent's version.) The woods were
ideal for those trains of thought that involved tedium and brood-
ing. Often when I went by myself I would climb a tree and just sit.

I could list a hundred pointless things we did in the woods.
Climbing trees, though, was a common one. Often we got "lost"
and had to climb a tree to get our bearings. If you read a story in
which someone does that successfully, be skeptical; the topmost
branches are usually too skinny to hold weight, and we could never
climb high enough to see anything except other trees. There were
four or five trees that we visited regularly — tall beeches, easy to
climb and comfortable to sit in. We spent hours at a time in trees,
afflicting the best perches with so many carved-in names, hearts,
arrows, and funny sayings from the comic strips that we ran out of
room for more.

It was in a tree, too, that our days of fooling around in the woods
came to an end. By then some of us had reached seventh grade
and had begun the bumpy ride of adolescence. In March, the
month when we usually took to the woods again after winter, two
friends and I set out to go exploring. Right away, we climbed a
tree, and soon were indulging in the spurious nostalgia of kids who
have only short pasts to look back upon. The "remember whens"
faltered, finally, and I think it occurred to all three of us at the

same time that we really were rather big to be up in a tree. Some of us had started wearing unwoodsy outfits like short-sleeved madras shirts and penny loafers, even after school. Soon there would be the spring dances on Friday evenings in the high school cafeteria. We looked at the bare branches around us receding into obscurity, and suddenly there was nothing up there for us. Like Adam and Eve, we saw our own nakedness, and that terrible grown-up question "What are you *doing?*" made us ashamed.

We went back to the woods eventually — and when I say "we," I'm speaking demographically, not just of my friends and me. Millions of us went back, once the sexual and social business of early adulthood had been more or less sorted out. But significantly, we brought that same question with us. Now we had to be seriously doing — racing, strengthening, slimming, traversing, collecting, achieving, catching-and-releasing. A few parts per million of our concentrated purpose changed the chemistry of the whole outdoors. Even those rare interludes of actually doing nothing in the woods took on a certain fierceness as we reinforced them with personal dramas, usually of a social or sexual kind: the only way we could justify sitting motionless in an A-frame cabin in the north woods of Michigan, for example, was if we had just survived a really messy divorce.

"What are you *doing?*" The question pursues me still. When I go fishing and catch no fish, the idea that it's fun simply to be out on the river consoles me for not one second. I must catch fish; and if I do, I must then catch more and bigger fish. On a Sunday afternoon last summer I took my two young children fishing with me on a famous trout stream near my house. My son was four and my daughter was eight, and I kidded myself that in their company I would be able to fish with my usual single-minded mania. I suited up in my waders and tackle-shopful of gear and led my kids from the parking area down toward the water. On the way, however, we had to cross a narrow, shallow irrigation ditch dating from when this part of the valley had farms. Well, the kids saw that little ditch and immediately took off their shoes and waded in and splashed and floated pine cones. My son got an inexplicable joy from casting his little spinning rod far over the ditch into the woods and reeling the rubber casting weight back through the trees. My daughter observed many tent caterpillars — a curse of yard-owners that year — falling from bushes into the ditch and floating helplessly along, and she decided to rescue them. She kept watching the water carefully, and whenever she spotted a caterpillar she swooped down and plucked it out and put it carefully on the bank. I didn't have the heart to drag the kids away, and as I was sitting in all my fishing gear beside that unlikely trickle, a fly fisherman about my age and just as geared-up came along. He took me in at a glance, noticed my equipment and my idleness, and gave a small but unmistakable snort of derision. I was offended, but I understood how he felt as he and his purpose hurried on by.

Here, I'd like to consider a word whose meaning has begun to drift like a caterpillar on a stream. That word is *margin*. Originally its meaning — the blank space around a body of type or the border of a piece of ground — had neutral connotations. But its adjective form, *marginal,* now has a negative tinge. Marginal people or places or activities are ones that don't quite work out, don't sufficiently account for themselves in the economic world. From the adjective sprouted a far-fetched verb, *marginalize,* whose meaning is only bad. To be marginalized is to be a victim, and to marginalize someone else is an act of exclusion that can cost you tenure. Today's so-called marginal people are the exact equivalents, etymologically, of the old-time heathens. A heathen was a savage, wild, un-Christian person who lived out on a heath. The heath was the margin of Christendom. No one today would ever use the word *heathen* except ironically, but we call certain people and activities marginal without a hint of irony all the time.

I've never been on a heath, but to judge from accounts of coal-smogged London in the days when *heathen* was in vogue, a windswept place full of heather and salmon streams sounds like the better place to be. And if the modern version of the margin is somewhere in western Nebraska, and the un-margin, the coveted red-hot center, is a site like Rodeo Drive, I wouldn't know which to choose. We need both, but especially as the world gets more jammed up, we need margins. A book without margins is impossible to read. And marginal behavior can be the most important kind. Every purpose-filled activity we pursue in the woods began as just fooling around. The first person to ride his bicycle down a mountain trail was doing a decidedly marginal thing. The margin is where you can try out odd ideas that you might be afraid to admit to with people looking on. Scientists have a term for research carried on with no immediate prospects of economic gain: "blue-sky research." Marginal places are the blue-sky research zones of the outdoors.

Unfortunately, there are fewer and fewer of them every day. Now a common fate of a place on the margin is to have a convenience store or a windowless brick building belonging to a telephone company built on it. Across the country, endless miles of exurbia now overlap and spill into one another with hardly a margin at all. There's still a lot of open space out there, of course, but usually it's far enough from home that just getting to it requires purpose and premeditation. As the easy-to-wander-into hometown margins disappear, a certain kind of wandering becomes endangered too.

On the far west side of the small western city where I live, past the town-killer discount stores, is an open expanse of undeveloped ground. Its many acres border the Bitterroot River, and its far end abuts a fence surrounding a commercial gravel pit. It is a classic marginal, anything-goes sort of place, and at the moment I prefer it to just about anywhere I know.

Army reservists sometimes drive tanks there on weekends. The camouflaged behemoths slithering across the ground would make my skin crawl if I didn't suspect that the kids driving them were having such a good time. The dirt-bike guys certainly are, as they zip all over, often dawn to dusk, exuberantly making a racket. Dads bring their kids to this place to fly kites and model airplanes, people in a converted school bus camp there for weeks on end, coin-shooters cruise around with metal detectors, hunters just in off the river clean game, college kids party and leave heaps of cigarette butts and beer cans and occasionally pieces of underwear. I fish there, of course, but remarkably I don't always feel I have to. Sometimes I also pick up the trash, and I pull my kids around on a sled in the winter, and I bring friends just off the plane to sit on the riverbank and drink wine and watch the sunset.

Soon, I'm sure, Development will set its surveyor's tripod on this ground and make it get with one program or another. Rumblings of this have already begun to sound in the local newspaper. I foresee rows of condominiums, or an expansion of the gravel pit, or a public park featuring hiking trails and grim pieces of exercise equipment every twenty yards. That last choice, in all its worthy banality, somehow is the most disheartening of all. A plan will claim the empty acres and erase the spotted knapweed and the tank tracks and the beer-can heaps. The place's possibilities, which at the moment are approximately infinite, will be reduced to merely a few. And those of uncertain purpose will have to go elsewhere when they feel like doing nothing in particular, just fooling around.

DAGOBERTO GILB

Victoria

FROM THE WASHINGTON POST MAGAZINE

I'LL EVEN BLAME the heat for my inability to remember which year it was — 1986, give or take. It was hot like never before, my skin so porous it was hard to distinguish which side of it I was on. Like I could sweat and become a puddle. A dirty puddle, because I'd absorbed that construction site. And because this was Los Angeles, and it was smoggy too. But you know what, it wasn't the smog or the dirt or the cement dust, it was the heat that seemed to drain all the color into an overexposed gauze. It was so hot. I'm talking about three digits, so don't think I'm exaggerating. It was so hot. It was so hot everybody had to say it again and again. So hot I don't remember if the heat lasted three weeks, a month, two, three. It was day and night hot, as forever and endless as boredom.

I remember the fan. That's what I had going in the apartment when I got back from the job. I can still hear its shuddering fizz as it rotated, the clacks as it teetered at far left and far right until it shifted direction. I'd rigged together electrician's tape and no. 9 tie wire to keep the plastic base joined to the plastic stem, too cheap to buy a new one. I carried it with me wherever I sat because I wanted it close. Right after work, that was on the couch, near the tube. I'd have already downed one beer, and I'd have already put three cans of an already refrigerated six-pack in the freezer, and I'd be almost done with the third when I would turn on my show to drink two more almost frozen: *Dallas* was on every weekday evening. It was going around probably a second time, and so some of the episodes I'd seen, but who knows why you hook onto a particular TV program. For me it had always been cop shows, so I can't explain my deal with *Dallas*. I didn't like the city of Dallas, did not want to live there and never had. There was nobody I identified with and nothing these Ewings owned that I dreamed of having. Besides Pam. Besides Victoria Principal. You see, I didn't watch television much, and when I did it was reruns, not prime time. I didn't flip through the *Star* or *People,* and I knew nothing about Hollywood even if my apartment was a few blocks from it. Obviously a woman as stunning as Victoria Principal had a past that brought her to the show, obviously everybody knew how beautiful she was. But since I'd never seen or heard of her outside either *Dallas* or my own television set, my brain didn't register obvious. And of course it didn't matter. I alone saw and discovered her, how sweet and gorgeous she was. I wouldn't even joke to my wife about my infatuation with her. Pale as she was, I wanted her to have Mexican blood — you know, like Rita Hayworth, Raquel Welch, even, I thought I heard, Vanna White. And if she didn't, well, I didn't care that much.

The job was called a Class-A high-rise, and it was a steel building going several stories up and a few down. We were pouring decks and nonstructural beams and wrapping columns. It was in Beverly Hills, and it was on Rodeo Drive. Which sounds good but isn't. It meant that, because of Beverly Hills noise ordinances, starting time was an hour later than a job anywhere else. Because of morning L.A. traffic, it meant getting there at the same time as any job and leaving an hour later than usual, right in the worst evening traffic. I needed the money bad. My first days — or was it weeks? — were at the bottom level, in dirt, sharing air with a Bobcat — a miniature backhoe, like a Go Kart compared with the real thing — whose purpose, as I recall, was to fuse abused earth and unfiltered exhaust fumes into, first, a paste that lathered my sweaty arms and face black, and, second, a dyeing agent for snot and phlegm whose blow and hack you don't want to read about.

It was down there where I first met the guy I remember only as Pretty Boy. He was sent to assist me a couple of times. I'm fairly sure we were doing the same work, together, those hours, but you wouldn't know it by looking at him. I think he maybe perspired some, but he did it in such a way that it could have been a spray-on. You know how they use those little misting bottles on wealthy beaches to keep cool, or on a movie set, where they dapple a V on the gray T-shirt between the pecs and shoulder blades? Pretty Boy had puffy blond hair like an Aryan, like a surfer, like a New York model. If he didn't have to wear a hard hat, I'm sure a head twitch would have sent a cute curlicue off his forehead. He loved Reagan. He had an apartment in Santa Monica. He was single. That is to say, he did not live with a wife, he did not have two children. He smiled much more than was acceptable and, unlike me and everybody else panting in the L.A. basin, said he didn't mind the heat. He'd admit it was hot, it was hotter than anything he'd lived through, but . . . But *what?* He just shrugged his shoulders, a smile more than a wink — he treated himself to colder air conditioning when he got home, turned it *way* down. That is to say, he had air conditioning. Do I remember that remark, its surrounding image lingering dreamy. He was such a short, thin pretty boy. What good would it do for me to reply? What good to beat him with my steel Estwing hammer?

My hammer brings up Modesto Rodriguez, he of somewhere a hundred kilometers or so from Acapulco, where he was a *mero mero,* a big cheese, in a village, not as in Los Angeles, where he was mostly unemployed and struggling. And a lot of that struggle was with the English language. He had been working on the job with a young laborer, Matthew, who was related to someone and so was allowed to do all kinds of jobs laborers aren't supposed to, like this union carpenter's work with Modesto Rodriguez. I'd been brought up from the darkness below to set beams on the first level because, though Matthew spoke Spanish, Modesto's wasn't the same — the suggestion being that Modesto's was "Mexican," not "Castilian" — and therefore they were having trouble communicating. The other laborers on this job were a Polish guy from Poland and a black guy from Compton. Modesto was very happy to be with me, because these other two were about as fluent in this "Castilian" Spanish as Matthew. That is to say, they went around saying *no problema* a lot. What nobody ever understood, thinking that Spanish alone is a lot to have in common, is how little Modesto and I had to talk about — unlike, for instance, me and that laborer from Compton. Modesto had great enthusiasm, though, and he wanted to know everything. If someone did come up to us to say something, he wanted it translated. He wanted everything anyone said translated, everything I said back translated. Once I started not doing that, it was often the topic of discussion while we were working. I told him it was too hot for talking, period.

I do remember clearly the beginning of the end of this job for me. It was before lunch, and the super was standing there. Modesto barked words of greeting in an overly voweled English, wagging energetically. The super was shaped like a heavily mustached and bearded and eyebrowed cantaloupe. You wouldn't be able to tell by staring whether he smiled or not. Take that back. He didn't smile. He never smiled around me, anyway. It could've been the heat. But then sometimes, for reasons unknown, or instinctual, or born of karmic resentments from previous lives, people don't like you. It could be the nose. Could be a hard hat worn backward, the bandanna under it. Could be the laugh. Could be the teeth, though not the silver ones in Modesto's mouth — I thought they were too glary in the sun, wondered if they got too hot when he grinned — because the super wasn't bothered, looking right at them when he wanted to know what we were doing. And he continued looking at them as I translated and then stepped forward, skipping the Spanish. He did not want to look at me while I explained why we were going about our project the way we were, which was not how it was being done before I got there. It's true, I made decisions, and I made one about installing these beam sides. I was a journeyman, and sometimes I knew what I was doing, and this saved time and made it easier on us. The super heard me explain. He knew it wasn't wrong, because we were putting them in and stripping them out much faster. He didn't like it anyway, because, probably, of my nose type.

It was just hot, I knew it. It was so hot. Nobody was in a good mood. Well, Modesto was okay. At lunch, we went up on the roof, where some Pacific breezes might pass by. Modesto would have another T-shirt and change into it and let the sweat-soaked one dry, then eat. A great idea I copied. Pretty Boy was up there, too. Miserable as it was, he'd be in a good mood. Why shouldn't he be, all those breezes going to him alone? Even his depressing stories didn't make him feel bad: He went to a nightclub on the Sunset Strip called Coconut Teasers. I'd been there once. It was one of those bright, pink-decorated places peopled by men and women who had their hair styled, who wore clothes with names and worked out in gyms with names on machines with names and drank colored drinks with names. Men as beautiful as Pretty Boy, buttons done and undone just so. Women with lots of cleavage and revealed thigh. A place, in other words, I went to once for a short visit. Pretty Boy liked to go there because he liked to sleep with lots of pretty girls and that was the place for him. He said he took pictures. What kind of pictures? You know. No, what kind? Of the women. Everyone you slept with? Yeah. He brought a photo another day to show me. A Polaroid. She was lying on a bed, and she didn't have anything on. She let you? They all do. Whaddaya mean, they *all* do? I take pictures of them all. I have a collection. You just ask them? He nodded. And they do this? He smiled. You just *ask* them? He nodded, smiling. And you have a collection? In a binder. He smiled.

Sometimes I didn't want to be there and watch the cool breezes billowing into him. And I was with Modesto all day. Sometimes I'm grouchy. I wanted to eat lunch alone sometimes. So I found a bench at the edge of the site, at a driveway at the back entrance of the I. Magnin department store — maybe we were building an addition to it. I liked sitting there, watching the rich ladies step out of their Jaguars and Mercedes and BMWs, all dressed like it was an opera night, then high-heel clicking those twenty-five feet into the autumn climate of the luxury store. The red-coated attendants sprinted up and down the parking structure, whistling like birds, those radial tires squealing like peacocks into the parking structure. I sat there one lunch break with my feet up on the bumper of a Bentley. I was sitting there this other lunch break when Victoria Principal came and sat next to me.

Victoria Principal, of *Dallas*. She sat down a yard from me. Maybe less when I think of it. Yes, less. Expert with a carpenter's tape, I assure you, reconsidering it now, it was less. Her precious hips were between sixteen and twenty inches from mine once she sat down. I saw her coming before she sat. It seemed like a mirage at first, bad eyesight. And I didn't want to stare while she sat there. I was eating. I can't remember what I was eating. Tacos? Yogurt? I think of both when I strain to remember. I said hi. She turned and she said hi back. Victoria. She was very pleasant about saying hi, not self-conscious or worried in the unnatural heat about sitting next to me, a sweaty, dirty construction worker. Of course I wanted to talk. We both watched the boys in the red coats sprinting, whistling. Did I want to offer her my food? I don't remember that. I didn't want to tell her I was a fan. I didn't want to tell her I watched the reruns. I almost did say something. All I could think of: I'm a carpenter here. That would've been the opening. Once we got to talking I would tell her more about me, that I wasn't just a carpenter, but a writer. Really. I never told anybody that, but I wanted her to know, to know that my working poverty wasn't without its other value — artistic, or spiritual, some higher implication like that. I would have to talk both casually and with sophistication. Instead I sat there. I did peek over at her a few times. I didn't want her to think I was a weirdo, but I couldn't resist. She was beautiful. And then her Jaguar Mercedes BMW appeared and she was getting up and I said bye. She turned to me and she said bye back. She was nice. Nice like a kiss is nice. Like a kiss that, even when you can only imagine it, makes you remember, right then, that you are happy to be alive.

Modesto didn't know who Victoria Principal was. Pretty Boy said he said hi to Kareem Abdul-Jabbar when he walked by a couple of weeks before and Kareem waved to him. What did Pretty Boy know about love? My brain was swollen with the vision of her, of her and me sitting there, saying hi, saying bye. I couldn't get it out of my mind.

Modesto and I had to haul some long sticks of two-by-four up several levels of stairs. This was a laborer's job, but Matthew didn't have to do this sort of thing. Somewhere along the way, my hammer fell out of its sling, and when we were done, I went up and down trying to find it. That's when the super decided to look me right in the eyes. What are you doing? he asked. I'm looking for my hammer, I told him. Why? Because I lost it somewhere. Where did you lose it? I couldn't believe he was actually staring at me, either. And I didn't know what else to say, except, if I knew where I lost it, it wouldn't be lost.

And that was the end, though I don't remember what happened after. Nothing specifically dramatic, I don't mean to imply that. I simply cannot remember whether I got my check, whether I quit, whether it was a day later or a week or two. I've had so many jobs, and I've been laid off and fired and quit so many times that no details stick. Just that it was the hottest, most miserable summer ever, and I hated this job. That on a bench near Rodeo Drive, at lunch, I sat so close to Victoria Principal we could have been holding hands, we could have been sharing tacos, or yogurt, talking, getting to know each other.

MARY GORDON

Still Life

FROM HARPER'S MAGAZINE

IN THE YEAR 1908, Pierre Bonnard painted *The Bathroom* and my mother was born. The posture of the young woman in the painting is that of someone enraptured by the miracle of light. The light is filtered through the lace curtains, and its patterning is reflected in the water that fills the tub into which she is about to step. Even the floral spread on the divan from which she has just risen is an emblem of prosperity and joy. Bonnard is famous for painting bathing women; in all her life my mother has never taken a bath. At three, she was stricken with polio, and she never had the agility to get in or out of a bathtub. She told me that once, after I was born, my father tried to lift her into a bath, but it made them both too nervous.

Ninety years after the painting of *The Bathroom,* ten days before my mother's ninetieth birthday, I am looking at the works of Bonnard at the Museum of Modern Art, a show I've been waiting for with the excitement of a teenager waiting for a rock concert. I was not brought to museums as a child; going to museums wasn't, as my mother would have said, "the kind of thing we went in for." It is very possible that my mother has never been inside a museum in her life. As a family we were pious, talkative, and fond of stories and the law. Our preference was for the invisible.

I can no longer remember how looking at art became such a source of solace and refreshment for me. Art history wasn't anything I studied formally. I think I must have begun going to museums as a place to meet friends. However and wherever it happened, a fully realized painterly vision that testifies in its full-

ness to the goodness of life has become for me a repository of faith
and hope, two of the three theological virtues I was brought up to
believe were at the center of things. It is no accident, I suppose,
though at the time I might have said it was, that I've arranged to
meet two friends at the Bonnard show at the same time that I'm
meant to phone the recreation therapist at my mother's nursing
home to plan her birthday party. Fifteen minutes after I arrive, I'll
have to leave the show. The therapist will be available only for a
specific half hour; after that, she's leaving for vacation.

Am I purposely creating difficulties for myself, a situation of false
conflict, so that I can be tested and emerge a hero? There is the
chance that I will not be able to leave the dazzle of the first room,
to resist the intoxication of these paintings, so absorbing, so satu-
rating, so suggestive of a world of intense color, of prosperous
involvement, of the flow of good life and good fortune. There's
the chance that I will forget to call the therapist. I do not forget,
but my experience of the first paintings is poisoned by the fear
that I will.

My mother has no idea that her ninetieth birthday is coming up.
She has no notion of the time of day, the day of the week, the
season of the year, the year of the century. No notion of the
approaching millennium. And no idea, any longer, who I am. Her
forgetting of me happened just a few months ago, after I had been
traveling for more than a month and hadn't been to see her. When
I came back, she asked me if I were her niece. I said no, I was her
daughter. "Does that mean I had you?" she asked. I said yes.
"Where was I when I had you?" she asked me. I told her she was
in a hospital in Far Rockaway, New York. "So much has happened
to me in my life," she said. "You can't expect me to remember
everything."

My mother has erased me from the book of the living. She is
denying the significance of my birth. I do not take this personally.
It is impossible for me to believe any longer that anything she says
refers to me. As long as I remember this, I can still, sometimes,
enjoy her company.

The day before I go to the Bonnard show, I visit my mother. It is
not a good visit. It is one of her fearful days. I say I'll take her out

to the roof garden for some air. She says, "But what if I fall off?" I
bring her flowers, which I put in a vase near her bed. She says,
"But what if they steal them or yell at me for having them?" She
asks me thirty or more times if I know where I'm going as we wait
for the elevator. When I say we'll go to the chapel in a little while,
she asks if I think she'll get in trouble for going to the chapel
outside the normal hours for Mass, and on a day that's not a
Sunday or a holy day. She seems to believe me each time when I
tell her that she won't fall off the roof, that no one will reprimand
her or steal her flowers, that I know where I'm going, that she will
not get in trouble for being in church and saying her prayers.

I have brought her a piece of banana cake and some cut-up
watermelon. There are only three things to which my mother now
responds: prayers, songs, and sweets. Usually, I sing to her as we
eat cake and then I take her to the chapel, where we say a decade
of the rosary. But today she is too cast down to sing, or pray, or
even eat. There is no question of going out onto the roof. She just
wants to go back to her room. She complains of being cold, though
it is 95 degrees outside and the air conditioning is off. It is not a
long visit. I bring her back to her floor after twenty minutes.

On my mother's floor in the nursing home, many people in
wheelchairs spend most of their days in the hall. There is a man
who is still attractive, though his face is sullen and his eyes are dull.
Well, of course, I think, why wouldn't they be? He looks at me, and
his dull eyes focus on my breasts in a way that is still predatory,
despite his immobility. I take this as a sign of life. It's another thing
I don't take personally. In fact, I want to encourage this sign of
life. So I walk down the hall in an obviously sexual way. "*Putana!*"
he screams out behind me. I believe that I deserve this; even
though what I did was an error, a misreading, it was still, I understand now, wrong.

In front of the dayroom door sits a legless woman. Her hair is
shoulder length, dyed a reddish color; her lips are painted red.
The light blue and white nylon skirts of her dressing gown billow
around her seat, and she looks like a doll sitting on a child's
dresser or a child's crude drawing of a doll.

My mother was once a beautiful woman, but all her teeth are
gone now. Toothless, no woman can be considered beautiful.
Whenever I arrive, she is sitting at the table in the common dining

room, her head in her hands, rocking. Medication has eased her anxiety, but nothing moves her from her stupor except occasional moments of fear, too deep for medication. This is a room that has no windows, that lets in no light, in which an overlarge TV is constantly blaring, sending images that no one looks at, where the floors are beige tiles, the walls cream-colored at the bottom, papered halfway up with a pattern of nearly invisible grayish leaves. Many of the residents sit staring, slack-jawed, open-mouthed. I find it impossible to imagine what they might be looking at.

It is difficult to meet the eyes of these people; it is difficult to look at their faces. I wonder if Bonnard could do anything with this lightless room. If he could enter it, see in these suffering people, including my mother, especially my mother, only a series of shapes and forms, concentrate on the colors of their clothing (a red sweater here, a blue shirt there), transform the blaring images on the TV screen to a series of vivid rectangles, and, failing to differentiate, insisting on the falseness of distinctions, of an overly rigid individuality, saying that we must get over the idea that the features of the face are the important part — would he be able to create a scene of beauty from this scene, which is, to me, nearly unbearable? He once told friends that he had spent much of his life trying to understand the secret of white. How I envy him such a pure preoccupation, so removed from the inevitable degradations of human character and fate. So he could paint wilting flowers, overripe fruit, and make of them a richer kind of beauty, like the nearly deliquescing purple grapes, the visibly softening bananas, of *Bowl of Fruit*, 1933. "He let the flowers wilt and then he started painting; he said that way they would have more presence," his housekeeper once said.

The people in the dining room are wilting, they are decomposing, but I cannot perceive it as simply another form, simply another subject or observation. I cannot say there are no differences between them and young, healthy people, no greater or lesser beauty, as one could say of buds or wilting flowers, unripe fruit or fruit on the verge of rotting. It is impossible for me to say that what has happened to these people is not a slow disaster.

And how important is it that when we read or look at a painting we do not use our sense of smell? The smells of age and misery hang over the common room. Overcooked food, aging flesh. My mother is kept clean, but when I bend over to kiss her hair, it smells like an old woman's. And there is the residual smell of her incontinence. My mother wears diapers. A residual smell that is unpleasant even in children but in the old is not only a bad smell but a sign of shame, of punishment: a curse. I cannot experience it any other way. My mother's body is inexorably failing, but not fast enough. She is still more among the living than the dying, and I wonder, often, what might be the good of that.

I thought that the women in the Bonnard paintings would all be long dead. As it turns out, at least one is still alive.

It is the day of my mother's birthday. Two of my friends, Gary and Nola, have agreed to be with me for this day. They are both very good-looking people. They are both, in fact, beauties. Gary is a priest; in another age, he might be called my confessor, not that he has heard my confession in the sacramental sense but because he is someone to whom I could tell anything, with no shame. Nola was my prize student, then she worked as my assistant for four years. We are proud that we have transformed ourselves from teacher/student, employer/employee, into, simply, friends.

When I thank him for agreeing to come to my mother's party, Gary says, "This will be fun." "No it won't," I say, "it won't be fun at all." "Well, it will be something to be got through. Which is, in some ways, not so different from fun." "It is," I say, "it is." "No, not really. It isn't really," he says, and we both laugh.

Gary's mother is also in a nursing home, in St. Louis, Missouri, a city I have never visited. She accuses his father, who is devoted to her, who has been devoted for years, of the most flagrant infidelities. All he says in response is, "I didn't do that, I would never do that." When we speak about our mothers, of our mothers' fears and sadnesses, particularly about the shape his mother's rage has taken, Gary and I agree that if we could understand the mystery of sex and the mystery of our mothers' fates we would have penetrated to the heart of something quite essential. We very well know that we will not. This is very different from Bonnard's secret of white.

Gary's father visits his mother in the nursing home every day. The end of Marthe Bonnard's life was marked by a withdrawal into a depressed and increasingly phobic isolation, so that the shape of a large part of her husband's life was determined by her illness, finding places for her to take cures and staying away from people whom she feared, who she thought were staring at her, laughing at her. In 1931, Bonnard wrote, "For quite some time now I have been living a very secluded life as Marthe has become completely antisocial [*Marthe étant devenue d'une sauvagerie complète*] and I am obliged to avoid all contact with other people. I have hopes though that this state of affairs will change for the better but it is rather painful."

Did this forced isolation, in fact, suit Bonnard very well; was it the excuse he could present to a sympathetic world so that he could have the solitude he needed for his work? What is the nature of the pain of which he spoke? What was the nature of her "*sauvagerie complète*"? In the painting in which he suggests Marthe's isolation, *The Vigil*, although she sits uncomfortably in her chair, in a room empty of people, alienated even from the furniture, unable to take comfort even from her dog, she appears still young, still attractive, still someone we want to look at. In fact, she was fifty-two, and someone whose misery, if we encountered it in person, might have caused us to avert our eyes.

I do not shape my life around my mother's needs or her condition. I try to visit her once a week, but sometimes I don't make it, sometimes it is two weeks, even three. If life is pressing on me, it is easy for me to put the visit off, because I don't know how much it means to her, and I know that she forgets I was there minutes after I have left, that she doesn't feel a difference between three hours and three weeks. If I believed that visiting my mother every day would give something important to my work, as the isolation required by Marthe Bonnard's illness gave something to her husband's, perhaps I would do it. But when I leave my mother, work is impossible for me; the rest of the afternoon is a struggle not to give in to a hopelessness that makes the creation of something made of words seem ridiculous, grotesque, a joke.

Two weeks before my mother's birthday, Gary celebrated the twenty-fifth anniversary of his ordination. His father couldn't be there; he wouldn't leave Gary's mother, even for a day. That was a grief for Gary, but most of the day was full of joy, a swelling of love, a church full of all the representatives of Gary's life — musicians, artists, dancers, writers, the bodybuilders he came to know at the gym where he works out, to whom he is an informal chaplain, as well as the parishioners he serves. The music was mostly provided by a gospel choir, who brought everyone to tears, and whose music blended perfectly with the parish choir's Gregorian chant, with which it alternated. It was a day of harmony, of perfect blending, but with high spots of color, like the paintings of Bonnard. I bought for the occasion a red silk dress with a fitted waist and an elaborate collar. I wore gold shoes. On the altar, flanked by red and white flowers in brass vases, I read the epistle of St. Paul to the Galatians, which assures that in Christ there is neither male nor female, slave nor free — a blurring of distinctions like the blurring of boundaries in Bonnard, where the edge of an arm melts into a tablecloth, a leg into the ceramic of a tub, flesh into water, the sun's light into the pink triangle of a crotch.

Nola has the long legs, slim hips, and small but feminine breasts of Marthe Bonnard. I know this because a certain part of our relationship centers around water. We swim together in the university pools; afterward we shower and take saunas. She has introduced me to a place where, three or four times a year, we treat ourselves to a day of luxury. A no-frills bath in the old style, a shvitz, a place where we sit in steam, in wet heat, in dry heat, in a room that sounds like something from the *Arabian Nights*: the Radiant Room. We spend hours naked among other naked women, women who walk unselfconsciously, women of all ages and all ranges of beauty, in a place where wetness is the rule, where a mist hangs over things, as in the bathrooms of Bonnard. The preponderance of bathing women in Bonnard's work has been explained by Marthe Bonnard's compulsive bathing. She sometimes bathed several times a day. This may have been part of a hygienic treatment connected to her tuberculosis. But whatever the cause, her husband used it triumphantly.

Nola has just come from a friend's wedding in Maine. She was seated at the reception next to a German student, who became besotted with her. He grabbed her head and tried to put his own head on her shoulder. "You must come and have a drink with me at my inn," he said to her. She refused.

"You weren't tempted by all that ardor?" I ask her.

"No," she says. "I saw he had no lightness, that there was no lightness to him or anything that he did."

Bonnard's paintings are full of light, but they are not exactly about lightness, and his touch is not light, except in the sense that the paint is applied thinly and wetly. But he is always present in his paintings, and his hand is always visible. He has not tried to efface himself; he has not tried to disappear.

When I walk into the dining room on the day of my mother's birthday, I see that she has already been served lunch. The staff has forgotten to hold it back, though I told them a week ago that I would be providing lunch. She hasn't touched anything on her tray except a piece of carrot cake, which she holds in her hands. The icing is smeared on her hands and face. I don't want my friends to see her smeared with icing, so I wet a paper towel and wipe her. This fills me with a terrible tenderness, recalling, as it does, a gesture I have performed for my children. If I can see her as a child, it is easy to feel only tenderness for her. Bonnard paints children most frequently in his earlier period, in the darker Vuillard-like paintings, in which it is his natal family that is invoked. In the brighter pictures, children do not take their place as representatives of the goodness of the world. That place is taken up by dogs. In the painting *Marthe and Her Dog*, Marthe and a dachshund greet each other ecstatically in the foreground. In the far background, faceless, and having no communication with the woman and her dog, children run, leaving lime-colored shadows on the yellow grass.

As I wipe my mother's face, I see that her skin is still beautiful. I hold her chin in my hand and kiss her forehead. I tell her it's her birthday, that she's ninety years old. "How did that happen?" she asks. "I can't understand how that could happen."

I have brought her a bouquet of crimson, yellow, and salmon-pink snapdragons. She likes the flowers very much. She likes the name. "Snapdragons. It seems like an animal that's going to bite me. But it's not an animal, it's a plant. That's a funny thing."

One reason I bought the flowers is that the colors reminded me of Bonnard. I don't tell my mother that. Even if she still had her wits, I would not have mentioned it. Bonnard is not someone she would have heard of. She had no interest in painting.

I have bought food that I hope will please my mother, and that will be easy for her to eat: orzo salad with little pieces of crayfish cut into it, potato salad, small chunks of marinated tomatoes. I have bought paper plates with a rust-colored background, upon which are painted yellow and gold flowers and blue leaves. I deliberated over the color of the plastic knives, forks, and spoons and settled on dark blue, to match the leaves. I am trying to make an attractive arrangement of food and flowers, but it's not easy against the worn gray Formica of the table. I think of Bonnard's beautiful food, which always looks as if it would be warm to the touch. It is most often fruit, fruit that seems to be another vessel of sunlight, as if pressing it to the roof of your mouth would release into your body a pure jet of sun. Bonnard's food is arranged with the generous voluptuous propriety I associate with the south of France, though Bonnard moved often, dividing his time between the south and the north. He places his food in rooms or gardens that themselves contribute to a sense of colorful plenitude. Yet it is very rare in Bonnard that more than one person is with the food; none of the festal atmosphere of the Impressionists, none of Renoir's expansive party mood, enters the paintings of Bonnard in which food is an important component. The beautiful colors of the food are what is important, not that the food is part of an encounter with people who will eat it, speak of it, enjoy one another's company.

Nola and Gary and I enjoy one another's company; I do not know what my mother enjoys. Certainly, the colorful food — the pink crayfish in the saffron-colored orzo, the red tomatoes, the russet potatoes punctuated with the parsley's severe green — is not a source of joy for her. Joy, if it is in the room, comes from the love of friends, from human communion — usually absent in the paintings of Bonnard. I do not think, though, that my mother feels part of this communion.

I talk about the food a bit to my mother, but she isn't much interested in descriptions of food. She never has been. She always had contempt for people who talked about food, who recounted memorable meals. She doesn't join us in saying the Grace in which Gary leads us. Nor does she join us in singing the songs that, two weeks ago, she still was able to sing: "Sweet Rosie O'Grady," "Daisy, Daisy," "When Irish Eyes Are Smiling." Nothing focuses her attention until the cake, a cheesecake, which she picks up in her hands and eats messily, greedily. I wonder if it is only the prospect of eating sweets that keeps my mother alive.

When we are about to leave, I tell my mother that I'm going on vacation, that I won't see her for three weeks, that I am going to the sea. "How will I stand that, how will I stand that?" she says, but I know that a minute after I'm gone she'll forget I was there.

I have bought the catalogue of the exhibition, and when I leave my mother I go home and look at it for quite a long time. I read that Bonnard once said that "he liked to construct a painting around an empty space." A critic named Patrick Heron says that Bonnard knew "how to make a virtue of emptiness." Illustrating Bonnard's affinities with Mallarmé, Sarah Whitfield, the curator of the show, quotes a description of a water lily in one of Mallarmé's prose poems. The lily encloses "in the hollow whiteness a nothing, made of intact dreams, of a happiness which will not take place."

Much of my mother's life is made up of emptiness. She does, literally, nothing most of the day. For many hours she sits with her head in her hands, her eyes closed, rocking. She is not sleeping. I have no idea what she thinks about or if she thinks, if she's making images. Are images the outgrowth of memory? If they are, I don't know how my mother can be making images in her mind, since she has no memory. And, if her eyes are mostly closed, can she be making images of what is in front of her? The beige walls and linoleum, her compatriots with their withered faces, thin hair, toothless mouths, distorted bodies? The nurses and caretakers, perhaps? No, I don't think so. I think that my mother's life is mostly a blank, perhaps an empty screen occasionally impressed upon by shadows.

Sarah Whitfield says that in the center of many of Bonnard's pictures is a hole or a hollow: a tub, a bath, a basket, or a bowl. A hole or hollow that makes a place for a beautiful emptiness. Nola once described her mother's life as having graceful emptiness so that a whole day could be shaped around one action. We both admired that, so different from the frantic buzz that often charac-terizes our lives. I am afraid that the emptiness at the center of my mother's life is neither beautiful nor graceful but a blankness that has become obdurate, no longer malleable enough even to con-tain sadness. An emptiness that, unlike Bonnard's or Mallarmé's or Nola's mother's, really contains nothing. And there is nothing I can do about it. Nothing.

I don't know what that emptiness once contained, if it once held Mallarmé's intact dreams; dreams of happiness, which, for my mother, will not now be realized. Perhaps she is experiencing the "emptying out" of which the mystics speak, an emptying of the self in order to make a place for God. I don't know, since my mother does not use language to describe her mental state. I try to allow for the possibility that within my mother's emptiness there is a richness beyond language and beyond visual expression, a truth so profound that my mother is kept alive by it, and that she lives for it. To believe that, I must reject all the evidence of my senses, all the ways of knowing the world represented by the paintings of Bonnard.

Bonnard's mistress, Renée Monchaty, killed herself. There are many stories that surround the suicide. One is that she killed herself in the bath, a punitive homage to her lover's iconography. Another is that she took pills and covered herself with a blanket of lilacs. I also have heard that Marthe, after the painter finally married her, insisted that Bonnard destroy all the paintings he had done of Renée. I don't know if any of these stories is true, and I no longer remember where I heard them.

In one painting that survives, *Young Women in the Garden,* Renée is suffused in a yellow light that seems like a shower of undiluted sun; her blond hair, the bowl of fruit, the undefined yet suggestively fecund floral background, are all saturated with a yellowness, the distilled essence of youthful hope. Renée sits, her head resting against one hand, a half smile on her face, her light eyes catlike and ambiguous; she sits in a light-filled universe, in front of a table with a striped cloth, a bowl of apples, a dish of pears. In the margins, seen from the rear and only in profile, Marthe peers, eclipsed but omnipresent. I am thinking of this painting as I stand in the corner of the dining room, watching my mother from the side, like Marthe, the future wife. How can it be, I wonder, that Renée — who inhabited a world of yellow light, striped tablecloths, red and russet-colored fruit, a world in which all that is good about the physical presented itself in abundance — chose to end her life? While these old people, sitting in a windowless room with nothing to look at but the hysterically colored TV screen, their bodies failing, aching, how can it be that they are fighting so desperately for the very life that this woman, enveloped in such a varied richness, threw away? I am angry at Renée; she seems ungrateful. At the same time I do not understand why these people whom my mother sits among do not allow themselves to die. Renée had so much to live for, to live in, and chose not to live. What do they have to live for? I often ask myself of my mother and her companions. And yet they choose, with a terrible animal avidity, to continue to live.

In a 1941 letter to Bonnard, Matisse writes that "we must bless the luck that has allowed us, who are still here, to come this far. Rodin once said that a combination of extraordinary circumstances was needed for a man to live to seventy and to pursue with passion what he loves." And yet the last self-portraits painted by Bonnard in his seventies are as desolate as the monologues of Samuel Beckett. *Self-Portrait in the Bathroom Mirror* portrays a nearly featureless face, eyes that are more like sockets, a head that seems shamed by its own baldness, the defeatist's sloping shoulders, arms cut off before we can see hands. In the *Self-Portrait* of 1945, Bonnard's mouth is half open in a gesture of desolation; his eyes, miserable, are black holes, swallowing, rather than reflecting, light. At the end of his life, Bonnard was deeply dejected by the loss of Marthe, of his friends, by the hardship of the war, which he includes in one of his self-portraits by the presence of a blackout shade. Is it possible that, despite his portrayal of the joy and richness of the colors of this world, despite his mastery and his absorption in the process of seeing, despite his recognition and success, his last days were no more enviable than my mother's?

A Week in the Word

FROM IMAGE

IF I NEGLECT to take my flashlight up to the monastery chapel for Vespers, I will regret it later when, sloshing blindly through puddles left in the rutted dirt road by the recent downpours, I stumble back in the dark to my — hermitage. The word interrupts with a medieval hiccup this — how do we describe this culture of ours? — this *postmodern* world, this banquet of possibilities. Just as this weeklong retreat interrupts my own life "down there," as I already think of home. I'm on a mountain, praying, thinking my thoughts — or, rather, trying not to think them for once. I am living not simply "away," in a geographic sense, but out of time, out of modernity, in this California monastery.

Meanwhile, our postmodern culture still revs along, inside me too — so many choices all jumbled together, and just one stomach. We have chosen the name for ourselves: we are no longer souls, as we once were, not even citizens; we are consumers, grasping at the disorder of life, all the *stuff.* Order is not our thing. *Only connect,* great grandfather (who was a Modernist) instructed. A few generations of only connecting, and here we are.

And what a strange *fin de siècle* it is. Not exuberant and brainy like the eighteenth century's mind bounding out of the Enlightenment looking for trouble, looking for progress, and not swooning like the nineteenth century, the Romantic heart sopping up sensibility with its Swinburne. We're not sad like that; we're sated.

Maybe we don't need memory here either. Like order, memory is selective, too constrained. Besides, it is parochial and specific, terribly local. We don't want memories. We'd rather have theories, constructs, opinions *about* memory. The littleness of real memories is a burden, also an annoyance. No things but in ideas — that's how it is with us. Memories (as distinct from "memory") are the sorry consolation of those who finger their cache of lavender-scented old stuff, fuddling over the past which, if *not* fuddled over, would leave the poor souls scorched with the truth: they're toast.

We — Americans — hate to be lassoed to the particular like that, like Europeans stuck with their dripping medieval real estate, the grimy pastel villas set prettily on sienna hills, the cobbled corners where their inflamed youth hurtle back and forth on unmuffled motorcycles, rattling the stained glass in the badly caulked basilica embrasures. The kids are trying to get out of there. We understand. Our tradition is to mistrust tradition.

The grotesqueries of leftover cathedrals, the doughty stone enclaves of ancient universities, armless statues, and Della Robbia wreaths — this isn't our kind of Disneyland either. There is no abstraction to it, no illusion of possibility. Especially, there is no freedom *from* it. It is beautiful, beautiful! But where is the trapdoor to the future? That is, to abstraction, to imagining oneself, rather than knowing oneself. For knowing oneself, we seem to know, implies acquiescence to limitations. We aren't ready, not quite, to give in to that — why should we? We're in charge, aren't we? "The only superpower left," we say, claiming our tough-guy trophy with meaty hands. The vanity of the imperial glitter rubs off on us, a gold dust all the world longs for and fears. We can't help preening: we've created ourselves. We're nobody's memory.

Strangely, after all this time of being a country — a "great" country — Americans still prefer the idea of the future to the idea of history. In a way, the idea of the future is our history, or at least a version of our cultural history. The filmy future is a can-do place, our natural habitat. But the past is distressingly complete, full of our absence. We seem to know if you take history too seriously, you'll never get out. In the place of national memory we have substituted the only other possible story form: the dream. And the essential thing required of the American Dream has always been that it remain a dream, vivid, tantalizing, barely beyond reach. Just the dreaming of it — which costs nothing, absolutely nothing except every cent of our imaginative attention — inflates the soul. Fills it, rather than fulfills it.

The specificity of memory, on the other hand, is humiliating:
you can buck that motorcycle up and down those *rues,* those *strasses*
and *borgos,* and still you're caught in your cul de sac, the stained
glass Madonna gazing down from her shuddering window with
maddening calm. We bolt from the iron apron strings of history.
We wish to be free — whatever that means — and we know that
memory, personal or civic, does not promote freedom. Memory
tethers.

But I am living — one week, maybe two, tourist time — in a niche
of memory. Cultural, not personal, memory. It is Lent, and I am
on retreat. This is my hermitage. It is a small trailer. Prefab, wood
paneled, snug. A cell, as the monks still call their own hexagonal
hermitages, which surround the chapel farther up the steep hill.
The idea is not prison cell but honeybee cell. The hive busy with
the *opus Dei,* the life of prayer.

I am following a way of life, balanced on a pattern of worship
trailing back to Saint Benedict and his sixth century Rule for
monasteries. And still farther back, into the Syrian desert where
the solitary weirdos starved and prayed themselves out of history
their own mystic way. Benedict's Rule drew all that eccentric urgency into the social embrace. Into history. He took the savage
hermitage of the Levant, and gentled it into the European monastery. He made a center out of the raw margin the early desert
recluses clawed toward. The convent, after all, says frankly what it
is: a convention, part of the social compact which claims order as
a minion of tradition.

The monastic day here in California at the end of the twentieth
century, like the monastic day at Monte Casino early in the sixth
century, is poised on a formal cycle of prayers that revolves with
the seasons. It is called the Office of Hours or the Divine Office.
It divides (or connects) the day (and night) by a series of commu-
nal prayer liturgies. This day, like all days, is a memory of the day
that preceded it. The day is a habit, the hours reinscribed as ritual.
Memory, habit, ritual — those qualities which do not perhaps sustain *life* (which is elemental, fiercely chaotic), but *a life.* A way of
life, specific, bound to time with the silken ties of — what else? —
words. The West murmurs, trying to locate itself; the East breathes,
trying to lose itself.

A simplistic distinction, not entirely accurate. After all, the heart of Western contemplative life is silence, and the East, in at least one central practice, chews the word, the mantra. Still, Christianity is undeniably a wordy religion. *Lectio divino,* sacred reading, the ancient practice laid down by the early patristic writers, is still alive today; it is part of the daily routine here.

Augustine, whose *Confessions* I've brought along on this retreat, is the most passionate exemplar of this practice. He is not simply one of the West's greatest writers, but its greatest reader. The year is 397, and he is composing the West's first autobiography, creating the genre which lies at the core of Western consciousness, substituting in place of the ancient idea of *a story,* the modern literary idea of *a life.* The omniscient authority of the tale told around the campfire turns to ash in the burning voice of the first person singular.

Augustine is, appropriately, hot with his subject, inflamed with the account of his fascinatingly bad life turned mysteriously good. But he only gives this story the first nine of the thirteen books of his *Confessions.* Then, without explanation or apology, as if it were the most natural thing in the world, the work elides smoothly into an extended meditation on the Book of Genesis as if this, too, were "his life."

In fact, the movement from his life to his reading is not smooth — it is ablaze. The narrative becomes more, not less, urgent. *His* story, for Augustine, is only part of the story. There is a clear logic dictating the form of the *Confessions,* which unites the account of his life with his reading of Genesis, though this is not a logic we in the late twentieth century see as readily as Augustine's late-fourth-century readers would have.

Having constructed himself in the first nine books of the *Confessions,* Augustine rushes on to investigate how God created the universe — how God, that is, created him. And all of us, all of *this.* Reading, therefore, is concentrated life, not a pastiche of life or an alternative to life. The soul, pondering, *is* experience. *Lectio* is not "reading" as we might think of it. It is for Augustine, as it was for Ambrose his teacher, and for these California monks in their late-twentieth-century cells, an acute form of *listening.* The method is reading — words on paper. But the endeavor is undertaken as a relationship, one filled with the pathos of the West: the individual, alone in a room, puts finger to page, following the Word, and attempts to touch the elusive Lord last seen scurrying down the rabbit hole of creation. *In the beginning God created . . .*

The voice of God is speaking on that page. Augustine, grappling with Genesis in his study, is no less heated — much more so — than Augustine struggling famously with "the flesh." He invents autobiography not to reveal his memory of his life, but to plumb the memory of God's creative act.

"My mind burns to solve this complicated enigma," he says with an anguish more intense than anything that accompanies his revelations about his own life. He understands his life as a model of the very creation that is beyond him — and of course in him. He writes and writes, he reads and reads his way through this double conundrum, the mystery of his own biography and the mystery of creation.

He makes the central, paradoxical, discovery of autobiography: memory is not in the service of the past; it is the future which commands its presence. It is not a reminiscence, but a quest.

Yet how bizarre the truncated modern notion of "seeking a self" would seem to Augustine. Autobiography, for him, does not seek a self, not even for its own "salvation." For Augustine, the memory work of autobiography creates a self as the right instrument to seek meaning. That is, to seek God. For what purpose? For praise, of course. For if God, the source, the creator, is found, what else is there to do but praise?

Augustine takes this a step further. On the first page of the *Confessions* he poses a problem that has a familiar modern ring: "it would seem clear that no one can call upon Thee without knowing Thee." There is, in other words, the problem of God's notorious absence. Augustine takes the next step West; he seeks his faith *with* his doubt: "May it be that a man must implore Thee before he can know Thee?" The assumption here is that faith is not to be confused with certainty; the only thing people can really count on is longing and the occult directives of desire. So, Augustine wonders, does that mean prayer must come *before* faith? Illogical as it is, perhaps not-knowing is the first condition of prayer, rather than its negation. Can that be?

He finds his working answer in Scripture: *How shall they call on Him in Whom they have not believed? . . . they shall praise the Lord that seek Him.* Praise, he decides, antedates certainty. Or rather, certainty resides in longing, that core of self from which praise unfurls its song. This is the same core from which streams the narrative impulse of memory: the wonder of a life lived. In the face (or, rather, in the embrace) of creation, there is no way to escape the instinct to cry out.

This is where the Psalms come in. They are praise. More: they are relation, full of the intensity of intimacy, the rage, petulance, and exaltation, the sheer delight and exasperation of intimate encounter. This is the spectrum of all emotion, all life. The Psalmist reaches with his lyric claw to fetch it all in words.

Words, words, words. They circle and spin around Western spiritual practice. They abide. They even sustain a way of life — this monastic one — which has careened down the centuries, creating families (the Benedictines, the Franciscans, the Carmelites, and others) with lineages longer and more unbroken than those of any royal house in Europe. The pattern of prayer, handed down generation to generation, has sustained this extraordinary lifeline.

Words have proven to be more protean than blood.

The monastic life of the West cleaves to the Psalms, claiming the ancient Jewish poetry as its real heart, more central to its day than the New Testament or even the sacraments. The Psalms keep this life going — the verbal engine running into the deepest recess of Christian social life, and beyond that back into the source of silence, the desert of the early hermits.

The idea here in this American monastery, based on a tenth-century reformation of the earlier Benedictine model, is to wed both traditions — the social monastery and the solitary hermitage, desert and city, public and private. It is a way of life based on a historical pattern.

Therefore, this life might be understood as a living memory. It is also a life lived, literally, within poetry. And as it happens, the name of this hermitage is Logos. The Word. The word made home. A week in the word.

Against one wall, the bed. I make it quickly like a good novice first thing every morning, pulling the dorm-room spread square. Suitcase stowed beneath — I'm here long enough to want to obscure the truth: I'm a visitor, passing through. I've never liked being a traveler: I take up residence. "I'm going home," I say instinctively, returning to my hotel the first day in a foreign city. So, here: Logos is my house.

Also here, a round table (eat, read, write, prop elbows on, sling leg over occasionally). Shelves niched in next to the tiny open closet space where I've installed my books, what I could lug on the plane: short stories by Harold Brodkey, a writer whose fiction I've sought out solely because of his searing AIDS memoir, drawn to the art by the life. Also a new novel by someone someone else said was good (not opened), poems I already love, one new book by Mark Doty, Augustine with his bookmark, Dawson's *Religion and the Rise of Western Culture,* plus a dictionary that didn't have the only word I've looked up so far, and Thich Nhat Hanh with yet another volume attempting to calm us Westerners down, out of ourselves: breathe, feel, exhale — there. And like everybody on a desert island, the Bible (the New Jerusalem version).

A rudimentary kitchen runs along another wall; bathroom beyond that, the only other room. And two windows, one to nowhere, hugged by two crowded eucalyptus trees and the vinca-covered curve of the steep eroded dirt road I alone seem to climb to the chapel. The other window, the window that counts, gives onto — paradise. The Western rind of America peels off far below into the extravagant white curl of Big Sur. Where the slant of the Santa Lucia range, where we are perched, cuts off the view of the coastline, the Pacific, blue as steel (it is overcast) or ultramarine (on sunny days), appears to be cantilevered below us, a blue platform leading to the end of the world. Sometimes, roughed up by wind and whitecaps, the ocean loses this quality of being architecture; it becomes expensive fabric, shimmering silver. Then, simply, what it is: the vast pool, brimming to the horizon.

This is where I have come. There was no crisis. No, at the moment, heartache or career impasse. No dark night except the usual ones. Doesn't everyone wake up maybe two nights a week, mind gunning, palms sweating? In the eyes-open misery of night, sensation gets mashed to a paste of meaninglessness — life's or one's own. No anguish beyond that to report. Every so often I just do this: go on retreat.

It is not uncommon in this supposedly secular age. Meditation, massage, monasteries, and spas — the postmodern stomach, if not its soul, knows it needs purging. Such places are even popular, booked months in advance. Down the coast the Buddhists are meditating, eating very intelligently. Esalen is nearby, too, and the place where Henry Miller discovered the hot tub. I could go to the Buddhists, cleanse in the silence, approach the big Empty which is the great source: I believe that.

But I come here, and follow the Christian monastic day laid out like a garden plot by Benedict at the close of the Roman era. I am Western; I like my silence sung.

In any case, the day itself is silent. The only words are the chanted ones in the chapel, unless I call home. My thin voice sounds odd, insubstantial. My husband carefully recites all the messages from my office answering machine. I ask if he's OK. He is. You OK? I tell him I am. I love you. Me too — I love *you*. Touching base. The telephone receiver clicks back into its cradle, and the mirage of news and endearments melts. It doesn't disappear exactly — I leave the telephone room, a little booth by the monastery bookstore, smiling, his voice still in my ear. It's just that conversation has become a bare tissue of meaning, a funny human foible, but not something to take seriously for once. The midday bell is ringing, and there is something I'm trying to remember.

That's wrong. I am not trying "to remember" something. I want to get this right, this odd experience of praying all day. More like this: I am being remembered. Being remembered into a memory — beyond historic to the inchoate, still intense trace of feeling that first laid down this pattern. It is a memory which puts all personal memory in the shade, and with it, all other language. In my experience, it is unique, this sensation of being drawn out of language by language which the Divine Office occasions. Praying, chanting the Psalms, draws me out of whatever I might be thinking or remembering (for so much thinking *is* remembering, revisiting, rehearsing). I am launched by the Psalms into a memory to which I belong but which is not mine. I don't possess it; it possesses me. Possession understood not as ownership, but as embrace. The embrace of habitation. Hermitage of the word.

In recent years, I have gone on several Vipassana Buddhist retreats, also silent, where the practice has been sitting and walking meditation. I will do that again because it was what it promised: cleansing, insightful. It felt like the rarest air it is possible to breathe. And its substance was exactly that: breath and its entrance, its exit. Though it was difficult, it was gentle. More: it was a relief. Perhaps especially so for a contemporary Western mind, wracked with busyness. It was not a hive, the cells humming.

But here in this Benedictine monastery, even though the day is silent (conversation has been abducted somewhere), the hours murmur. The first morning bell rings at 5:30. I walk up to the chapel in the dead-night dark for Vigils, the first round of daily prayers. The chapel is stark, perhaps to some eyes severe. Not to me: the calm of the place is an invitation. I bow, as each of the monks does when he enters, toward the dark sanctuary. A candle burns there. The honey-colored wood chairs and benches, ranked on two sides, face each other. They form two barely curved lines, two choirs deftly passing the ball of chant back and forth across the arched room as, somewhere beyond us, the sun rises and the world begins to exist again.

It is important that this not sound ecstatic. I must leach the exaltation out of the description. Here is what happens in the chapel: old news is revisited, peeves and praise ritualized (the Psalms don't just exult; they grunt and groan). The call to the elusive One, polished with plainchant, is handed back and forth across the ranks of the honey-colored chairs like an imaginary globe of blown glass passed by men wearing cream-colored habits over their jeans and work shirts, scuffed Reeboks visible below their chapel-robe hems. It sometimes seems improbable, ridiculous.

And my mind wanders. There are the monks, looking very much alike in their cream-colored robes, and yet I manage to wonder — is that one gay? The one with the clipped accent — from Boston maybe? The one on the left looks like a banker, could have been a CEO, why not? The guy over here looks like a truck driver. On and on it goes, my skittery mind. Meanwhile, the Psalms keep rolling. A line snags — *More than the watchman for daybreak, my whole being hopes in the Lord* — and I am pulled along.

It can also be boring. What happens in the chapel partakes of tedium. It must. The patterns repeat and return. Every four weeks the entire Book of Psalms, all 150 poems, is chanted. And then begun again, and again, and again. *Sing to the Lord a new song,* we have been saying since David was king. This new song rolls from the rise of monotheism, unbroken, across the first millennium, through the second, soon to enter the third, the lapidary waves of chant polishing the shore of history. There are men here — there are men and women in monasteries all over the world — repeating this pattern faithfully in antiphonal choirs, softly lobbing this same language back and forth to each other. What *is* this invisible globe they are passing across the space?

Worship, of course. But what is worship? It is the practice of the fiercest possible attention. And here, at the end of the millennium, the ancient globe of polished words, rubbed by a million anxious hands down the centuries, is also the filmy glass of memory. We touch it. But this is memory understood not as individual story, not as private fragment clutched to the heart, trusted only to the secret page. Even in the midst of high emotion, the rants and effusions that characterize the psalmist's wild compass, there is a curious nonpsychological quality to the voice. This is the voice of the intense anonymous self. It has no mother, no father. Or it borrows, finally, the human family as its one true relation. This is the memory of the world's longing. Desire so elemental that its shape can only be glimpsed in the incorruptible storehouse of poetic image — *he sends ice crystals like bread crumbs, and who can withstand that cold? Our days pass by like grass, our prime like a flower in bloom. A wind comes, the power goes. . .*

Paging through a picture book of Christian and Buddhist monasteries in the bookstore, stopped by this cutline accompanying a photograph of a beautiful Buddhist monastery, a remark by a dogen: "The only truth is we are here now." The humility of living in the present moment. The physical beauty of the place is eloquent, revealing the formal attentiveness of a supreme aesthetic: mindfulness. The human at its best. And the food is famous there. They are living their profound injunction, honoring the fleet moment, and the smallest life: Buddhist retreatants are asked not to kill the black flies that torment them. Here, when I told the monk at the bookstore that ants were streaming all over the kitchen counter of Logos, he handed me an aerosol canister, and I was glad. I sprayed, mopped, discarded the little poppy seeds of ant carcasses. I sat back satisfied, turning again to Augustine and the mind of the West, figuring, figuring. The sweetish spume of bug spray hung in the air for a day.

Lord, do we need the East. The bug spray has to stop, we know that. Contemplative nuns have told me that without the introduction of Buddhist meditation practice, they wouldn't be in the monastery anymore. "It's thanks to Buddhism that I'm a Catholic," one of them said. I have never been to an American Christian monastery that did not have Buddhist meditation mats and pillows somewhere in the chapel. The gentle missionary work of the East, its light, blessedly unecclesiastical heart, the absence of cultural imperialism, the poetry of its gestures: the bell is never "struck," never "hit." In the Buddhist monastery, it is invited to sound.

But still this handing down of words, still this Western practice I cannot abandon, would not wish myself out of. *The only truth is we are here now.* I don't believe we are *only* here. How could I, transfixed by memory as I am, believing in the surge of these particular words down the channel of the centuries? We are here — for now. My conception of this is not of a heaven (and hell) in the future, but rather of an understanding of existence which encompasses history as well as being.

I will ponder the story of your wonders. Imagine that. Imagine living one's life entirely around, within, through, over and under the chanting of poetry. Maybe it is another way, the West's way, of saying *we are here now.* Out of this recitation of the ancient words to reach the stillness of the present moment. The Psalms are an intricate web of human experience, reminding us that we live in history, and that history is the story of longing. Its pulse races.

We enter the dark sanctuary, bow to the flame, assemble in the honey-colored chairs again, two halves of the human choir. Some mornings at Vigils, before first light, it feels strangely as if our little band — fifteen monks, a handful of retreatants — are legion. The two facing choir lines curve slightly, two horizon lines, an embryonic globe forming anew.

We are greeting first light, we are entering dark night. It is all very old, a memory of a memory. And it is new as only the day can be new, over and over. The day is a paradox, and we enter it possessed by time's tricksy spirit, history and the present instant sublimely transposed.

We are here now, the East is chanting from its side of the monastery.

Oh yes, the West chants in response, the antiphon rising as it has all these short centuries, out of the endless memory we inhabit together, *Sing a new song, sing a new song to the Lord.*

BARBARA HURD

The Country Below

FROM THE YALE REVIEW

A NUMBER OF YEARS AGO, I had a dream. The car I was driving had in its trunk an art treasure, something wrapped in black velvet. I had been given instructions to drive to the wettest fringes of town, to carry the treasure through twilight muck, to lean over and press it into the trembling ground until the earth redraped its covers and buried it completely. I never knew what the treasure was, but the image of its burial is clear to this day — that lowering of something that could keep for years if need be, rocking and swaying two feet deep in the dappled soddenness of bog. It was the kind of dream you cannot shake off, that clings to the skin. You notice it at the oddest moments, your arm vaguely green as you reach through a patch of morning sun for the Cheerios box on the kitchen table. Or in those moments, barefoot in the garden, when your toes disappear in a profusion of potato plants.

Like most everything from glaciers and meringue to humans and their relationships, from a distance a bog looks solid. From the air over Cranesville Swamp what you see in autumn is plush umber dotted with tufts of cotton grass, acres of nap rubbed the wrong way, the fuzzed yarns of velvet gold. It looks firm enough, as if you could, in an emergency, throttle your engines back, lower the wing flaps and landing gear, and ease your small plane down in this large clearing between forested ridges of western Maryland, bumping and skidding across a runway of dying weeds and hardened mud. It's an illusion, like the solidity of glaciers. Once in Alaska, I made my way, gingerly, across a glacier, astonished at how hard I had to work to avoid millwells and tunnels, crevasses large

enough for people and dogsleds to fall into, rubble and rock
fragment, the debris of high-country canyons. I thought about
John Muir galloping and yahooing his way across glaciers like a
big-pawed puppy skidding over hardwood floors. Wasn't he afraid
of falling in? Doesn't intimacy always reveal the pores, the loosely
woven, the invitation to go below, the way the bog invites, gurgling
and swaying and rearranging itself around your by-now-somer-
saulted plane, its tousled layers of sphagnum and cranberry rising
over your upside-down windshield?

The psyche of Western cultures is dampened by bog monsters
and the swamp lights of aliens. In high school English classes all
across the country, we follow Beowulf down into the murky, de-
mon-infested waters of Grendel's lair. We have grown up with the
Swamp Thing lurching through gnarled cypress trees, its breath
like wind from Hades, with the Creature of the Black Lagoon, with
bog elves and flickering lights luring innocent humans to live
burials in quaking mires. Even our language is soaked with its
doom: we are "bogged down" in too much work, "swamped" by
debts, "mired" in triviality. Once I visited an elementary school and
had my students writing poems about landscapes. One of them
wrote about swamps, about green ooze, about wishing he could
fling a bully cousin into the middle of a burpy crypt of slippery
slime. When he read his poem to his classmates, they squirmed in
their seats and cried "Oh, yuck!" and reveled in the image of the
brute up to his ears in muck, algae dripping from his pimples.
What is evidently worse punishment than being stripped, desert-
style, of unnecessary accouterments, as Moses and his people were,
is being immersed in all of them. All the endless variety of bullfrogs, bog orchids, swamp beacons, skunk cabbage. All the sinking,
slurping, lumpy conglomeration of mud and plant and water. This
is an onslaught on the senses, where even what you stand on is
solid one minute and liquid the next. The Western mind loves
lines and categories, the neat logic of syllogisms, clear and indis-
putable as Mount Hood against a summer sunset. Meanwhile, in
the slow backwater, in pools between scum-slicked swamps, above
the bowl-shaped leaves of *Nelumbo lutea* floats the American lotus,
the yellow blossom of the water lily, upon which the Buddha sits,
contemplating the paradox voiced by a zookeeper in Dublin who,
when asked for the secret of his unusually successful breeding of

lions, answered, "Understanding lions," and, when asked for the secret of understanding lions, replied, "Every lion is different."

I love the names of swamps, how they are as varied as their origins: Great Dismal, Four Holes, Big Thicket, Mingo, LaRue, Callahan, and Honey Island. Some of them oozed into being in high shallow bowls as glaciers withdrew their icy fingers. Some of them formed as the ancient Atlantic slid off an inland continental shelf and land rose behind it and rainwater flushed salt out of the pocket left behind. Concerning the origins of Lake Drummond in the center of Dismal Swamp, some scientists speculate about the impact of a giant meteor. Others suggest that the swamp might have been formed by hundreds of years of a giant underground peatburn. I like this theory. It reminds me of a friend I used to know who tried working as a hairstylist, who spent his days clipping and curling and chatting. All the while his underground was smoldering. You could feel it if you got too close, layers and layers of compressed decay smoking and smoldering, collapsing into themselves like hot coals into ash. He liked to read Goethe, who praises what longs to be burned to death. But imagine the surprise if, after years of such smoldering, what happens next is not the great transformative fire but an underground collapse, a sinking depression, slow filling with rainwater and nearby flooding rivers, the ignominious creep of moss and duckweed and the gradual silence of the swamp.

Having opted today for the boardwalk that crosses Cranesville, I feel conspicuous, too upright in this bog where almost everything else spreads sideways. Sphagnum moss stretches its vast network of cells, living and dead, out across the acres. It reaches from the edge of the pond in toward the middle. It will someday take over. It creeps like a thick raft, its underbelly always dying, its sun-soaked surface a dense sponge of pale green tentacled stems. The term *quaking bog* comes from this characteristic sponginess — you can actually step onto the sphagnum, jump up and down, and feel the ground sway under your feet. It would be, I suppose, a way to give a chicken like me some semblance of surfing — holding the feet steady, keeping knees bent and flexible, riding the waves of sphagnum and hair-cap moss. I step back onto the boardwalk and lie down on warm planks to watch the size-nine boot-shaped pools of black water I have left in the bog disappear. I stare and stare. I want not just the overall effect of the vanished but the cause and exact moment of change. I want to see this clump of bog moss, that strand of sphagnum straighten and stretch, link tentacles with another, fill in the footprint. But all I get are the quick sparkles of sunlight as plant and water rearrange themselves. If I look away, even for five seconds, and then back, I can see change, how the instep and heel have filled in. But if I keep my eyes glued to the footprint, nothing seems to happen.

It is July and I have come looking for what is buried here and have found, instead, a sundew dissolving an ant. The sundew glistens, like the palm of a wet hand ringed with dozens of diamonded finger-stubs. The ant, attracted by the promise of something sweet, had wandered in and gotten its leg stuck in sticky secretions. The sundew's enzymes, acting like a miniaturized blender, pureed the ant, whose body began to shrink, wrinkling, collapsing into itself like a black leather balloon with a slow leak. Moments before, I had been watching a dragonfly in the final stage of its metamorphosis. Its four wings unfolded like veined and moist cellophane as it inched along the boardwalk, unsteady, dragging its newly unpacked tail like a drunken bride with a too-long train of tulle. Saint Philip says that truth comes to this world clothed in images. Are we to undress it? Become costume managers in reverse, hanging veils and black leather in wardrobes, sending the truth naked onto the stage before an audience who yawns at the dreariness of abstractions? I am as interested in truth as everyone else, but my faith is in imagery, in the scandalously particular sight of this ant and that dragonfly, in this drama taking place on the floating mat of sphagnum and cranberry.

It is impossible to spend any time belly down on the boardwalk, face to face with that wobbly cover, and not eventually reach over and push your fingers in. We are drawn to what's below. From the safety of whatever boardwalks we have chosen, we linger at the edges, testing the mire with the tips of galoshes, a long stick, a hand. Do we dare? Do we dare? When I was ten, I loved the scabs on my legs. I scratched mosquito bites until they bled and walked around all summer, lifting the hard crusty edges of scabs, the way I might have lifted manhole covers in a city street. I loved the moistness underneath. I loved imagining my shins dotted with shallow ponds the size of lentils, complete with sedgy fringes and the chorus of spring peepers, the possibility of lowering myself into a labyrinth. I lived, at that time, in a neighborhood whose northern edge abutted a small swamp. I remember that swamp only in winter. I remember the icy hummocks we used as hassocks, half-sitting, half-leaning against them when we bent over to tie our skates on, the still, shallow water solidly frozen and skimmed with white, the swamp edges solid as playground benches. A swamp that to my child's mind had no depth, only white flatness, a slick surface to glide across. But when geese flew north and the ice thinned until blackwater showed through again, the swamp dropped out of my psyche. In my mind, I must have pleated the land there, drawn one side of the neighborhood up against the field on the other side and left the swamp dangling in the fold underneath.

Thoreau would have us unpleat that fabric, draw the swamp up to our front doors, enter it as *sanctum sanctorum*. Those were my days of being a religious scavenger. I checked out churches the way a person does flea markets, browsing the tables of old toasters and chess sets. Or the way potential home buyers scan the real estate section and spend a Sunday afternoon raising eyebrows at yellow vinyl flooring, clucking at sun-bleached drapes, admiring the view from a kitchen window. I entered churches fingering the oak pews, scanning hymnals, waiting to see if it was here that some grace would waft down on me. I was sure that Catholic girls wore mantillas on their heads when they went to Mass for just that reason — to protect their pageboys from the disarraying blast of holy light. The fact that I sometimes joined them, bareheaded, and emerged with hairdo intact did nothing to dissuade me from that notion. I was, after all, an outsider in their church and figured my hair stayed put because I knew nothing of their concepts of sin or of their rising and kneeling on the swells and storms of Catholic seas. What I did know, even then, was the ardor with which they knelt and closed their eyes as something silent and robed-winged brushed by and touched their tongues. I knew it first, not in a church, but in a swamp somewhere in the South. The canopy of cypress and gum trees arched overhead; altar cloth of florescent moss draped over cypress knees. On the few higher spots grew green-fly orchids, resurrection ferns, and crimson cardinal flowers. Everywhere the cathedral was flooded with the wine of the sacrament, tannin-stained and clean and home to cottonmouths and water moccasins. An honest church where the spirit might just as easily sink its fangs into your leg as stream down through glass-stained windows, where what is holy only increases the appetite. It is a clever trick. You are going along living what you think is your life. Something drifts by and enters your body, gets in through the holes it bores in your skin or through your eyes, or maybe it tracks a hair shaft down to the pale softness of skull-flesh, follows the root on in. And you know, even as you open your mouth, as you open whatever you can to feed, that this is a hunger that will never be filled.

Once I walked all afternoon in a bog high on Meadow Mountain. I was headed north, skirting and crossing, dipping into and out of the red plush of rugosa sphagnum. I was thinking about the German poet Rainer Maria Rilke and how, on the page, his poems look like poems. They have titles and they sit still when you close the book and return it to the shelf. But his language is more like a steep slope. Or like the well on my grandmother's farm. If you lean over far enough, you fall in, and once you do, that tremendous thirst begins. I was thinking about those lines of his, in which he feels himself pushing through solid rock. I show him this bog. I want to know if he's ever been in such a place, if his dark god with its webbing of roots began in a swamp, the way Horus did after Isis hovered above her dead husband in a swamp until out of that ooze enough rose up that she conceived him. I show him the Nile goose, that swamp bird who laid the cosmic egg. He leads me out of the swamp and into the flintlike layers that surround him, where "everything close to my face is stone." I want him to practice what he knows about hunger, to begin wherever he is, pressing his teeth into the rock beneath his lips, his tongue against the ore, to see what happens when darkness meets an appetite. He wants me to know what makes us all small. He hands me a stone. This is your life, he says, sometimes a stone deep inside you, sometimes a star.

One summer I became obsessed with finding the edge of a nearby bog. I hiked its perimeter with a long stick, jabbing it into the muck every ten feet or so. I spent a week in a seminar, learning how the government delineates wetlands. We learned about obligate hydrophytes, facultative plant life, about hydrology and soil samples and soil maps. The government's guide to finding the edge of a swamp is fifty pages long, complete with graphs and soil

maps you need a magnifying glass to decipher. We spent hours
mucking in the field with spades and buckets and Munsell soil
color charts, the same bog I had crisscrossed with my long stick of
maple. At the end, I understood how trying to define a bog is like
trying to put a neatly folded shadow into a dresser drawer. What
and where the bog is is inseparable from who we are. And who we
think we are not. In the Cameroons, the shadow is sacred. Its
length is a sign of power. Its absence is a sign of death. Our efforts
to define these places are efforts to separate ourselves from them,
from their shifting boundaries, their reminders of decay, where
what sways beneath the feet is both itself and its opposite at the
same time.

From the Cranesville boardwalk today, I watch the ant die and
the dragonfly dry and I push my fingers down into the bog as deep
as I can. They disappear. There's no telling what they will encounter down there or what will spy my five-pronged flesh shoved
through the baroque ceiling of its world, groping around in dark
rooms below. When I can push no further, it's not because my
fingers have hit solid ground. What stops them is a net whose
weave gets tighter and tighter the deeper you go. Down there, out
of sight, my stubby fingers try tearing holes in the net, spreading
apart the woof and the warp enough to push an index finger
further. I can't. I'm down three inches and can go no more. I pull
my fingers out, the bog slurping and slavering, and insert a pointed
stick half an inch in diameter. Standing on the edge of the boardwalk, I lean on it, pushing slowly down. I am a medieval surgeon
probing the body of a patient. The stick goes down three inches,
ten, twenty. Two feet down, it breaks off and I almost fall in. The
water slips over its fractured tip, the sphagnum straightens, and
the buried half disappears.

What's below remains, for the most part, out of sight. Cousteau's
Calypso has yet to sail across the undulating layers of upland bog,
his men stepping backward off the deck with flippered feet and
high-tech, under-bog cameras to film for us *The Private Life of the
Bog*. I can only see what's underneath if I reach down, grab a
chunk, and rip it up into the air and sunlight — tangle of mud-
slicked roots of hair-cap and sphagnum mosses, cranberry, high-
bush blueberry, and wild raisin braided, twisted, and curling.

A man I know, a wetlands expert, once sank to his chest in a bog more loosely woven than this one, sank until his toes were five feet under, his heart nestled among the green shoots of cotton grass in a place known as Hammel's Glade. He said it was good, good to stand there with the earth up to his shoulders, sepia pools and sedges drifting in waves. Thoreau would have loved him, both of them at home in the swamps, both aware that in between the big events, the graduations, weddings, births, and death, lies a damp profusion of chaos and contentment. Thoreau says, "I derive more of my subsistence from the swamps which surround my native town than from the cultivated gardens in the village. There are no richer parterres to my eyes." Perhaps it is, as Thoreau says, the tenderness of swamps that draws us. Here are places in the earth you can enter without backhoe and chisels and dynamite, without ropes and helmets and lanterns. All it takes is a step off the edge, the willingness to imagine being buried alive, which is how the wetlands man described it, standing in Hammel's Glade while the bog floated its beds under his chin. And that's the rub. Anticipating death is hard enough, but how to go at it in slow motion, immersed in the decay of last century's plant life with nothing to do but chronicle the way one's bones become almost visible beneath flesh?

The man got out, of course, had lunch somewhere, went home. Not everyone does. Bogs are famous burial grounds. There are stories in Ireland, in Germany and Denmark and England, of hundreds of men, women, and children buried in bogs, some of them lured into the misty muck by flickering lights, by bog elves, some of them minus their ears, lips, the skin torn off their backs. The highly acidic water in a bog means that the usual microorganisms that decompose a body are all but absent. Add in the very cold water and what you have are ideal conditions for preservation. In 1450, German peasants found the upright body of a man hundreds of years old buried to his neck in a bog. Concerned about a proper interment, the peasants went to the local priest, who forbade his burial in the churchyard. The reason? The priest believed that the man had been lured into the mire by bog elves. Evidently anyone susceptible to such spirits wasn't worthy of the sacraments. But maybe there's something else here. Maybe the priest saw the man as someone who had stood too long in the doorway between two worlds. Who knows what his death was like? Perhaps he fell in, got his feet stuck, then his thighs, found that wriggling only made matters worse. Perhaps he stood there in the bog for weeks, contemplating his death. I heard a story once of a husband and wife hopelessly lost in a cave. After days had passed and they had given up hope of rescue, they began to confide in each other as they had never done. They revealed extramarital affairs, the disdain each felt for the other's naiveté, impatience with the way one left tea bags on the counter, how the other liked the left foot to stick out of the covers at night. On and on they went, unwrapping secrets, lifting layers off their life together, until they lay weak and spent on the damp cave floor in an intimacy they had never known. Of course they were rescued. Hauled out of the labyrinth and returned to their kitchen, where they could no longer stand the sight of each other. Knowing more than they could bear, they divorced, went their separate ways. Perhaps the priest feared what the bog man had learned during his weeks of dying and didn't want such knowledge in the ground outside his church.

Burial in unconsecrated ground was thought to prevent hauntings. In the eleventh century, a woman who died in childbirth was sometimes buried in a bog so that she couldn't return to the world of the living and drag her surviving child back to the grave with her. It's a quirky solution, given that the mother's body might last for hundreds of years in a bog, far longer than the child who grows up and dies with a more traditional burial. There is a story in Vermont about a dead hollow tree at the edge of a swamp and a raccoon being chased by a young boy's dog. The coon scoots through the hollow tree; the dog, fatter, follows and gets himself wedged inside. Years later, a farmer comes along with a chain saw, drags logs out for his sugar camp, and loads them on the back of his pickup. By happenstance, the dog's former master, now a grown man, is in a car following the truck down the road. He finds himself staring at the face of his lost, long-dead dog, framed in the hollow of a log. Things decay slowly here. What is down there may reappear, bounding over dirt roads in the back of a pickup, combing the German villages for a child. Some cultures believe that when you die, your doppelgänger appears, your opposite, your shadow. It stands there with you at the place where your soul departs from this world. If in a swamp you take your dying slow, then everywhere here must be half-formed doppelgängers, stuck between worlds, restless and roaming through muck, leaning on the giant leaves of skunk cabbage, drumming their fingers on the green pads of lilies, waiting for you to get on with it. If it's a long wait, perhaps they pass the time by amusing themselves. On the peninsula of Djursland in Denmark is an ancient cauldron-bog called Huldre Fen. A huldre is a fairy who lures wanderers into the fen, captivates them with dance and song, bewitches them until they forget all else, much like the sirens of Ulysses' day. It beats skidding crockpots across kitchen counters or jiggling the bed in the middle of the night, the way modern poltergeists do, bored by the interminable wait.

There are other risks with bog burials, notably that chances are you won't be found. Most of the 150 or so bog bodies we know of were discovered by peat-cutters who just happened to look down in time to see a foot or a head moments before their spades and machines cut into soft ground. Imagine how many more didn't look down. There must be thousands of bodies entombed in peat across England that have never been unearthed. And never will, now that the peat-cutting machines have passed over, now that the peat has been bagged and sold and spread over the roots of those luxuriant English gardens.

We like our burials satin-wrapped and coffin-clad. The earth kept at a respectable distance. Too much intimacy and it seems we're all afraid. I have a cracked crock that belonged to my grandmother. When I run my fingers over it, I try to imagine her fingers, bony and gnarled from work on the farm, hauling water from the well, twisting clothes through the wringer, her fingers lifting this crock, maybe filling it with daffodils, setting it on a table before dinner. I'm after those moments when I can't tell whose fingers these are, when the difference between her hand on the big scoop she kept by the well and mine on the faucet in my kitchen is a matter of tilting the surface. Loren Eiseley says the door to the past swings open. It's a one-way street and you can only go backward. But sometimes the playing field tips. The past sloshes into the present, floods the ground you stand on. Once, lying in bed and looking at an old photograph of myself, I knew not only my face, the dress, but just for a moment, how I had felt, exactly, at that age when my father would appear in the middle of the night, closing bedroom windows in a storm, drawing the bedspread up under my chin. How that room of ivory walls and gingham curtains was suddenly here, and I stretched my feet under the covers as far down as my knees now reach. And then it was gone, that moment, in a sudden displacement, as if the past had bulged up through the ground and sunk again and I knew in the aftershock that the past is still alive, still everywhere around, separated from this moment by a skim of amnesia. It isn't all we have — this present where we live our whole lives, this tiny dribble of time pushed over the edge. All it takes is a slight wobble of the field for land and water to start sliding into one another, green and brown and fluid swallowed in fold after fold of water and moss and mud, the whole place a sodden mirror, the reflections vaguely familiar. Why wouldn't we be afraid? When Tollund man was unearthed in Jutland in 1950, one of the men lifting the body and knocking off chunks of surrounding peat looked at the well-preserved face, had a heart attack, and died. Tollund man's chin is stubbled with whiskers, his eyes closed, lips pressed gently together in an almost tranquil expression. He lived more than two thousand years ago, but in the photographs he looks like any number of men I know after a week of camping. His final meal of willow herb seeds, black bindwood, and mustard was still evident. Surely the past lumbers just behind us, or just below. What separates us from the dead and dying can be measured in the seconds it takes to drop through a skim of algae. Below us, the swamp gurgles, rolls over, the bog sways, its bulges and sighs visible from the boardwalk.

It is a truism in many religions that you must face your fear. If you go to therapists today instead of priests, they will tell you the same. Go straight to it, look it in the face. In fact, put your face right into it, the practitioners of certain Germanic tribal rites might have added. It was their custom to take a man who had been accused of cowardice to places like the Hingst Fen near Hanover and make him lie face down in waterlogged earth. They made sure he kept his gaze steady, eye to eye with the bog, by crisscrossing sticks over his body, plunging the ends deep into the mire, until he lay fastened to the bog as if by a pile of pick-up sticks. What to make of this? Was the guy supposed to learn something useful, to get up the next day and slosh back to the village, wringing bog water from his shirt, and tell the tribal elders he'd stared death in the face and was no longer afraid? Of course, they knew he would die there. The question is, did they, in the first century A.D., also know that his body might outlast civilizations, that he might in the 1900s be unearthed, carted over soggy fens, his teeth counted, his stomach carefully rinsed, his head removed and preserved in a mixture of toluene and wax? Was he supposed to teach us, staring at his actual face two thousand years later, something about courage?

What we learn from the bog burials has to do with who we have been. And still are. Not just our diets of barley and bristle grass, not just our intolerance of cowardice, adultery, the ways we punish thieves and murderers, our ancient need to make sacrifices to whatever brings the harvest. When we go to the Silkeborg Museum in Denmark and stare into the dark face of Tollund Man, the bog becomes an antechamber and the door is still open. What goes there in its dying might float back into the present, its face tanned and almost smiling. We may be used to the presence of the dead in cemeteries, in the leaf debris of forests, in the somber faces of daguerreotypes. We think they're on a one-way street headed away from us. But a bog is more like those rotaries I hate in Massachusetts, where you might circle for hours while other cars zoom into and out of your orbit, where whiskers on the face of a bog man brush by, your dead dog's face grins from its log frame in front of you, where you can imagine your own face unearthed from a peatbed a thousand years hence. What will they note? Your grin? Your diet of Big Macs and yogurt? The way your skin seems so real?

By afternoon, the ant is long dead, the dragonfly has disappeared, and a light rain at Cranesville has become a downpour. This water will eventually slip south, tumble over Muddy Creek Falls, thrash through Class V rapids of the Youghiogheny, and flow into the waters that drift by Pittsburgh's Three Rivers Stadium, into the Mississippi and the Gulf of Mexico. If, as some psychologists tell us, our memories are locked into the cells of our bodies, is it true for live water, too? Does the river in New Orleans remember days like this when a week of rain is like a coveted hall pass in high school — permission to leave the confines of its corridors and wander to the far edge of the building where seniors with more privilege or chutzpah pool into stairwells and smooch and feel each other up, the wild abandon of brushing the hairy stems of lady slippers, fringed petals of blue gentians? I have heard people say that rivers can heal memories, but can they hold them? Can this water dribbling from a slightly tilted bowl high in the Appalachians later slip under traffic backed up on the Huey Long Bridge and disappear into the endlessness of the gulf without losing the memory of bullfrogs bellowing from its seepy start? Can we slip through our lives without losing sight of our fingers plunged into this clogged sink of the earth, our own memories teeming with egg cases and larvae, blue damselflies and lady's slippers, the smell of blueberries and decay? Here there is room for the elusive, the paradox, for what rocks and sways below the surface. Here the holes in the sieve of your mind open wider. Chunks of unrecognizable matter drift in. You notice your skin, how the pores themselves can open and close like millions of tiny fish mouths. You lean against the sloped sides of an invisible vortex and music pours down from the sky and you kneel in the wet bulging earth, algae clinging to your thighs, and pray that at least once in your life your own pores will open, that what knows no boundary between land and water will know no boundary at the edge of your body, that what lies riddled and pocked and hungry within you will fill and fill and fill.

JOHN LAHR

The Lion and Me

FROM THE NEW YORKER

ON NOVEMBER 6, twenty-six years after *The Wizard of Oz* was last released and on the eve of its sixtieth anniversary, a spiffy, digitally remastered print of the film arrived in eighteen hundred movie theaters throughout the land. With a rub rub here and a rub rub there, *The Wizard of Oz,* which never looked bad, has been made to look even better. Dorothy's ruby slippers are rubier. Emerald City is greener. Kansas, a rumpled and grainy black-and-white world, has been restored to a buff, sepia Midwestern blandness. And, since everything that rises nowadays in America ends up in a licensing agreement, new Oz merchandise will shower the planet like manna from hog heaven.

The last time I watched *The Wizard of Oz* from start to finish was in 1962, at home, with my family. My father, Bert Lahr, who played the Cowardly Lion, was sixty-seven. I was twenty-one; my sister, Jane, was nineteen. My mother, Mildred, who never disclosed her age, was permanently thirty-nine. By then, as a way of getting to know the friendly absence who answered to the name of Dad, I was writing a biography — it was published, in 1969, as *Notes on a Cowardly Lion* — and I used any occasion with him as field work. This was the first time we'd sat down together as a family to watch the film, but not the first time a Lahr had been secretly under surveillance while viewing it. The family album had infrared photographs of Jane and me in the mid-forties — Jane in a pinafore, me in short pants — slumped in a darkened movie house as part of a row of well-dressed, bug-eyed kids. Jane, who was five, is scrunched in the back of her seat in a state of high anxiety about the witch's monkey henchmen. I'm trying to be a laid-back big brother: my face shows nothing, but my hands are firmly clutching the armrests.

Recently, Jane told me that for weeks afterward she'd had nightmares about lions, but what had amazed her most then was the movie's shift from black-and-white to Technicolor, not the fact that Dad was up onscreen in a lion's suit. Once, around that time, while waiting up till dawn for my parents to return from a costume party, I heard laughter and then a thud in the hall; I tiptoed out to discover Dad dressed in a skirt and bonnet as Whistler's Mother, passed out on the floor. That was shocking. Dad dressed as a lion in a show was what he did for a living, and was no big deal. Our small, sunless Fifth Avenue apartment was full of Dad's disguises, which he'd first used onstage and in which he now occasionally appeared on TV. The closet contained a woodsman's props (axe, jodhpurs, and boots); a policeman's suit and baton; a New York Giants baseball outfit, with cap and cleats. The drawers of an apothecary's cabinet, which served as a wall-length bedroom bureau, held his toupees, starting pistol, monocle, putty noses, and makeup. In the living room, Dad was Louis XV, complete with scepter and periwig, in a huge oil painting made from a poster for Cole Porter's *Du Barry Was a Lady* (1939); in the bedroom, he was a grimacing tramp in Richard Avedon's heartbreaking photograph of him praying, as Estragon, in *Waiting for Godot* (1956).

Over the decades, the popular memory of these wonderful stage performances has faded; the Cowardly Lion remains the enduring posthumous monument to Dad's comic genius. While we were growing up, there was not one Oz image or memento of any kind in the apartment. (Later, at Sotheby's, Dad acquired a first edition of L. Frank Baum's *The Wonderful Wizard of Oz*.) The film had not yet become a cult. Occasionally, a taxi driver or a passerby would spot Dad in the street and call out, "Put 'em up, put 'em *uuuhp!*" Dad would smile and tip his tweed cap, but the film's popularity didn't seem to mean as much to him as it did to other people.

As we grew older and more curious, Mom had to prod Dad out of his habitual solitude to divulge tidbits of information to us. So, as we assumed our ritual positions around the TV — Mom propped up with bolsters on the bed, Jane sprawled on the floor with our Scotch terrier, Merlin, me on the chaise longue, Dad at his desk

— the accumulated knowledge we brought to the movie was limited to a few hard-won facts. To wit: Dad had held out for twenty-five hundred dollars a week with a five-week guarantee, which turned into a twenty-six-week bonanza because of the technical complexities of the production numbers; in the scene where the Lion and Dorothy fall asleep in the poppy field and wake to find it snowing, the director, Victor Fleming, had asked for a laugh and Dad had come up with "Unusual weather we're havin', ain't it?"; his makeup took two hours a day to apply and was so complicated that he had to have lunch through a straw; he wore football shoulder pads under his twenty-five-pound lion suit; and his tail, which had a fishing line attached to it, was wagged back and forth by a stagehand with a fishing rod who was positioned above him on a catwalk. It was only memories of the Munchkins, a rabble of 124 midgets assembled from around the world, that seemed to delight Dad and bring a shine to his eyes. "I remember one day when we were supposed to shoot a scene with the witch's monkeys," he told me. "The head of the group was a little man who called himself the Count. He was never sober. When the call came, everybody was looking for the Count. We could not start without him. And then, a little ways offstage, we heard what sounded like a whine coming from the men's room." He went on, "They found the Count. He got plastered during lunch, and fell in the latrine and couldn't get himself out."

Dad, in his blue Sulka bathrobe, with the sash tied under his belly, was watching the show from his Victorian mahogany desk, which was positioned strategically at a right angle to the TV. Here, with his back to the room, he sat in a Colonial maple chair — the throne from which, with the minutest physical adjustment, he could watch the TV, work his crossword puzzles, and listen to the radio all at the same time. Except to eat, Dad hardly ever moved from this spot. He was almost permanently rooted to the desk, which had a pea-green leatherette top and held a large Funk & Wagnall's dictionary, a magnifying glass, a commemorative bronze medal from President Eisenhower's inauguration (which he'd attended), various scripts, and the radio. On that afternoon, long before Dorothy had gone over the rainbow and into Technicolor, Dad had donned his radio earphones and tuned in the Giants' game. "Bert!" Mom said. "Bert!" But Dad didn't answer.

This was typical. At dinner, after he finished eating, Dad would

sometimes wander away from the table without so much as a
fare-thee-well; at Christmas, for which he never bought presents,
the memories of his unhappy childhood made the ritual exchange
of gifts almost unbearable, so he'd slip back to his desk as soon as
possible. Now, just as his ravishing Technicolor performance was
about to begin, he'd drifted off again, retreating into that private
space.

That was irrefutably him up there, disguised in a lion's suit,
telling us in the semaphore of his outlandishness what he was
feeling in the silence of his bedroom. It was confusing, and more
disturbing than I realized then, to see Dad so powerful onscreen
and so paralyzed off it. "Yeah, it's sad believe me missy / When
you're born to be a sissy / Without the vim and *voive*," Dad sang,
in words so perfectly fitting his own intonation and idiom that it
almost seemed he was making them up. In a sense, the song *was*
him; it was written to the specifications of his paradoxical nature
by E. Y. (Yip) Harburg and Harold Arlen, who had already provided him with some of his best material, in *Life Begins at 8:40*
(1934) and *The Show Is On* (1936).

"I got to the point where I could do him," Arlen told me. And
Harburg, who once said that he could "say something in Bert's
voice that I couldn't with my own," saw social pathos in Dad's
clowning. "I accepted Bert and wanted him for the part because
the role was one of the things *The Wizard of Oz* stands for: the
search for some basic human necessity," he said. "Call it anxiety;
call it neurosis. We're in a world we don't understand. When the
Cowardly Lion admits that he lacks courage, everybody's heart is
out to him. He must be somebody who embodies all this pathos,
sweetness, and yet puts on the comic bravura." He added, "Bert
had that quality to such a wonderful degree. It was in his face. It
was in his talk. It was in himself."

When the song began onscreen, Dad swiveled around in his
chair to watch himself; once the song was over, he stepped forward
and switched over to football.

"Dad!" we cried.

"Watch it in Jane's room," he said.

"Is it gonna kill you, Bert?"

Dad's beaky profile turned toward Mom; his face was a fist of
irritation. "Look, Mildred, I see things," he said. "Things I coulda

. . . I'm older now. There's stuff I coulda done better." Mother
rolled her eyes toward the ceiling. I returned us to Oz. Dad pulled
the headphones up from around his neck and went back to the
hand of solitaire he'd started. His performance was enough for
the world; it wasn't enough for him.

Onscreen, the Lion was panic-stricken but fun; his despair was
delightful. ("But I could show my prowess / Be a lion, not a
mouesse / If I only had the *noive.*") The Lion had words for what
was going on inside him; he asked for help and got it. At home,
there were no words or even tears, just the thick fog of some
ontological anxiety, which seemed to have settled permanently
around Dad and was palpable, impenetrable — it lifted only occasionally, for a few brilliant moments. "I do believe in spooks. I do.
I do. I do" is the Cowardly Lion's mantra as the foursome approach
the Wicked Witch's aerie. In life, Dad was constantly spooked, and
his fear took the form of morbid worry. It wasn't so much a state
of mind as a continent over which Dad was the bewildered sovereign. Onstage, Dad gave his fear a sound — "*Gnong, gnong, gnong!*"
It was a primitive, hilarious yawping, which seemed to sum up all
his wide-eyed loss and confusion. Offstage, there was no defining
it. The clinical words wheeled out these days for his symptoms —
"manic depressive," "bipolar" — can't convey the sensual, dramatic, almost reverent power of the moroseness that Dad could
bring with him into a room, or the crazy joy he could manufacture
out of it onstage. It was awful and laughable at the same time. We
couldn't fathom it; instead, we learned to live with it and to treat
him with amused affection. He was our beloved grump. He was
perpetually distracted from others, and, despite his ability to tease
the last scintilla of laughter from a role, he had no idea how to
brighten his own day. "I listened to the audience, and they told
me where the joke was," he told me backstage at S. J. Perelman's
The Beauty Part (1962) after he'd got a howl from a line that
had no apparent comic payoff. Why couldn't he listen as closely
to us?

When you kissed Dad on the top of his bald head — it smelled
deliciously like the inside of a baseball glove — he didn't turn
around; when you talked to him, he didn't always answer; sometimes he even forgot our names. That was the bittersweet comedy

of his self-absorption. But the Lion confessed his fears, he looked people in the eye, he was easy to touch (even Dorothy, in their first fierce encounter, puts a hand on him); he joined arms with the others and skipped off down the Yellow Brick Road. At the finale, their victory was a triumph of collaboration. In private, as even our little family get-together made apparent, Dad never collaborated; he never reached out (in all the years I went off to camp or college, he wrote me only one letter, and it was dictated); he never elaborated on what weighed him down and kept us under wraps. But there was a gentleness to his bewilderment, which made both the audience and the family want to embrace him. His laughter was a comfort to the world; in his world, which was rarely humorous, we comforted him. All the family forces were marshaled to keep Dad's demons at bay and "to be happy," an instruction that translated into specific behavior that would generate no worries — good humor, loyalty, gratitude, obedience, and looking good.

If Dad had had a tail, he would have twisted it just as the Lion did; instead, he had to make do with his buttons and with the cellophane from his cigarette packs, which he perpetually rolled between his fingers. What was Dad afraid of? We never knew exactly. Things were mentioned: work, money, Communists, cholesterol, garlic, the "Big C." Even a fly intruding into his airspace could bring a sudden whirlwind of worry as he tried to stalk the pest with a flyswatter. "The son of a bitch has been hit before," he would say, lashing at the fly and missing. Dad's global anxiety seeped into the foundation of all our lives; it was hard to see, and, when it was finally identified, it had to be fortified against. One of the most efficient ways to do this was to treat Dad as a metaphor — a sort of work of art, whose extraordinary and articulate performing self was what we took to heart instead of the deflated private person who seemed always at a loss. Any lessons Dad taught about excellence, courage, perseverance, discipline, and integrity we got from his stage persona. His best self — the one that was fearless, resourceful, and generous, and that told the truth — was what he saved for the public, which included us; otherwise, as every relative of a star knows, the family had to make do with what was left over. Even at the end of our Oz viewing, Dad brushed aside our praise, which seemed only to increase his anxiety. As he shuffled into the kitchen to get some ice cream, he glanced over at

Mom. "If I'd made a hit as a *human being*, then perhaps I'd be
sailing in films now," he said.

When *The Wizard of Oz* opened in New York, on August 17, 1939,
fifteen thousand people were lined up outside the Capitol Theatre
by 8 A.M. Dad's photograph was in the window of Lindy's, across
the street, and the *Times* declared his roar "one of the laughingest
sounds since the talkies came in." "Believe me it was a tonic for
my inferiority complex which is so readily developed in Hollywood," Dad wrote to Mildred, who would become Mrs. Lahr in
1940. As an animal, in closeup, and eight times as large as life, Dad,
with his broad, burlesque energy, was acceptable; there was no
place for his baggy looks and his clowning, eccentric mannerisms
in talking pictures except on the periphery of romantic stories. Despite his huge success, Metro soon dropped his option. He signed
for a Broadway musical, *Du Barry Was a Lady*. "Well, how many lion
parts are there," Dad said as he departed from Hollywood.

Over the years, especially after my son was born, in 1976, I'd
catch glimpses of Dad as the Lion, but, perhaps out of some
residual loyalty to his bias, I could never sit through the film. The
hubbub around the movie irritated me, because the other accom-
plishments of the performers were swept away in the wake of its
unique and spectacular success. I think Dad knew that he was a
hostage to technology: a Broadway star whose legend would go
largely unrecorded while, by the luck of a new medium, performers who couldn't get work on Broadway would be preserved and
perpetuated in the culture. Nowadays, the general public doesn't
know about the likes of Florenz Ziegfeld, Abe Burrows, Ethel
Merman, Bea Lillie, Billy Rose, Walter Winchell, Clifton Webb, and
Nancy Walker, whose stories intersected with Dad's.

What lives on is the Cowardly Lion. When I watch him now, I
don't see just the Lion; I see the echoes — the little touches and
moves — of those long-forgotten sensational stage performances
that Dad condensed into his evergreen role. His floppy consonants, slurred vowels, malapropisms, and baritone vibrato all derived from the collection of sophisticated operatic sendups he'd
developed first for Harburg and Arlen's "Things" (from *Life Begins
at 8:40*) and "Song of the Woodman" (from *The Show Is On*), to be
perfected in "If I Were King of the Forest":

> Each rabbit would show respect to me,
> The chipmunks genuflect to me,
> Tho' my tail would lash
> I would show compash
> For ev'ry underling
> If I, if I were king.
> Just king.

The Cowardly Lion's boxing bravado ("I'll fight you both together if you want! I'll fight you with one paw tied behind my back! I'll fight you standin' on one foot! I'll fight you wit' my eyes closed!") and his woozy body language (the shoulder rolls, the elbows akimbo, the bobbing head) were grafted onto the Lion from Dad's portrayal of the punch-drunk sparring partner Gink Schiner, in his first Broadway hit, *Hold Everything* (1928). And when the Wizard awards the Cowardly Lion his medal for courage, even Dad's vaudeville act, "What's the Idea" (1922–25), came into play: he swaggered like the policeman he had impersonated while trying to both arrest and impress the hootchy-cootchy dancer Nellie Bean. "Read what my medal says — 'Courage,'" the Lion says. "Ain't it de truth. Ain't it de *trooth*."

In later years, one of the many canards that grew up about the film was that there was a feud between the old pros and the young Judy Garland — that they had tried to upstage her and push her off the Yellow Brick Road. "How could that be?" my godfather, Jack Haley, who played the Tin Man, told me. "When we go off to see the Wizard, we're locked arm in arm, and every shot is a long shot. How can you push someone out of the picture with a long shot?" Although Garland wasn't pushed out, her "Over the Rainbow," which became the anthem of a generation, was almost cut from the movie three times. According to Dad, Harburg hadn't liked the original tune, which he found too symphonic and heroic. Years later, when I was working on a book about Harburg's lyrics, Arlen explained the deadlock, which Ira Gershwin had finally been called in to arbitrate. "I got sick to my stomach," Arlen told me. "I knew Ira didn't like ballads. He only liked things with a twinkle. Ira came over, listened, and said, 'That's a good melody.' I knew the heat was off. Yip tried out a few musical notions and came up with the lyric." Another of their favorite numbers, written for *Oz*, was one called "The Jitter Bug," in which bugs bite the travelers, who begin to dance with the trees and flowers. It was cut for reasons of pace and of balance, and though it gave Dad a big dance number, he never expressed regret over the loss of the material. What he remembered was the hard work and the offscreen hacking around. "Smith's premium ham!" the old pros yelled at one another before takes. "Vic Fleming had never experienced guys like us," Dad told me. "Some legitimate directors can't imagine anybody thinking about something else and when he yells 'Shoot!' just going in and playing." He went on, "We'd kid around up to the last minute and go on. You could see he got mad and red-faced. Some actors try and get into the mood. They'll put themselves into the character. I never did that. I'm not that — let's say — dedicated."

Dad died on December 4, 1967, the day I finished my book about him. He had never read any part of it. I saw him again in a dream on January 25, 1977. I'd been arguing about comedy with the distinguished English actor Jonathan Pryce, and had stepped out of his dressing room to cool off, and there was Dad in the corridor. "He was wearing his blue jacket with padded shoulders," I wrote in my diary. "He smelled of cologne, and he felt soft when I hugged him. I said, 'I love you.' I can't remember if he answered. But it felt completely real, with all the details of his presence — smell, feel, look, silence — very clear. I woke up sobbing." I added, "When will we meet again?"

So far, he has not reappeared in my dreams; but, in another sense, as the reissue of *The Wizard of Oz* only underscores, he has never really gone away. He's a Christmas ornament, a pen, a watch, a beanbag toy, a bracelet charm, a snow globe, a light sculpture, a bedroom-wall decoration. (Neiman Marcus's Christmas catalogue includes Dad in the *Wizard of Oz* bedroom — "the ultimate child's bedroom" — which, at $150,000, is more than twice as much as he was paid for the movie.) In the space of only two days this fall, on the merchandise channel QVC, a new offering of Oz paraphernalia sold about a million and a half dollars, which seems to prove the claim on the Warner Bros. fact sheet that "*The Wizard of Oz* has Universal Awareness." I should be outraged by all this, I suppose, since Dad's estate gets no money. I should deplore the trivialization of him as an artist and bemoan the pagan impulse to make household gods of mortal endeavor. (When Dad took up painting, in his last years, and realized that there was a market for Cowardly Lion artifacts, even he got the franchise itch, and stopped doing flowers and vegetables in order to churn out lions, which he signed and sold to friends.) But, if I'm honest with myself, these tchotchkes comfort me. They are totems of Dad's legacy of joy, and of his enduring life in the century's collective imagination.

I'm an orphan now, but I'm full of gratitude for the world that made me. I get letters from older readers who knew my parents, and who tell me in passing how proud Dad was of Jane and me. It's nice to know. I think Dad loved us, but it was in the nature of his way of loving that the knowledge is not bone deep. So the marketed trinkets work for me like Mexican *milagros* — talismans that are extensions of prayer and are tacked by the prayerful onto crosses in thanks for the miracle of survival. I'm pushing sixty now, but I find that the conversation with one's parents doesn't end with the grave. I want Dad back to finish the discussion — to answer some questions, to talk theater, to see me now. Almost anywhere in the city these days, I can turn the corner and run into him. I stroll past a novelty store on Lexington Avenue, and there's Dad as a cookie jar. I steal a peek at the computer of a young woman in the Public Library, and, by God, there he is as a desktop image. I go to buy some wrapping paper at the stationery store, and his face stares at me from the greeting-card rack. "Hiya, Pop," I find myself saying, and continue on my way.

Making It Up

FROM THE OHIO REVIEW

MY COPY OF *Robinson Crusoe* is an edition published in 1887 by Estes and Lauriat of Boston, and it was given to me by a man named George Iles on August 28, 1935. Mr. Iles lived a couple of floors above my father's rooms at the Hotel Chelsea, and he had befriended me as I rode up and down the hotel's rickety elevator — one of my favorite pastimes in those summers when I traveled from Kansas City to New York; when the season seemed to turn my father, mother, and me into a traditional family unit.

> Hilary Masters from George Iles
> with every confidence in his success
> New York, August 28, 1935.

Mr. Iles's celluloid collars were of such rigid construction around his thin neck that I often expected his spectacled head to pop off like a cork from a bottle, but his formal attire in the elevator was a disguise for the bibliographic chaos of his rooms. Books. And then more books. He was a collector of books, and their jumble went from wall to wall and, to my seven-year-old wonder, all the way to the high ceilings. Laid up like bricks, the musty volumes formed a maze in which I could get lost as I inhaled the toxic fumes of their ancient bindery, become mesmerized by the embossed calligraphies along their spines. I walked through aisles of literature, and to this day my mind automatically puns his memory when I encounter the word. What I'm saying is that Mr. Iles provided me a stunning sensual experience, and though this transfer of knowledge upon innocence can become a scarifying episode (but sometimes with profitable consequences as a dreary memoir), this Edwardian gentleman's seduction left me only eager for more ravishment; a normal life forsaken. Mr. Iles's gift of *Robinson Crusoe* made me a writer.

Back to my grandparents' house in Kansas City at summer's end, I came down with whatever infection was making the rounds of the second grade at Scarritt School. Let's say chicken pox. Quarantined to my bed and strengthened by my grandmother's oxtail soup and egg custards, my incurable boredom turned me to the brownish volume only just unpacked from my suitcase. "With twenty illustrations by Kaufman" the title page fraudulently claims, because there are no pictures and no evidence that any had ever been bound into the pagination, but my initial disappointment was quickly overwhelmed by the first sentence.

I was born in the year 1632, in the city of York, of a good family, though not of that country, my father being a foreigner, of Bremen, who settled first at Hull: he got a good estate by merchandise, and leaving off his trade, he lived afterwards at York, from where he married my mother, whose relations were named Robinson, a very good family in that country, and from whom I was called Robinson Kreutnaer; but, by the usual corruption of words in England, we are now called, — nay, we call ourselves, and write our name, Crusoe; and so my companions always called me.

Whew! Talk about convoluted prose and cluttered punctuation! But the coils of language, the lassos of references held me face to face with several intriguing likenesses. *Though not of that country:* what country could I claim? Kansas City? New York? *My father being a foreigner:* my father was a strange figure to me, a mysterious man of puzzling importance whom I only saw in summer. And to change one's family name called up a recurrent fantasy that I was an orphan and had been adopted by this kindly old couple who kept and fed me nine months of the year. The status of illegitimacy was not within my seven-year-old ken, but the sense of the condition was.

Moreover, the confident, first-person voice that speaks so casually and candidly from the page beguiled me. Trust and belief are immediately secured. I could hear that voice, carried it in my mind; a plain sound but sometimes with an offhand guile that tickled me with its timbre, a note later to be identified with irony. I was hooked, and flipping through the early pages, their headings only drove the fluke deeper. "Misfortunes at Sea." "Captured by Pirates." "Escapes from Slavery." The man had a natural tabloid talent for grabbing a browser's interest. And these incidents some thirty pages before the famous shipwreck on the deserted island off the coast of South America and where my ultimate corruption procured by George Iles would commence.

But, in the meantime, Defoe's own story strikes out on its own interesting course. Perhaps an excusable divergence here. It should be comforting to all of us who dare to write to know that this progenitor of the modern novel was something of a hack. He was born about 1660 (different biographies give or take a year), but almost thirty years after his fictional creation. He also changed his name of Foe to Defoe, thinking the Frenchified version had a little more class. Good for business. His father was a butcher who urged him toward the pulpit along with the fairly good education that went with the calling, but young Daniel wasn't called, preferring to set himself up in the hosiery business. In the seventeenth century, it's to be remembered, probably more men wore stockings than women, and the incipient author did well for a while, trading in Spain and Portugal, traveling through France, making it in London. Then his business failed and he declared bankruptcy, but his political interests had been sharpening his quill in the meantime, eventually to change his course again as it was to affect our literary forms.

Born the year after the Restoration (Milton was still alive, blind and fuming), the ex-hosiery salesman pulled on a variety of opinions as a pamphleteer. He was enormously prolific — some count over three hundred tracts, pamphlets, and essays published under his name, not to mention the scads of journals he wrote for anonymously, or edited. He somehow escaped punishment for his participation in the Monmouth Rebellion, but he did serve time twice and was even pilloried for his published opinions on religious freedom. He was convicted of libel once. His tracts ranged widely, advocating changes in highway construction, prison conditions, and bankruptcy laws, and even recommending higher education for women. His ideas were usually far in advance of the period and often got him into trouble.

A satire called "Memoirs of Sundry Transactions from the World in Moon" is said to have given Swift the idea for *Gulliver's Travels,* while "A History of the Plague" amply proves Defoe to have been a first-class journalist. He had an eye for detail, he was a man on whom nothing was lost, as Henry James might have said, but more times than not, his eye was on the mark, because he wrote for money, for advancement, and would take on any point of view that paid for it.

A satiric ode defending Dutch King William against the xenophobic whine of the Jacobites attracted the Court's attention, and Defoe was appointed the royal mouthpiece. While in this cushy post, he also wrote anonymous anti-Royalty pieces for the Jacobite journal *Mist*, but recent scholarship suggests he was serving as a double agent in much the same way the CIA infiltrated the left-leaning editorial policies of *Encounter* magazine in the 1950s. Nor did he neglect his domestic rituals, laying down his pen now and then to father seven children. He became very prosperous, with a fine town house and a country estate, but was to die in mysterious circumstances in 1731, having spent the previous year in hiding for reasons yet to be known. However, a dozen years before, in 1719, lightning struck him at the age of fifty-eight.

Or at least a meeting struck, with one Alexander Selkirk, a sailor who had actually been marooned on a deserted island and who apparently handed over his journals of that experience to Defoe. No surprise that this classic of fiction is based on an actual event, hasn't that always been the case? Of course lately, the written life comes to us unadorned by invention, plainly out of the fire, uncooked if not unleavened and hastily served to appetites that prefer the dish not so much deconstructed as unconstructed. We seem to have lost the taste for reality put together piece by piece; perhaps a final counterrevolution against modernism's piecing, but that's another digression, for another time.

So, this brief synopsis of Defoe's extraordinary life, some of which is to be found in the introduction of my Estes and Lauriat edition, but, prickly with chicken pox, I have no mind for it as I suffer confinement on Roberts Street. Especially because I have by now reached page 31, "The Ship Strikes Upon the Sand." Here the magic commences as does my apprenticeship.

The morning after the storm that has wrecked the ship and drowned his companions, Crusoe wakes on shore with only a pocket knife, a pipe, and a tin of tobacco. He swims out to the

hulk, pulls himself aboard, and starts to put together the reality of
his next twenty-eight years, two months, and nineteen days. He
begins to make new entities, fabricate items from a salvaged past.
First a raft made of broken spars and planks to transport the usable
stores he can find aboard the derelict. Corn, grain that had been
intended for the chickens that had perished. Muskets, powder, and
shot. Some tools, clothing, rum, and cordials — these last from the
captain's cabin — this is all he was able to bring ashore that first
day. In an irony that we must credit Defoe with, the ship had been
on a slaving venture, so that its small cargo was composed of
trinkets intended to trade with "Negroes" for other human beings:
mirrors and strands of beads and such, and all useless for a man
trying to survive on an island. Except for crates of hatchets, that
handy item of hardware for which many a tribe bartered away its
land and existence. Crusoe brings off dozens of these.

The issue of slavery and colonialism, hinted at in these early
pages and to be amplified in the person of Friday later, can only
be scarcely mentioned here to avoid a digression from the headway
I'm trying to make. Because, in the meantime, Crusoe has made
several trips out to the wreck, bringing back canvas sails, lengths
of chain and rope, pens and ink, Bibles of both persuasions (but
never to crack either one of them), shovels, needles, thread —
even the ship's dog swims ashore with him on the second trip, as
the crew's two cats gingerly cling to the bobbing raft. Bit by bit, he
has assembled the materials to put his life together, piled them up
around himself on this uncharted shore, all the ingredients for
survival — to make a good story. He even creates more company
for himself, in addition to the dog and cats, by training a local
parrot to talk to him, teaching it to say, "Poor Robin Crusoe. Where
are you? Where have you been? How came you here?" thereby
lending the bird a droll insight into the human dilemma it might
not have come on if left to itself, eating nuts and berries.

Downstairs, my grandfather, Tom Coyne, rattles the glass panels
of the bookcase and takes out a volume of the *Encyclopaedia Britan-
nica* — let's say Volume 7, "Damascu to Edu." But he's looking up
"Diesel," not "Defoe," or maybe he's turning to "Dredging" or
"Docks." This self-educated immigrant is obsessed by such research, and he glories in human invention, not the least his own.
He had studied civil engineering by army correspondence school

while riding herd on the Sioux, and he had put this minimal book learning to practical use building railroads in Mexico, Central America, and Peru. To read about the mechanics of human ingenuity and effort somehow reflected the picture of himself that he so vainly tried to hang in the American gallery.

For it was with such pieced-together knowledge and hard work that my grandfather confronted the hazards of this wilderness on whose shores he found himself at the age of fourteen, cut off from his family and his native Ireland. With no identity. Isolated. To say he coped would be an understatement, though the word's primal meaning describes his constant struggle: a continuous setting up of defenses against the unknown and the unseen — even within his marriage and paternity. The continual preparation and repair of defenses is the life's work of the immigrant; it is a castaway's regimen even though an enemy may never show up. The labor of putting up walls, of making the fortress sound becomes more important than the fortification — even its purpose lost. Moreover, to erect a fortress around a property — even a picket fence — is to define the property and make it more valuable, which, in turn, reflects upon the value of the work involved. Indeed, if no enemy threatens, the worth of the defense has been proved and the work of it justified. And its cost. Working hard is the success story of the alien; no other rewards are really necessary, and, in any event, are rarely handed out.

The stakes and pales that the industrious Crusoe hews and pounds into the ground around his domain make such a fence, never to be attacked, though he fears the natives who occasionally barbecue their captives on one of his beaches. The first of these picnics is the occasion when he rescues Friday, but it is Crusoe who attacks the natives — a peremptory strike we might call it, slaughtering them with the instruments of his imported technology: the flintlock musket and pistol. But he is never satisfied with his security and constantly builds more fences, each new stockade enlarging his holdings, as if he doesn't have the whole island in the first place. It does not occur to me, at age seven, that the subtext of *Robinson Crusoe* is work, nor that this castaway shares the fear of being unrelated to his surroundings that all outsiders fear — like Tom Coyne downstairs reading the encyclopedia. The construction an exile puts upon his reality not only is meant to defend the particular plot he has staked out, but acts as a sort of tether that keeps him from floating away from it.

But I do remember wondering why the man never took up fishing, a much easier source of food than the hardscrabble farming he threw himself into. A never-ending supply of food swam just off shore, but, of course, that would have been too easy. He planted and harvested corn, barley, and rice, learning how to conserve seed and manage his crops. He gathered and dried grapes to make raisins for winter meals. The wild goats that fortunately inhabited the place were domesticated for meat and milk. He even taught himself how to make butter.

Obviously, these are slim pickings, not the usual tropical island fantasy or the la-la land Odysseus sometimes washed up upon, but the isolated province of a philosophy that preached that acceptance by a community, not to mention the Almighty, only came through hard work. Defoe surely carried the rigors of his Cromwellian youth, but the lesson was lost on me, my imagination awash in Defoe's quick-paced narrative.

The twenty-eight years plus pass in a couple of winks; one event comes fast upon the other. The guy could tell a good story, and he keeps the action moving, continuously. No modernist he, and the reader is given little opportunity to reflect or look around the narrative and wonder about time and space. Also, sensual details are totally absent, for Crusoe seems to have lost his appreciation for beauty along with his identity papers. He may look at the ocean, but it is to study its currents and tides, not to glory in its metaphysical splendor, and there isn't a single description of a sunrise or a sunset, and they must have been humdingers.

But that doesn't matter. I am caught up with the details of him putting his life together, as the story is put together, and my grandmother worries that I am straining my eyes. She's heard that certain childhood diseases can affect the eyesight, and in a way, she is right, for I will never look at the world the same way again. By now, the shipwreck has planted a large square post on which he notches the elapsed time of his abandonment. He invents a method that keeps track of weeks and months as well as days. His habitat consists of a reinforced cave, and a second home for the dry season; a country estate, if you will, made of the ship's sails. He's discovered how to fire the island's soft clay into pottery for storing grain and boiling goat stew. He's built boats and taken up tailoring, using the dressed skins of animals. He's rather proud of the jaunty cap he's designed and sewn together — just a little vanity left over from pre-Cromwellian times — so he's not a complete drab. He bakes his own bread, making up a way to grind the corn and sifting its meal and then putting together an oven from fired clay bowls heaped over with hot coals. He must do without yeast, but then he's not making Wonder Bread — the process itself is a wonder.

Once Friday runs pell-mell into his life, escaping consumption to become a factor of consumption, bells begin to ring in my fevered head. I had just read *Huckleberry Finn,* and that young exile's journey down the Mississippi, with his own Friday, seemed very similar to the one I am reading, written two hundred years before. The raft that Jim and Huck shared was a sort of island set adrift, and they were left to their own resources to make do. To make up their identities. Surely, there must be a ton of theses somewhere on this likeness. But there is a difference. Twain backs away from the conclusion toward which his feelings are steering him, but his courage or his venality got him no further than the stunning metaphor for our national predicament, and maybe that's enough. But Defoe finished his novel with Crusoe continuing as the wandering loner, especially after Friday's death, to head out for the territories of China and Siberia, to return to England at age seventy to prepare for his "final journey," emphasis on *prepare.*

But another lesson has been teaching my imagination. I had already pictured myself as an orphan, set adrift nine months of the year from my parents; perhaps a prince forced into mufti. Kansas City was not quite a desert island, but something told me it wasn't where I should be. And here, in *Robinson Crusoe,* I came upon the plans and the methods to reconstruct my reality, to overcome my sense of isolation. Defoe was loaning me some of Crusoe's tools to create my own shelter and circumstance. The shipwrecked sailor showed me how to bring together scraps of happenstance; how the debris of the past and the present can be salvaged to make up a different identity, a new worth in the work of its own making.

JOHN MCNEEL

On the Fedala Road

FROM THE VIRGINIA QUARTERLY REVIEW

THE THIN LIGHT of the approaching daybreak always seemed to emphasize the strangeness and foreignness of our battalion's bivouac area on a country road outside Casablanca. Every morning a heavy mist covered the land just before the sun rose. Then, as the light grew, odd-looking shapes and things came slowly into view. The trees and vegetation were especially strange to us. Dotted over the little plain which lay across the road in front of our camp were fig, olive, and some kind of thorn trees, none of which I had ever seen before. Their limbs seemed blasted into weird, almost tortuous attitudes, as though in despair and supplication.

Dim, moving figures behind the mist, dressed in ghostly white, materialized as Arabs perched upright on the hindquarters of spindly donkeys or walking along the road. In the pre-reveille silence of the sleeping camp, the men on guard duty could hear a low, chattering hum of voices through the fog; daylight would show, across the plain about a hundred yards away, a cluster of squalid huts built of reeds and mud. Women and children moved about among the huts, milking goats and tending to cooking fires. Robed men bent over prayer mats, rising and falling, rising and falling in the immemorial genuflection to Mecca. Travelers on the road into the city climbed down from their donkeys to spread prayer mats beside the road. On the other side of the bivouac area, away from the plain and the highway, lay a more familiar sight, high sand dunes which hid the Atlantic from view but which did not drown out the welcome roar of its surf; this sound plainly said, this way, across this sea lies the suddenly enticing safety of home.

We arrived in Casablanca in late January 1943, pulling into port alongside a French battleship, the *Jean Bart,* which had been sunk at its pier during the British-American invasion of North Africa a short while before. We debarked from our troopship about midnight, walking across the *Bart's* deck, which was now level with the pier. We could see no sign of the structural damage shells and bombs would have wreaked on the great warship; apparently, she was scuttled by her crew.

It was for nearly all of us the first step onto a foreign shore. In the darkness, it was impossible to keep to any marching formation, much less keep in step, and so we stumbled our way along the pier and out into the city streets. We could hear the sounds and smell the spicy, exotic odors of an oriental city, but in the rigorously enforced blackout we could see almost nothing. From time to time we became aware of strange, spectral shapes floating toward us out of the darkness, uttering shrill, high-pitched cries, and it took us some time to realize that they were Arabs (Ayrabs to the Southerners among us) trying to sell us bottles of wine. As we marched along the darkened city streets out into the countryside, our full field packs soon became burdensome; we were out of shape after three idle weeks at sea. The march was a slow one, and we did not reach our bivouac area, about eight miles out of the city, along the road to Fedala, until nearly 4 A.M. A kitchen truck was already on hand when we arrived; for the first (and last) time, C rations were a welcome spread.

The next morning we could see that our pup tent encampment was situated around the rim of a shallow crater or depression in the sandy soil of the beach area. The battalion was divided into two parts: my company of about ninety men was located on the southern edge of the depression, on the side toward Casablanca, with the main body, more than seven hundred men, on the north rim and strung out along the road. A low ridge cut off our view of the sea, but the sound of the surf was plainly audible, at least at high tide. The crater was about seventy yards across and some twelve feet deep on its deepest side toward the sea; from the back, the sides sloped downward to the highway. During those first days few of us noticed a row of what looked like short fence posts lined up against the back wall of the depression.

We had little to do in the weeks we were in this camp. Afternoon passes into Casablanca were freely available, and on clear days we often went to the beach. Occasionally, squads of men would be taken by truck into the port area to help unload supplies from the ships streaming in from the States. We resented these duties because, as with all green troops, we valued the distinction between supply and combat men, which is what we were supposed to be. We were not even drilled or given any instructions in weapons handling, which in view of what lay ahead should have been done. These were in fact lazy, carefree days, which we would come to look back on with pleasure and longing. Today's jaded tourists may see Casablanca as a somewhat humdrum place, but to us it was endlessly fascinating. The "exotic East" was still a fresh and meaningful perception to us, and we were thrilled to see actual camel caravans coming in from (we supposed) the Sahara. That desert, of course, was hundreds of miles away.

The city was full of people of different races and nationalities, wartime European refugees rubbing shoulders with Arabs, Berbers, Senegalese Goums (with whom we were to become acquainted a year later in the mountains of Italy), and men of other African nationalities serving in the French colonial army. The Moroccan Arabs seemed to be divided into two distinct classes, the very rich and the very poor. There was no gasoline available to the civil population, and most cars were powered by clumsy, charcoal-burning apparatuses that gave off a noxious black smoke. Some residents found a slower but more romantic means of transportation; they removed the engines from prewar Citroens, Renaults, and Fords and hitched them to teams of horses. These vehicles drew elderly dowagers or dignified government officials slowly along the boulevards with a queer kind of stately elegance.

The streets were full of military personnel, and one quickly became aware of the often slovenly appearance and movements of American troops in general, the draftees and citizen-soldiers in particular. All of us were seeing for the first time representatives of a breed alien to us, the European professional military man. The contrast between them — the soldiery of France and, later, England, Germany, and Italy — and us, the conscripts of American farms, cities, and villages, was to me striking. I don't remember ever seeing European soldiers of any nation walking down a street out of step, or, unless they were drunk on furlough, in an untidy state of dress. By comparison, many Americans were often sloppily dressed, slouching in deportment, awkward in movement, in short unmilitary. It seemed to me that our uniforms, while of top quality materially, were not designed with military purposes in mind, were simply civilian articles of attire that had been dyed brown. Groups of soldiers on a city street looked somewhat like grocers or Kiwanis members on a tourist junket, all dressed in brown slacks and shirts.

Within days of our arrival we began to hear rumors about the sinister use to which the little coastal depression was put by the French military. French officers came out from Casablanca to inspect the site and to confer with our colonel, an unpopular, fussy martinet who treated the visitors with what seemed to us as obsequiousness, even officers inferior to him in rank. For the first time, we saw the row of posts along the back wall of the hole, to which, we heard, men were tied to be shot.

I find it difficult now to understand why our officers were so unwilling to tell us anything about the intentions of the French, but it must have been a direct order from our commanding officer, Colonel Zimmer. There was no reason for secrecy; it can only have been that he had adopted the attitude of the French officers, who were, in those days, a medieval lot; they seemed to feel that giving any kind of information that was not strictly necessary to enlisted men was beneath them. All we were told was that one morning soon we were to have visitors not on mercy bent. It became the custom for the sergeant of the guard to warn those pulling sentry duty around the perimeter of the camp to keep an eye on the road to Casablanca, especially in the early morning hours, and to sound the alarm if any vehicles were seen coming our way.

And that actually was how it happened. We were awakened before dawn one morning by someone banging on a mess kit. Far down the road we could see, in defiance of blackout regulations, the lights of a truck convoy of four vehicles moving slowly toward us. Along the beach area, one could see for long distances, and it seemed an age before the convoy reached our bivouac area. The reveille bugle sounded just as the first truck turned off the highway, but no one paid it any attention; there would be no roll call on this morning. Besides two troop trucks, there was a command car and a small van, the rear door of which, we noticed, was secured by a large padlock. The four vehicles were lined up and parked with military precision against the south wall of the depression, just beneath where the men of my company were lined up watching. (I can't remember that a single man refused to watch the proceedings, but a subsequent execution drew a slim audience from among us.) Two soldiers jumped down from one of the trucks and took up guard posts at the rear of the van. The others remained sitting, at attention it seemed to us, in the trucks.

Colonel Zimmer and Sergeant Charette, one of the few French-speaking men in the battalion and who acted as an interpreter at battalion headquarters, walked down the sloping side of the depression toward the command car just as a French major and two lieutenants got out. The major was dressed in riding trousers and leather leggings, a formal military jacket, and all three officers wore the round, billed kepi, made familiar by many a Hollywood epic, such as *Beau Geste.* Colonel and major saluted and shook hands, the major introducing his colleagues to Colonel Zimmer; they saluted but did not shake hands. All three French officers were tall, slender men, while the colonel was rather short and squat in build; Charette, too, was somewhat short. To us, it seemed that Colonel Zimmer did most of the talking, with Charette interpreting. The three Frenchmen showed polite interest, but they seemed aloof, almost disdainful; they stood erect and hardly moved. The colonel, on the other hand, could not keep still. He fidgeted, gesticulated, stood first on one leg and then on the other, folded his arms across his chest, moments later jerking his hands down to his hips in an aggressive, arms akimbo stance. He seemed almost fawning in his attitude.

Presently, the conversation came to an end, and colonel and sergeant climbed up to where the other battalion officers were standing. Charette came over to join the enlisted men, and we were finally given at least a quasi-official report on what was about to take place. He said the van contained a prisoner, an Arab, who had been caught looting the bodies of dead and wounded French soldiers during the American attack on the coast near Casablanca. He was to be shot. He warned those few men who had cameras that the French would permit no picture-taking. After the execution, Charette said, the French officers, on Colonel Zimmer's invitation, were to have breakfast in the officers' mess.

Down in the crater, French noncoms were directing the proceedings. The three officers stood apart chatting, completely ignoring the activity in front of them and also ignoring the American officers standing just above them. At a shouted command, the French soldiers came out of the trucks, jumping over the tailgate onto the rough, sandy ground; they were joined by the two soldiers who had been guarding the van. We saw thirty fit-looking, sunburned men in the uniforms of the colonial army lined up in two columns being dressed off by a corporal. There came another command, and the columns moved off at quickstep toward the sandstone cliff at the rear of the depression. To raw, barely trained troops such as ourselves, the precise movement of these superbly trained men was little short of dazzling. We were not able to follow the corporal's commands, and it seemed like magic that the thirty fast-moving soldiers ended up, without a misstep, in six five-men squads, three squads facing the other three across an interval of a few yards directly in front of one of the low posts just out from the cliff.

The sergeant in command walked to the rear of the van and unlocked the door. A Roman Catholic military chaplain and two guards stepped out, turning as they touched the ground to help the prisoner down. But there was no further movement; in a moment, the sergeant reached inside and, not unkindly, pulled the man out by the arm. We could see a short, rather bulky figure dressed in a dirty, brown cloak topped with a rough hood. The hood, looking somewhat like a monk's cowl, completely covered the prisoner's face. His hands were manacled in front of him, and the cloak was not quite long enough to cover the leg chains. He seemed on the point of collapse, and the two guards, slinging their rifles, took him by the arms. At a command from the sergeant, the guards moved forward, half dragging, half carrying the prisoner, whose head barely reached the shoulder level of the tall Europeans. Slowly, the little party, prisoner, guards, sergeant, and priest, walked between the rifle squads, who stood at rigid attention, toward the post. On reaching it, the prisoner was turned to face the riflemen, and his hand manacles were removed. Silent until that moment, he suddenly let out a long, shrill scream, and his hands shot up, knocking the hood away from his head.

"Jesus!" It sounded as though the hundreds of soldiers lining the rim of the crater had given a collective gasp of astonishment.

"He's only a kid!" And it was true, he did seem very young, to most of us he appeared to be no more than fifteen or sixteen years old. Now that his head and shoulders were exposed, we could see that his body was malformed, and he looked as if he was mentally defective. His head was too large, even for the chunky body; it was a misshapen head, pulled down on the right shoulder, which was several inches lower than the left one. His rough features were contorted with fear. The shrill wail, once started, never ceased. It rose and fell unevenly, now rising to a near-scream and then falling back to a low, keening wail. For a few moments, the priest, holding a breviary in one hand, tried to gain the boy's attention; failing, he gave up and joined the three officers standing to one side.

The boy was alone now with the two guards and a corporal. The latter offered a cigarette, but he was past heeding. In this last extremity, he must have felt a desperate loneliness, as well as terror. In his final moments on earth, he was cut off from the men of his own race and religion, surrounded by his killers, a priest of an alien faith and several hundred curious strangers from across the sea.

Fifteen minutes passed, then thirty, then forty-five, the soldiers standing at ease. The sun was now well up from the horizon, but still the officers stood talking and laughing together. Did they possibly hope for a reprieve? The road to Casablanca, though full of the usual inbound traffic, was empty of vehicles headed toward our camp. Then, suddenly, the execution was under way, though none of us had heard a spoken command. Two corporals walked up to the post, grabbed the boy's hands, and tied them behind his back. He gave one last desperate scream and was silent, except for heavy, labored breathing. The noncoms forced him to his knees in front of the post, lashing him to it with a piece of rope around the chest and using the leg irons to secure the bottom part of his body. A black hood was dropped over the misshapen head and a black target patch covered the left breast. Then noncoms and guards walked away to one side.

One of the lieutenants stepped forward, in front of and to one side of the rifle squads. The sergeant barked out a command, and the middle squad on the right side of the post made a quick right face, almost at the same moment moving off at double time. As the head man in the squad came level with the lieutenant, he executed a left turn, the others following without breaking stride. Within seconds they were halted and given a right face. Another barked order and the second and fourth man dropped to the kneeling position; at the same instant, all five men raised their rifles to the firing position. The lieutenant lifted his right arm, made a sudden slashing move downward, the volley crashed out, and the figure at the stake leaped forward, straining for a few seconds against the bonds before falling limp. Drawing his revolver, the lieutenant walked over to the stake and pulled the hood away from the boy's head; with cool proficiency, he held the gun in both hands against the top of the still head and pulled the trigger. Without a backward glance, he walked away, blowing into the barrel of the gun before replacing it in the holster at his belt, and joined the other officers and the priest.

To the watching Americans, the shooting had been accomplished with stunning rapidity and efficiency. For a few seconds none of us stirred, except for one Pennsylvania boy who lay vomiting in the sand. I don't think it is in any way an exaggeration to say that in this brief time we lost not a little of our New World innocence. In straggling groups, men began moving back toward the tent area, while others stayed to the end, watching the French soldiers place the body in a rough, wooden coffin and nail the lid shut. They lifted it into one of the trucks, then all the vehicles except the command car turned into the road to Casablanca.

The French officers and the priest climbed up the side of the crater to join Colonel Zimmer and his staff. The two groups bowed, shook hands, then walked together toward the officers' mess tent, with Sergeant Charette in attendance. During the meal, he said later, Colonel Zimmer toasted the French on the successful and skillful completion of their mission, and he presented each officer with a carton of Lucky Strikes as a token of his esteem.

BEN METCALF

American Heartworm

FROM THE BAFFLER

I

I PROCEED FROM RAGE: rage at those whose ignorance, either God-given or self-consciously homespun, has excited in them a wrongheaded desire to peddle as the font of all that is virtuous and productive and eternal about our nation that shallow and putrid trough we call the Mississippi River. For generations we have suffered such fools to create unworthy riverside wetland areas and disappointing overlook sites and unventilated paddleboat museums and disturbing amusement parks on the theme of the American frontier; to form historical societies so that we might come to think a great deal more than we should of a rill no deeper in places than a backyard swimming pool and far less apt to hold its water; to lay bicycle paths along the levees so that we might crack open our heads within sight of chemical wastes bound for the Gulf of Mexico; to clutter the calendar with steamboat festivals and "Big Muddy" days so that we might pay a premium for corndogs and warm cola, and grow red and sullen under the Midwestern sun, and slap our children before a congregation of strangers acquainted with the impulse and approving of the act. Yet as much as I detest those who would pound the pig iron of history into the tinfoil of folklore, and despite the ease with which I could build a case against these people, and ascribe all that is trumped-up and harmful and loathsome about their region to a native failure to work the algebra of decency and taste, my hatred of the river itself is greater still, and conscience will not let me sight the lesser target.

For what manmade entity has worked more evil upon the land

than has this accident of nature? What other waterway has been the seat of more shame, or has inspired us to greater stupidity, or has inflicted more brutal and embarrassing wounds upon our culture? Have not the basest qualities to be found in the people of the middle states been quickened by the river's example, or by its seeming impulse for self-promotion? And have not these lessons been learned so well that the region now has little more to recommend it than the various log-cabin homes of Abraham Lincoln (hundreds of these), a handful of competing grain-based gasoline concerns, and the fat substitute olestra? But I hardly mean to confine myself to generalities here: My grievances against the river are specific and they are personal, for so thoroughly have the ideals it teaches laid waste to the soul and imagination of my own family, the Metcalfs of southern Illinois, that a high degree of emotional suffering and moral decay has become almost a point of pride among its members as they walk life's dreary dirt road.

II

The Mississippi's lessons are not "hard" in the familiar sense, wherein some touching bit of wisdom is had for a nominal fee, payable in humility and gratitude; they are hard precisely because, being wholly bad lessons, they exact a cost in wisdom, and because the river's students pay a dear tuition in sanity and health and self-esteem for the privilege of learning that which can only harm them further. Moreover, history records an almost conscious effort by the "old man" to clear his classroom of all those who recognize bunk when they see it and to gather in those who do not, a task accomplished in large part through the importation of white men. The first of these, De Soto, saw the river in 1542 but was of a reasonable bent and did not think the discovery worth bragging about; the river killed him. One hundred and thirty-one years later came Marquette the priest (now a Wisconsin basketball power) and Joliet the salesman (now an Illinois prison), who canoed downstream despite being asked not to by the local Indians and who, along with La Salle et al., set in motion a process by which the hospitable natives of the area became first trinket wholesalers, then Christians manqué, and finally a market to saturate with whiskey and firearms. Once this last goal had been achieved, the Choctaw helped the French annihilate or enslave the Natchez, while the Ojibwa scattered the Sioux, drove off the Winnebago, and ran the Fox, already shot full of holes by the French, into the desolate reaches of northeastern Wisconsin, where the Packers now play. Then arrived the European smallpox in 1782, ably ferried from village to village by the obliging Mississippi, and what few natives the plague left breathing were thereafter loath to crane their necks around the bend for fear of what was coming to get them next.

I imagine that after such a convincing bit of treachery only the stubborn or the foolish would not make some effort to get as far away from the river as they possibly could. One of those who stayed, or was born of those who stayed, was my great-great-great-grandmother "Grutch," most likely a Chickasaw, who married Joshua Metcalf, a widowed southern Illinois farmer, and bore him a son, Frank, to complement the lot his dead wife had left him, and who died herself, along with the first wife's children and those of a neighboring farm couple who had asked her to baby-sit, when at lunchtime one day she poured out tall glasses of milk laced with rat poison. The neighboring parents were never seen again, and it is assumed that they poisoned the milk and the children much in the same way that an animal chews off its own foot to be free of a trap, the trap in this instance being the river and all that it had cost them.

Young Frank did not fancy milk and drank only half of what was in his glass, enough to stunt and disfigure him but not enough to discontinue the line. In spite of his flaws, and his half-breed hair and features, the boy managed to secure a local farm girl for a mate and to avoid her outraged brothers, who had sworn vengeance not for the insult of the seduction but because a general by the name of Metcalf had once enthusiastically slaughtered their Irish cousins at the behest of the English crown. Frank tilled the soil in southern Illinois as had his father before him, leaving only briefly to make some ranching money in the Indian Territory (later Oklahoma) but returning when the Arkansas, a tentacle of the Mississippi, dried up one summer, as did the sum of his herd and profit.

My great-grandfather, Otto, was just a boy when he watched his father's fortune blow away in the Oklahoma dust, and when he grew into manhood all the obstinacy of his forebears, and all the bitterness and disappointment this trait had sowed over the generations, took full root in him. Otto sought to revisit his father's dream without leaving Illinois, *without leaving the river,* and because he could not afford the acreage required to graze even a moderate herd there, and because this circumstance served only to affirm his small place in the world, he made a habit of reversing the inevitable stampedes with shotgun blasts; all that could not be controlled in this manner he struck out at with his fists.

His firstborn, Max, tolerated these outbursts and the whippings because he believed, incongruously, that his place in the world was not small but large. He rode boxcars and flew cropdusters and caroused and married and in the end could no more escape the river's gravity than had his ancestors. Max's large place in the world had convinced him to people it as best he could, and with thirteen mouths to feed, my father's wide among them, he was forced at last to take work along the river as a conductor on the same north-south freight trains that as a young man he had jumped and that a century earlier had killed off the steamboats, which had killed off the keelboats, which had killed off the flatboats, which had killed off the Indians. After nearly two decades of sitting idle in cabooses, catching sight now and then of the Mississippi and all the while smoking tobacco, trade in which the river had graciously abetted, my grandfather was stricken with cancer and found himself being driven, in what the clownish side of circumstance had arranged to be a De Soto, across the muddy water to a hospital in St. Louis, where, after a devastating operation, he would taste the painkillers that in time would weaken first his will, and then his heart, and then his earthly grip.

III

In the mid-seventies an aunt and uncle were part of a Ma Barker-esque gang whose sad tale ended one afternoon with a raid on a warehouse by local authorities and a standoff in which my pregnant, foul-mouthed, shotgun-wielding aunt used up what social credit was still being extended to the family in those days. My own father has said, with some regret in his voice, that he once passed up the opportunity to help rob the Denny's between Charleston and Mattoon, Illinois. He had no moral qualms with the plan but could not find the energy to participate, or to do much else over the next twenty-odd years, once he understood how little a week's take at the only place in the area worth robbing would improve his ability to feed and clothe his children.

What tripped up my aunt and uncle, and I suspect would have undone my father as well, was an irrepressible urge to brag about what had been stolen and to exaggerate its worth well beyond the bounds of good sense. The police might not have troubled themselves with the warehouse, which of course had been left unlocked, had they not been led to believe that they would find there countless stolen Cadillacs, bags full of laundered mob money, and stacks of Fort Knox gold. As it was, and no doubt owing to the truculent stupidity the river had bred into the Metcalfs over the generations, my aunt made her stand over a few broken-down refrigerators and a lone pig.

Most of America's national resources, and the despoliation of same, have their mythic personifications: the Northwestern forests have Paul Bunyan, who, like the trees he felled, was immensely tall and who, if we are to believe the American lumber industry, created all that we now see before us; the Great Plains have Pecos Bill, whose bronco rides were apparently so intense that they whipped up the tornadoes that now regularly flatten trailer parks filled with Metcalfs; and I suppose all of America lays claim to John Henry, who represented the railroad, which has always wanted us to regard it as a natural resource. To this list the Mississippi adds an unmedicated schizophrenic named Mike Fink, a flatboat pilot who, to hear him tell it, was "half horse, half alligator" and could eat "you for breakfast, your folks for supper, and all of your cousins for a snack in between," which is to say that the river is personified, and aptly so, by a stunted and belligerent liar.

The damage done to my family by this monster Fink, and by Huck and Tom, those young liars Fink prefigured, is close to immeasurable. When my father speaks of a youthful altercation, he does not say that both parties were injured some, as is the usual way with fights; rather he says, "I hit that motherfucker so hard he actually complimented me on it later — said he was shitting teeth for a week." When I hear the tale of how my great-uncle Walter threatened my grandfather with a knife, I am not told that there was some nod toward calm, or some recognition that Walter was mentally ill and needed to be dealt with accordingly; I hear that "Max had that silly fucker on his knees before he could blink and told him, 'If you ever pull a knife on me again, you sonofabitch,

I'll stick it so far up your ass you won't have to cut your meat come suppertime.'"

I do not know exactly what led Walter to draw on Grandpa. By all accounts Walter was a miserable drunk who spent his days whitewashing clapboard houses that eventually would rot because of the flooding and the humidity, and would collapse into sticks if a twister came near, but could not be built of stone or brick because the boy in Mr. Twain's story had painted a *wooden* fence, and so Walter, who might have made a decent and sober bricklayer, was forced instead to cover house after wooden house with the whitest paint he could find, which contained an extraordinary helping of lead, which may or may not have given him the bone cancer that would eventually spread to his skull and torture him there until he died but certainly did not help his sanity or intelligence in the meantime and may or may not have been a factor in both the drinking and the knife pulled on Grandpa. I do not know. What I do know is that Walter might have lived and died beyond humiliation's shadow if the river had not driven him to drink, and Tom Sawyer had not poisoned him with lead, and Mike Fink had not encouraged him to pull a knife on a man three times as fast, ten times as smart, and fully twice his size.

IV

I used to consider it odd that the word most often called upon by those compelled to describe their feelings for a river that had just washed away their crops, or their homes, or their livestock, or their neighbors, was "respect," because to my mind a river worthy of respect put up a fight against the rain, and made some show of absorbing what fell, and did not run its banks at the first sign of darkening clouds and heat lightning. I did not know then that to the river's victims, "respect" is but a theatrical means of invoking the notions "fear" and "helplessness," and that so familiar are these notions to the river-warped mind as to render a more direct reference to them absurd.

Fear in the Midwest bears relation not only to the river's senseless attacks but to the flattened land beyond its banks, which promises the paranoid (and the river has made many of these) that he will be able to see Armageddon coming a long way off but reminds him always that there will be precious little barring its way.

My father has said that when lazy old Basil Metcalf, my great-great-great-great-great-grandfather, reached the Mississippi somewhere in the lower half of Illinois, he stopped there simply because it was the first thing he had encountered since leaving the East that could not be walked around or over; he intended to press on, the story goes, but perished before he could decide whether to head north or south. His son Reuben, an uncommonly bleak and wary soul, father of Joshua, in time would see a son taken away by the Union Army and would sit outside his farmhouse and scan the horizon until one morning he spotted what he took to be a visitor far across his fields and by evening held a note informing him that his son was dead, shot through the eye at Vicksburg, the body being sent upriver to Cairo. Reuben set off to claim the boy's remains, sure now that fate and the landscape had conspired against him, and promptly vanished. He may have reached Cairo and kept going, having concluded too late that his father's course need not have been stayed by such a petty obstacle, but more likely he was murdered somewhere along the river's banks, a common occurrence in those days and not unheard of in these. At any rate, the river failed to make delivery on either corpse.

The Midwestern strain of helplessness is in part a function of the river's exaggerated capacity, for although much is made of the fact that it attains a width of 3,000 feet (generally rounded to "a mile") and a depth of 200 feet (also "a mile"), this holds true only if one attempts to swim across in the vicinity of New Orleans; upstream the soundings are less impressive: from Baton Rouge to St. Paul a shipping channel of just nine feet is maintained. It is well worth asking what chance those feet have against a flow of the sort reported in 1993, when eleven times the volume of Niagara Falls threatened St. Louis, and it is equally well worth asking what chance is afforded even inland trailer homes against a river so ill-equipped to contain the water, or to teach by its example anything more hopeful than that weakness and chaos are the natural law.

The power of this lesson is made clear to me when I learn that a cousin of mine has burned down his high school because a bully told him to do so, or has molested a child for his own reasons, or has run off with his brother's wife (and offered his own in recompense), or has deserted his pregnant girlfriend for a woman old enough to buy him beer, or has somehow managed to electrocute himself, or has tattooed an infant, or has been beaten so badly that her kidney was removed, or has not spoken to her aunt since her aunt married the man who ruined the kidney, or has rolled a car because his father never taught him to slow down on corners (and because the thought never occurred to him privately), or has attempted to run down his wife and her lover in a combine, or has been shotgunned at close range but is "too ornery to die," or has been arrested for growing marijuana *in the front yard,* or has made no effort to pay the telephone bill and must now communicate solely by CB radio, or has become some sort of humorless Christian, or has been delivered of yet another child so that this jug band of woe might play on.

I can no more doubt that the river has turned and perverted my cousins' lives than that it has done the same to its own course, at will and at random, over the eleven thousand or so years since it was brought into existence by what looks to have been an honest mistake on the part of a glacier. In his book *The Control of Nature,* Mr. McPhee writes that "southern Louisiana exists in its present form because the Mississippi River has jumped here and there within an arc of about two hundred miles wide, like a pianist playing with one hand. . . . Always it is the river's purpose to get to the Gulf by the shortest and steepest gradient." Although I concur with the notion that the river's selfish meanderings have cursed us with southern Louisiana, I prefer the image of a drunken blind man carelessly whipping his cane back and forth in unfamiliar surrounds to that of a tasteful pianist. And I do not think that the river's purpose is "to get to the Gulf" so much as it is to cause the greatest amount of suffering on the way there. Consider the river's capricious disregard for the boundaries between our states: Arkansas has been forced to sue Tennessee on numerous occasions (1918, 1940, 1970) in order to retrieve land and taxpayers carved from its eastern flank by the river and handed over to the Volunteer State. Louisiana has sued Mississippi (1906, 1931, 1966) for like cause, and Mississippi has sued Louisiana, and Arkansas has sued Mississippi, and Missouri has sued Kentucky, and Iowa has sued Illinois, and Minnesota has sued Wisconsin, until the very identities of these states have been eroded, and the wisdom of entrusting their shapes to a slithering and deceitful border impeached.

This epidemic of strife and distrust has spread elsewhere, to other rivers and other states (e.g., *Texas v. Louisiana, Missouri v. Nebraska, Nebraska v. Iowa, Indiana v. Kentucky, Virginia v. Tennessee, Maryland v. West Virginia, Rhode Island v. Massachusetts*), and has so intensified our citizenry's penchant for litigation that judges in many fluvial districts no longer have even the time required to perform a marriage or to entertain a bribe. In those areas directly scarred by the Mississippi, neighbors sue one another with a frequency and a fervor that belie the small gains to be had, having learned at the foot of the river hard lessons in desperation that have left them suckers for the bittersweet lies of the American justice system. I consider it a mere accident that to date, and to the best of my knowledge, no Metcalf has sued another Metcalf, and I do not doubt that this fact will reverse itself soon. Already the Midwestern milieu is such that involvement in a petty lawsuit is held to be the height of glamour and achievement and therefore suitable excuse not to hold down a job.

My grandmother once spoke proudly to me of a cousin who had finally "growed up a little." The cause of the improvement was not parenthood, for he was a father many times over and by numerous women; nor was it some semblance of a career, for he was minimally employed at that time and, as far as I know, since. What impressed my grandmother was that he had found the gumption to sue someone (or to do something that got him sued; I cannot remember which, nor does it particularly matter) and at last stood to make a man of himself. He failed, of course, even on these terms. Petition lost, courtroom fees owed and unpayable, he ceded control to the panic that was his birthright and fled to Missouri, across the river but really no farther from it, where I suppose he became, at least until the next chance to play the river's fool* presented, a child again.

---

*Mr. Russell "Rusty" Weston Jr., late of Valmeyer, Illinois, and a small pied-à-gulch in Montana, who in July of 1998 allegedly took it upon himself to gun down a dozen cats and two Capitol Police officers before being shot himself, was so perfect an example of Mississippi victimhood that I wondered at the time of his spree if he did not have some Metcalf blood in him. Here was a man who had seen his town washed away in the 1993 floods and (stubbornly, pointlessly) rebuilt just a stone's throw to the east to await the river's next assault, who was terrified of television sets and satellite dishes (this is common even among Midwesterners who own and enjoy them), who believed that the president of the United States had

V

There runs through this continent a river worthy at least of the
praise heaped upon the paltry Mississippi; that drains 9,715 square
miles of Canada without once crossing the border, as well as
523,000 square miles, or fully one-sixth, of these United States;
that rises up out of the Continental Divide in Montana and wends
its way across the American heartland, flowing in places north and
elsewhere east and in the balance south, having decided its course
a long time ago and having for the most part stuck to it; that at
2,315 miles is without challenge the longest stream around and if
allowed by mapmakers to claim its southernmost leg (that is, "the
Mississippi River" below St. Louis) would reach 3,495 miles, a
length bested only by those great rivers of the tropics, the Nile and
the Amazon. I refer, of course, to the Missouri River.

In addition to doing its own job, the Missouri drains nearly
three-quarters of the upper Mississippi basin, leaving the rest not
to the Mississippi, which is incapable of doing what by rights should
come naturally to it, but to the Iowa, the Illinois, the Des Moines,
the Wisconsin, the Minnesota, the Meramec, the Kaskaskia, and
the St. Croix, fine rivers all. That they, along with the White, the
St. Francis, the Salt, and the Rock, should be deemed "tributaries"
of the Mississippi I can only regard as fraud of the highest order,
considering that the Mississippi, which receives nearly half of its
annual flow from the Ohio alone, and a good deal of the remain-
der from the Missouri, is but where these streams happen to collide
and not, as is commonly supposed, the mythic force that draws
them together or, more ludicrous still, created them.

The Mississippi is in reality a thin creek issuing from a nonde-

---

sent a Navy SEAL to kill him (the SEAL is an unusual variation here, but the claim
of persecution at the hands of the president certainly is not), and whose acute
schizophrenia deviated so slightly from the Midwestern norm that his father
thought it sufficient to offer the following gloss to the *Miami Herald:* "His mind
doesn't work real good." More familiar still, and what finally locates Mr. Weston Jr.
on the middle bands of the riverine behavioral spectrum, is his comfort with, and
obvious flair for, the lawsuit. In addition to considering a suit against the Secret
Service, who had questioned him regarding threats he had made against the
president, Mr. Weston Jr. is known to have sued a pickup-truck dealer in Illinois
and to have fought his eighty-six-year-old landlady, who he claimed had beaten him
with a cane, all the way to the Montana Supreme Court, where, in true Mississippian
fashion, he lost.

script pond in Minnesota and would likely trickle away to nothing before it reached St. Louis if on the way it did not loot every proper river in sight. Even availed of the extra water, the Mississippi is so wasteful with the stuff, and so fickle with its bearings, that only the constant attentions of the Army Corps of Engineers enable it to reach the Gulf at all. Unaided, it would pour off into the Louisiana swampland known as Atchafalaya and form a fetid inland sea. Should it therefore surprise us that the Mississippi's pupils have developed a habit for public assistance unrivaled even by that to be found in our decaying coastal cities; that there is scarcely a household in my extended family that does not have at least one potential breadwinner sitting it out on some sort of "disability"; that there are stores in these people's communities where a food stamp is met with less suspicion than a five- or ten-dollar bill?

Some years ago an uncle made a break with family tradition and found work in the oil fields near his house, doing so not because he saw any need to improve himself or his situation but because the job allowed him to tell people he was an "oilman," which he thought had a ring to it. He did not care much for the actual work, though, and began to send his eldest son out in his stead, a practice tolerated by my uncle's employers only because they considered it unlikely that the son could be any lazier than the father. The boy soon opened their minds, and one afternoon he arrived home to tell his father, "We've been fired." My parents visited shortly after the incident and found the entire household in good spirits. My uncle had been angry at first, and he did express concern that his son might never learn how to hold down a job, but now he believed that things might work out after all: as he saw it, both he and the boy were now eligible for unemployment. My parents did not disabuse him of the notion.

VI

Having taught the Midwesterner to freeload, and to lie, and to steal, and to work violence against his brother, the Mississippi now rings its doleful school bell once more. My father heeds the call as he always has, emptying the family bank account and driving to one of several riverboat casinos tethered off the coasts of Illinois, Iowa, and Missouri, where he plays at blackjack and roulette until he has entirely lost what sum my mother has managed to save up since his last unfortunate visit. He goes not because he believes that the river will make a winner of him, for he surrendered that fantasy long ago, if indeed he ever entertained it at all. He goes because he believes, or needs to believe, that one day the river might look more kindly upon its son than it has in the past, and teach him some lesson not predicated on havoc and despair, and allow him just once to recoup the losses that have imperiled both his future and his sanity.

And of course it never will.

Ecce Mississippi. We might well ask how much longer the republic can stand with a worm such as this slithering through its heart.

ARTHUR MILLER

Before Air Conditioning

FROM THE NEW YORKER

EXACTLY WHAT YEAR it was I can no longer recall — probably 1927 or '28 — there was an extraordinarily hot September, which hung on even after school had started and we were back from our Rockaway Beach bungalow. Every window in New York was open, and on the streets venders manning little carts chopped ice and sprinkled colored sugar over mounds of it for a couple of pennies. We kids would jump onto the back steps of the slow-moving, horse-drawn ice wagons and steal a chip or two; the ice smelled vaguely of manure but cooled palm and tongue.

People on West 110th Street, where I lived, were a little too bourgeois to sit out on their fire escapes, but around the corner on 111th and farther uptown mattresses were put out as night fell, and whole families lay on those iron balconies in their underwear.

Even through the nights, the pall of heat never broke. With a couple of other kids, I would go across 110th to the park and walk among the hundreds of people, singles and families, who slept on the grass, next to their big alarm clocks, which set up a mild cacophony of the seconds passing, one clock's ticks syncopating with another's. Babies cried in the darkness, men's deep voices murmured, and a woman let out an occasional high laugh beside the lake. I can recall only white people spread out on the grass; Harlem began above 116th Street then.

Later on, in the Depression thirties, the summers seemed even hotter. Out West, it was the time of the red sun and the dust storms, when whole desiccated farms blew away and sent the Okies, whom Steinbeck immortalized, out on their desperate treks toward the Pacific. My father had a small coat factory on Thirty-ninth Street then, with about a dozen men working sewing machines. Just to watch them handling thick woolen winter coats in that heat was, for me, a torture. The cutters were on piecework, paid by the number of seams they finished, so their lunch break was short — fifteen or twenty minutes. They brought their own food: bunches of radishes, a tomato perhaps, cucumbers, and a jar of thick sour cream, which went into a bowl they kept under the machines. A small loaf of pumpernickel also materialized, which they tore apart and used as a spoon to scoop up the cream and vegetables.

The men sweated a lot in those lofts, and I remember one worker who had a peculiar way of dripping. He was a tiny fellow, who disdained scissors, and, at the end of a seam, always bit off the thread instead of cutting it, so that inch-long strands stuck to his lower lip, and by the end of the day he had a multicolored beard. His sweat poured onto those thread ends and dripped down onto the cloth, which he was constantly blotting with a rag.

Given the heat, people smelled, of course, but some smelled a lot worse than others. One cutter in my father's shop was a horse in this respect, and my father, who normally had no sense of smell — no one understood why — claimed that he could smell this man and would address him only from a distance. In order to make as much money as possible, this fellow would start work at half past five in the morning and continue until midnight. He owned Bronx apartment houses and land in Florida and Jersey, and seemed half mad with greed. He had a powerful physique, a very straight spine, a tangle of hair, and a black shadow on his cheeks. He snorted like a horse as he pushed the cutting machine, following his patterns through some eighteen layers of winter-coat material. One late afternoon, he blinked his eyes hard against the burning sweat as he held down the material with his left hand and pressed the vertical, razor-sharp reciprocating blade with his right. The blade sliced through his index finger at the second joint. Angrily refusing to go to the hospital, he ran tap water over the stump, wrapped his hand in a towel, and went right on cutting, snorting, and stinking. When the blood began to show through the towel's bunched layers, my father pulled the plug on the machine and ordered him to the hospital. But he was back at work the next morning, and worked right through the day and into the evening, as usual, piling up his apartment houses.

*

There were still elevated trains then, along Second, Third, Sixth, and Ninth Avenues, and many of the cars were wooden, with windows that opened. Broadway had open trolleys with no side walls, in which you at least caught the breeze, hot though it was, so that desperate people, unable to endure their apartments, would simply pay a nickel and ride around aimlessly for a couple of hours to cool off. As for Coney Island on weekends, block after block of beach was so jammed with people that it was barely possible to find a space to sit or to put down your book or your hot dog.

My first direct contact with an air conditioner came only in the sixties, when I was living in the Chelsea Hotel. The so-called management sent up a machine on casters, which rather aimlessly cooled and sometimes heated the air, relying, as it did, on pitchers of water that one had to pour into it. On the initial filling, it would spray water all over the room, so one had to face it toward the bathroom rather than the bed.

A South African gentleman once told me that New York in August was hotter than any place he knew in Africa, yet people here dressed for a northern city. He had wanted to wear shorts but feared that he would be arrested for indecent exposure.

High heat created irrational solutions: linen suits that collapsed into deep wrinkles when one bent an arm or a knee, and men's straw hats as stiff as matzohs, which, like some kind of hard yellow flower, bloomed annually all over the city on a certain sacred date —June 1 or so. Those hats dug deep pink creases around men's foreheads, and the wrinkled suits, which were supposedly cooler, had to be pulled down and up and sidewise to make room for the body within.

The city in summer floated in a daze that moved otherwise sensible people to repeat endlessly the brainless greeting "Hot enough for ya? Ha-ha!" It was like the final joke before the meltdown of the world in a pool of sweat.

JOYCE CAROL OATES

After Amnesia

FROM GRANTA

WE ENTER THE WORLD as purely physical beings and leave it in the same way. In between, through our lifetimes, we labor pridefully to establish *identities, selves* distinct from our bodies. Not *what* we are but *who* we are. This is the crux of our humanity.

I had reason to believe myself established in my identity. I had been a professional woman for more than twenty years, and had been attached to Princeton University for some time; a woman who had earned, it might be argued, the privilege of being no longer a *woman* exclusively but a *person*. Of course, I didn't think of such things. It would not have occurred to me to think of such things. I had assimilated these assumptions over two-thirds of my lifetime the way food is broken down and assimilated into the body's bones, flesh, and blood.

This episode, this humiliating experience, occurred in March 1984. I told no one about it afterward, failing to find an adequate language in which to transpose it into an entertaining anecdote, and not wanting to embarrass others, in any case. For perhaps eleven years I did not think of it. I had not so much forgotten it as dismissed it — a cluster of blurred, vaguely malevolent images, and smells; a dreamlike event to which confused emotions were attached, perhaps not even my own.

The occasion was a guided tour through a New Jersey prison facility. The Millstone County Detention Center, I'll call it, named for a river that flows nearby in an anonymous urban area not unlike the outskirts of Newark, New Jersey. Less than an hour's drive from Princeton, where I live, but so wholly unlike Princeton as to seem a separate state. (It's part of my amnesia that I'm unable to recall who arranged for me to visit the facility. I'm sure I didn't make a personal request. More likely, a friend of a friend, or a professional acquaintance, had arranged for the invitation. I've said yes to most invitations of a seemingly "broadening" and "enriching" nature out of a dread of saying no to the one crucial invitation that might make a difference in my life.)

From the outside, the Millstone County Detention Center did not appear conspicuously different from the old weather-worn factories, warehouses, and train yards in the vicinity, which I had only glimpsed from time to time, in passing, from an interstate highway. The walls were high, ten or twelve feet of gray, discolored concrete that appeared to be exuding an oily damp, topped with "razor wire" in sinuous coils. When I parked my car in the visitors' parking lot, which was almost empty, I smelled a sharp odor in the air as of coins held in a sweating palm, that might have been blown from a chemical factory near the river, but was concentrated in the area around the detention center.

As soon as I entered the building through a metal detector checkpoint, past uniformed guards from the Millstone County Sheriff's Office, I thought *This is a mistake: turn back.* But of course I did not turn back. Pride and curiosity in equal measure would never have allowed me to turn back. The tour group was small, only five or six of us. A professor from Rutgers-Newark Law School, a visiting criminologist, lawyers from the New Jersey State Department of Public Advocacy. My identity that day was not "writer" but "professor of humanities, Princeton University." I'm unable to remember the names, even the faces, of these other visitors, except that they were all men, and, like me, Caucasian. The fact of race would not seem significant outside the context of a state prison in which so many inmates are black; "Caucasians" rarely feel any binding principle otherwise. Majority populations take themselves for granted as the norm; not accident, still less historical privilege, but "nature" would seem to define us.

Our tour guide was an officer from the New Jersey State Correctional Facility, wearing a bright coppery badge that identified him as a sergeant and an instructor of firearms. An affable, smiling, stocky-muscled man of vigorous middle age with a flushed face and a habit of winking, or seeming to wink, as he spoke; eyes like transparent blue glass, alert, intelligent, yet cast for the most part over our heads. You could not tell if he took pride in his role,

guiding civilian visitors through the facility, or if he merely tolerated it, and us. His uniform was pale blue and around his waist he
wore a smartly gleaming leather holster conspicuously missing a
pistol.

Here was the first ominous note, though the sergeant explained
the situation with a smile. Outside the security checkpoints, county
sheriff's guards were armed; inside, guards in beige-brown uniforms carried no weapons, or even holsters. One of us inquired
about the policy and the sergeant said, matter-of-factly, "If guards
carry guns there's the possibility the inmates will take the guns
from them." He paused, his manner mildly teasing, as if a joke
hovered in the air close about us and he was the only one to
discern it. Seeing the expressions on our faces, he went on, "Millstone is a maximum security facility and once the alarm goes off,
if it goes off, you couldn't get out in a tank. Every door, every gate,
every elevator is bolted electronically. And there's no windows —
you'll notice there's no windows to the outside."

One of the men in our group asked what would happen if
someone was taken hostage. The sergeant smiled, peering over our
heads, and with the air of one who has uttered certain words many
times and has yet to be disappointed in his listeners' reactions,
said, "Policy is, if they take you, they take you. If they take me, they
take me. No negotiations with inmates at Millstone. No hostages."

The tour began, no turning back. Checkpoints, beady blinking
camera-eyes overhead, ponderous metallic doors like those in
spaceships in sci-fi movies of the 1950s. Without my handbag,
which had to be checked at the front desk, my hands were loose
and empty. Entering the maximum security unit, we had to be
frisked, but because I was female none of the male guards could
touch me; the sergeant telephoned the women's unit on the seventh floor to summon down a matron. She was a black woman in
the same beige-brown uniform who briskly patted my body up and
down and passed me on with a murmured "OK," not a glance of
acknowledgment. It struck us as odd that the sergeant too was
frisked by a guard. He said, with his affable smile, a just-perceptible
hint of a wink, "A county officer might smuggle in contraband,
like anybody else. Like some lawyers have been known to do, eh?"

We were marched along a windowless corridor. Instructed *You will not speak with any inmate, you will not make eye contact with any inmate, you will not follow me closely at all times and direct any questions exclusively to me.* The odor of coins in a sweating hand grew more intense, a greasy odor beneath, a faint stench as of overripe oranges. We were told a brief history of Millstone, "old" facility and "new." Statistics, dates. The sergeant informed us in a clipped voice that there were four categories of inmates in the facility: those who'd been arrested and couldn't make bail; those presently on trial; those who'd been convicted and were awaiting sentencing; and overflow from other state facilities. The women's unit was segregated, of course. Don't feel sorry for any inmate. Most of them, they've worked damn hard to get in here. All kinds of crimes: theft, arson, drugs and drug-dealing, armed robbery, rape, manslaughter, murder. Drunk and disorderly, wife-beating, child-beating, child molesters. No "white-collar" crimes — the perpetrators can make bail. A serious sex offender, like that guy raped the little girl a few weeks ago, they're segregated from the general population.

Before one of the hefty metal doors the sergeant called, "Key up!" A black guard appeared with a key to let us into the kitchen unit, which was an older unit, the sergeant said, with a door still manually operated, by key rather than TV monitor and code. The door swung open, we were led inside and abruptly found ourselves in the presence of inmates. A number of men, dark-skinned, working in the kitchen, a cavernous fluorescent-lit space. There was a hum of ventilators and fans but the air was thick with smells of grease, yeasty baked rolls, scorched tomato sauce, cleanser, ammonia, disinfectant. Smells of hair oil, perspiration. The kitchen workers wore baggy uniforms, coveralls, of the green hue of stagnant water. As we civilians entered in suits, ties, blazers, and polished shoes their eyes shifted to us and away in a single swerve of a motion as if seeing and not-seeing were simultaneous. In his rapid, affable, overly loud voice the sergeant continued to speak as if the inmates could not hear him, and indeed they appeared oblivious of us as if on the other side of a plate glass barrier. It was embarrassing, awkward, unnatural, and yet clearly routine. White visitors, "professionals"; black inmates, "criminals." Yet how close we were, only a few yards separating us. A lanky black man of about thirty with his springy-woolly hair caught tight in a hairnet was scouring the interior of a badly crusted giant baking tin; another was unpacking a cardboard box of what appeared to be gallon-sized cans of Montco peaches; another, heavyset, with a raddled black face and wearing an upright dazzling white chef's hat like a figure in a cartoon, worked at a giant stove. *You will not make eye contact with any inmate* and so I did not, fixing my attention on the canned food which was stacked on counters and shelves. These were comically oversized cans of familiar brand names, Hunt's Tomato Sauce, Heinz's Pork & Beans, Campbell's Chicken Noodle Soup, Montco Sliced Peaches, like a pop artifact by Andy Warhol. I could see, though I tried not to look at him, the inmate in the hairnet watching me out of the corner of his eye as, with a fist-sized clump of steel wool, he scoured, scoured, scoured the baking tin in furious circles.

"At Millstone, inmates feed in their cell blocks," the sergeant was saying. "A big dining hall isn't looked to be practical here."

Uneasy in our professional clothes and Caucasian skin the five or six of us were led through the kitchen unit as if on a march across a special ramp laid down in a swamp — you wouldn't wish to step off that ramp, not for an instant.

Next we were taken through the laundry unit, which was another cavernous, windowless, fluorescent-glaring space, warm as a slow oven and smelling of damp laundry, disinfectant, and oily male sweat. A half-dozen inmates were working, dark-skinned, silent, all with sizable stomachs. Except for their sullen faces and their reso-lutely downcast eyes, these men too gave not the slightest sign of being conscious of their observers. They might have been per-formers in a long-running play at which we, visiting tourists, were just another audience. The sergeant talked, the inmates went about their work. Folding sheets, towels, and uniforms; hauling more laundry out of enormous dryers. Their faces oozed sweat. They moved mechanically, yet with no perceptible beat or rhythm. There could be no pleasure in such work, nor even the angry satisfaction of displeasure. Within minutes the laundry unit be-came unbearably warm. We visitors were uncomfortable in our winter clothes, our "professional" uniforms. I wore dark wool, a blazer and a long skirt, and my clothes weighed heavily on me. It was becoming increasingly difficult to concentrate on the ser-

geant's relentless voice. How mixed up with the glaring fluorescent
light, that voice of seemingly casual authority. I too had begun to
sweat inside my clothes. Like the other visitors I dared not look
too closely at inmates who so stonily, with such dignity, refused to
look at us. I was thinking *We didn't put you here! We aren't the ones.*

We ascended in an elevator and were led briskly along a corridor
and through an electronically monitored checkpoint (the sergeant
punched in a code to open the door) and invited then to contem-
plate through a wire-enforced plate glass window the "volleyball
court" — a flat asphalt roof with a lank net strung up, and no
players. An icy rain had begun to fall. A half-mile beyond the
facility's concrete wall was the expressway, and beyond that the
river, only barely visible, of the color this morning of stainless steel
cutlery. Recreation for most inmates was two hours a day when
practical, the sergeant was saying, but now that the gym was used
for beds there was a problem, the prison population being mainly
young men, blacks and some Hispanics, eighteen to twenty-five
years of age on the average, street kids, lots of energy they got to
work off. Lots of anger.

We stared at the deserted volleyball court for a while. We were
then led back through the checkpoint and to the elevator. One of
the men in our group asked about violence in the facility, and the
sergeant said affably, "Violence? Here? Nah," but this was a joke
evidently, for he went on to say, still more affably, "Sure, there's
always a problem in any prison facility. Inmates extorting other
inmates, like they do on the street. A detention center is basically
the street with walls around it. It's a population can't make bail.
It's a population where everybody knows everybody else. You're
connected, or you're not. There's guys hitting up other guys for
money, ganging up on them in the showers. Five minutes in, a
guy's weak, without connections, everybody knows it. It's in the
showers they're vulnerable. Beatings, rapes. Nobody ever informs
on anybody. Unless he's finished anyway. They make a 'woman' of
him, he's dead meat from then on." The sergeant paused and then
added, "Sometimes a certain class of white guy, not segregated,
he'll have a serious problem. Other white guys, you'll be seeing
them, can handle it OK."

We were not to be taken through the segregated unit on the

fourth floor but were allowed to peer into it through another wire-enforced plate glass window in a guard station, as the sergeant explained the circumstances of "segregation." It seemed to be an important term to him, a category of distinction. We saw little except a long brightly lit corridor with cells opening off it, at the far end of which two guards stood talking together. The cells had canvas padding, the sergeant said, and the guards here knew first aid. Inmates who lost control in their cell blocks, attacked their attorneys, for instance, or attacked guards — they were brought here and closely monitored. The protective-custody unit was next door, only a few inmates in it at the present time, including the white guy who raped and killed a little girl.

In one of the cells we could see, dimly, a figure lying on a cot. This was a "suicide watch cell" where inmates were watched twenty-four hours a day. No suicides at Millstone, not if they could be prevented. The facility had a high rating in this respect. Still, sometimes an inmate will surprise everybody, the sergeant said, shaking his head. Sometimes they can kill themselves in the damnedest ways if they're desperate. We watched the motionless figure in the cell.

One of the lawyers in our group persisted in asking about violence in the facility, rape, for instance. The sergeant said with a shrug that sure it happened, men going after men, healthy young guys of that age, late adolescence but with the emotional age of children, what would you expect? We were in an elevator in which a guard accompanied a stony-faced black man in handcuffs, both of them ignoring our presence. A woman in such company, I assumed the attitude of an honorary man. A professional woman, in a sense, *is* an honorary man. So I, too, had questions to ask of the sergeant: what did he think of the newly revived death penalty in New Jersey? Wasn't it the case that there was a disproportionate number of black men sentenced to death throughout the United States, compared to the general prison population? The sergeant said, shrugging, "That's how the system works out."

Adding, as if reluctantly, "There's advantages and disadvantages to the death penalty. The advantage is, you put away a dangerous criminal for a long time, all these guys on Death Row, and society is protected. The disadvantage is, for law enforcement officers, you encounter a more dangerous type of criminal. What's he got to lose, he's thinking. And probably he's right." The sergeant's voice was still resolutely affable. "Some of these guys, their lives aren't worth much to them. Like it's a match they lit and they can blow out any time. That's the type of inmate you're basically dealing with in Millstone."

We were not to be taken through the women's unit on the seventh floor, but on our brief tour through the infirmary unit we encountered a number of female inmates waiting to see the doctor, supervised by a matron. The matron was black, and it seemed that all of the women were black, and of varying ages though mainly young, several looking no more than sixteen. They wore baggy coveralls or dresses of the same washed-out sickly green as the male inmates. Like the men, they did not look at us after the initial sullen glance. One young woman was bloated with pregnancy; another, her hair braided in dozens of delicate cornrows, had a bruised-looking face and furious eyes. *What you lookin' at, you!* The sergeant was saying matter-of-factly that the female population at Millstone was between eight and ten percent of the male, but it was going up, like it was going up nationally. The crimes were mainly drug-related, prostitution, bad checks. Mostly the crimes were tied in with male perpetrators. Though sometimes you'd be surprised, women were turning up for armed robbery, assault, murder. All across the country.

Women didn't mind incarceration the way men did, the sergeant said. The worst thing was being deprived of their children if they had children but, overall, they were protected in the facility — "Protected from the men."

Was this meant to be funny, or ironic? A few of us laughed uncertainly.

The air about us was becoming thick, more difficult to breathe, as though too many breaths had already been expelled into it. Now we were in the interior of the facility, where the prison population was housed. We stared through another wire-enforced window in a guard station on the fifth floor, into a scene of disconcerting intimacy, a gym made over into a "temporary dorm" for newly arrested prisoners. The "temporary dorm," the sergeant said, had been in use for over a year. Mattresses were spread out in almost uniform rows on the hardwood floor of the windowless fluorescent-lit space — "The lights are never turned off," the sergeant said. What a shock: dozens of men in dull green baggy clothes amid rumpled sheets, towels, clothes, shoes, toiletries. Nearly all were black or swarthy-skinned but there was one man with the look of a skinned rabbit, bloodless-pale amid his fellows, with a dome of thinning white hair. Most of the men were of ordinary height and girth, but there were several who were as tall and solid as horses. Unaware of being observed, or indifferent, the inmates seemed to be pantomiming "real" people. Some lay on mattresses asleep in the glaring light or comatose, and others sat sorting through their possessions as if they'd been doing so for a long time; still others stood motionless as if arrested in thought, or walked about aimlessly like somnambulists, or stood talking together in small groups. Near the guard station was a long table at which inmates sat conferring with men in civilian clothes — their attorneys. Over all was an air of passivity, withheld power. No sound penetrated the plate glass window through which we looked, adding to the atmosphere of strangeness. There was a heraldic simplicity about the inmates, as if they were figures in a twelfth-century fresco, charged with a symbolic meaning of which they themselves were ignorant, and wholly without self-consciousness. The sergeant was saying, "Your average inmate in the system, if he's in for a prison term, would be waiting, about now, for lunch. Mainly they're waiting for the next meal. These men are waiting to be moved somewhere else. If they get lucky, they could be back on the street tomorrow. If not, not. Whatever it is, they're waiting. Lots of them got scores to settle so they think about that. What they don't like, what pisses them off, is a glitch in their routine."

The pointlessness of it. The futility. I would not ask about remorse, conscience — I did not want the sergeant to laugh at me. It might be argued that the human condition was not tragic after all, nor even spiritual. A matter of waiting, eating, settling scores. Not that the inmates in the "temporary dorm" were estranged from common humanity but that this, in its starkest, least sentimental essence, *was* humanity. If we could observe ourselves through wire-enforced plate glass windows twenty-four hours a day.

If the tour had ended at this point, my impressions would have been disturbing, even depressing, but not annihilating, in no way personal. The dominant sensation was physical: extreme fatigue, eye ache. I was not thinking any longer of injustice — or justice — or of the tragic inequities of black and white America — but only of the anticipation of my own release. Within the hour! — freedom.

But, unfortunately, the tour did not end at that point. We were observing a cell block on the fifth floor, one of numerous thirty-man cell blocks in the facility, the "heart" of the modern prison system, the sergeant explained, replacing the old-style tiers of cells that you'd see in the movies. The thirty-man block was structured with cells arranged around an open space like a common room, containing tables and chairs; the fourth wall of this rectangular space was an elevated guard station in which a window, wire-enforced as usual, was inset. No privacy for these men except at the very rear of their cells, and these cells measuring six feet by eight. The effect was like that of a zoo enclosure or an aquarium. Here as elsewhere the dominant majority of the population was dark-skinned and young. There was more movement here, more restiveness, than in the gym. *Don't make eye contact with any inmate* an inner voice admonished even as I drifted close to the window. Perhaps I was trying to ease away from the sergeant's droning voice. Perhaps by this time I was not thinking very coherently. I might have come to assume that, in my Caucasian skin, protected by plate glass, I was invisible. Certainly I'd grown dazed. And in this state I was careless, and met the startled gazes of two young inmates standing near the window, about ten feet below. They were husky black men in their mid-twenties. They were frowning at me, staring at me, as if they'd never seen anything quite like me before in their lives. Their faces showed consternation, resentment, fury. It was a reflexive act on my part: I was confused, and smiled.

The most natural of female reactions: the first impulse, frightened of the male, you smile. Not with the eyes, which show fear, but with the mouth, promising compliance.

Now came an immediate, extraordinary reaction — as if I'd flung open a window to call attention to myself, as if I'd waved a flaming torch.

A ripple of excited interest passed among the inmates. Suddenly everyone was looking at me. *A woman! There's a woman!* In the instant of knowing my blunder, already it was too late. I'd been sighted, discovered, and exposed, there could be no discreet withdrawal. My skin flushed, my heart beat rapidly with a rush of adrenaline. I would have liked to cringe from view and did in fact look to see if I could position myself behind the sergeant's stocky frame, as a child might, but, perversely, I'm sure it was coincidentally, the sergeant had seated himself on the edge of a desk; the first time since the tour had begun that he'd taken a seat.

Excited calls and cries spread through the cell block, muffled behind the soundproof glass. Even older inmates slouched dispiritedly at the margins of the enclosure were roused to life. Others leaned out of their cells to stare. In idle-seeming but purposeful eddies, younger men began to drift boldly forward to within a few feet of the window. They bared their teeth, grinned, and rolled their eyes. Their mouths shaped words I could not hear. I stood paralyzed, stricken with embarrassment and mounting panic. Males, in a pack. The female terror of becoming an object of male sexual desire, prey. Multiple rape, rape to the death, a frenzy of propagation. The life force gone wild, blocked-up seed yearning only to be spilled. Why didn't the sergeant, or the guards in the station, notice? Didn't my tour companions notice? Yet the sergeant continued to speak. Citing statistics, the names of New Jersey politicians. How could he keep us here, talking with such calm, maddening persistence, as agitation built up in the cell block?

Certain of the younger, more emboldened inmates were flashing outright grins and their hands moved suggestively. *White bitch! White cunt!* They appeared about to break into a rowdy dance, like mocking children. Yet I could not look away, as if I'd been hypnotized. Perhaps I was still smiling, in my terror, a ghastly fixed smile like a death's head. It was as if I stood naked before strangers, utterly exposed and in such exposure annihilated. A woman in her mid-forties — too old! But that was not the point. Sexual desirability was not the point, nor even attractiveness. Mere sexual identity was all that mattered. *A woman: cunt.* What these eager men would do to me, if they could get hold of me: that was the promise of their eyes, their mouths. How I would beg, plead, scream. How I would sacrifice in an instant all that remained of my dignity, if only I could be spared. *But this isn't me! I am so much more than what you see.*

The episode could not have lasted more than a few minutes, and yet those few minutes were excruciating. As I was the lone woman in the inmates' mocking and enraged eyes, so I was the lone woman in the guard station. Was it possible the sergeant and the other officers were unaware of the inmates' excitement? Yet no one intervened, nor even glanced at me. No one offered to lead me out, to spare me the humiliation I was obviously enduring. Maybe I deserved it? Maybe the ravening inmates deserved it? For the one, a lesson of knowing, *This is just to show you what you would experience except for us, your protectors.* For the others, *This is your punishment, what we've deprived you of, behind bars — the female body.*

So at certain junctures of experience we who are women are made to realize, as no man would ever be made to realize in quite the same way, that our identities as individuals are provisional. A professional woman, particularly one who associates herself with an institution, or has a public reputation substantial enough to characterize her, believes that, by having distinguished herself from others of her category (that is, her sex), she might have achieved a distinctive identity; through this identity, she might be in possession of some measure of power. (For what is "identity" but our power to control others' definitions of us?) In this, she is mistaken. A woman's "identity" is one granted her by men; it is a neutral identity, an honorific. The fiction is *We grant you your putative identity apart from being merely female; but we retain the privilege of revoking it at any time.* In this fiction, the "professional woman" is a desexualized female. But a desexualized female is an impossibility. Never in any plausible scenario could a professional man be unwillingly divested of his identity in such a way, becoming, in others' eyes, a sheerly sexual being; a genitalia-bearing body. To be reduced to a body is to be contemptible, because anonymous, mass-produced.

Of course I was not thinking of such speculative matters that morning in March 1984; nor would I think of them in the intervening years. Shame is the emotion that most effectively blocks memory. Amnesia is the great solace, the most available form of self-protection. For one to whom anger, let alone rage, is not an option, what recourse but forgetfulness?

Only years later would I begin to remember. My memory triggered by another woman saying, with an air of bemusement: Why do we instinctively smile when men stare at us? insult us? threaten us sexually? Only then, after eleven years. How like actual mist the amnesia seemed as it lifted and dissolved.

*

The tour was over, or nearly. Two hours and five minutes had passed, leaving us as drained as eight or twelve hours might have done. The sergeant smiled at us, looking at us directly for the first time. "Tired, eh?" We were on the ground floor, toward the rear of the facility, in the control center, where officers sat smoking and drinking coffee and staring at TV monitors in a double row on a concrete wall. Now that the adrenalin rush had subsided, my head throbbed with pain. I must have looked sickly. Every drop of pride and integrity had been drained from me; it was my great accomplishment simply to have finished the tour. Not to have broken down in my companions' eyes.

As we left the facility, the sergeant called, teasing, after us, "Be sure to come back again soon, eh?"

Now that I had my handbag and my coat, I felt more possessed of myself. I departed the oppressive building quickly, ahead of my male companions, without a backward glance. If someone called goodbye to me, I did not hear. Free! A fine icy rain was being blown slantwise by the wind, smelling of the river. But how wonderful the icy rain, the chemical odor! I smiled in relief and gratitude as I unlocked my car, giddy as if my life had been spared; better yet, as if I'd slipped away unapprehended from the scene of a shameful crime.

CYNTHIA OZICK

The Impious Impatience of Job

FROM THE AMERICAN SCHOLAR

The riddles of God are more satisfying than the solutions of men.
                                                    — G. K. Chesterton

TWENTY-FIVE CENTURIES AGO (or perhaps twenty-four or twenty-three), an unnamed Hebrew poet took up an old folktale and transformed it into a sacred hymn so sublime — and yet so shocking to conventional religion — that it agitates and exalts us even now. Scholars may place the Book of Job in the age of the Babylonian Exile, following the conquest of Jerusalem by Nebuchadnezzar — but to readers of our own time, or of any time, the historicity of this timeless poem hardly matters. It is timeless because its author intended it so; it is timeless the way Lear on the heath is timeless (and Lear may owe much to Job). Job is a man who belongs to no known nation; despite his peerless Hebrew speech, he is plainly not a Hebrew. His religious customs are unfamiliar, yet he is no pagan: he addresses the One God of monotheism. Because he is unidentified by period or place, nothing in his situation is foreign or obsolete; his story cannot blunder into anachronism or archaism. Like almost no other primordial poem the West has inherited, the Book of Job is conceived under the aspect of the universal — if the universal is understood to be a questioning so organic to our nature that no creed or philosophy can elude it.

That is why the striking discoveries of scholars — whether through philological evidence or through the detection of infusions from surrounding ancient cultures — will not deeply unsettle the common reader. We are driven — we common readers — to

approach Job's story with tremulous palms held upward and un-
laden. Not for us the burden of historical linguistics, or the torrent
of clerical commentary that sweeps through the centuries, or the
dusty overlay of partisan interpretation. Such a refusal of context,
historical and theological, is least of all the work of willed ignorance; if we choose to turn from received instruction, it is rather
because of an intrinsic knowledge — the terror, in fact, of self-
knowledge. Who among us has not been tempted to ask Job's
questions? Which of us has not doubted God's justice? What human creature ever lived in the absence of suffering? If we, ordinary
clay that we are, are not equal to Job in the wild intelligence of his
cries, or in the unintelligible wilderness of his anguish, we are, all
the same, privy to his conundrums.

Yet what captivates the scholars may also captivate us. A faithful
English translation, for instance, names God as "God," "the Lord,"
"the Holy One," "the Almighty" — terms reverential, familiar, and
nearly interchangeable in their capacity to evoke an ultimate Presence. But the author of Job, while aiming for the same effect of
incalculable awe, has another resonance in mind as well: the dim
tolling of some indefinable aboriginal chime, a suggestion of immeasurable antiquity. To achieve this, he is altogether sparing in
his inclusion of the Tetragrammaton, the unvocalized YHVH —
the root of which is "to be," rendered as "I am that I am" — which
chiefly delineates God in the Hebrew Bible (and was later approximately transliterated as Yahweh or Jehovah). Instead, he sprinkles
his poem, cannily and profusely, with pre-Israelite God-names: El,
Eloah, Shaddai — names so lost in the long-ago, so unembedded
in usage, that the poem is inevitably swept clean of traditional
pieties. Translation veils the presence — and the intent — of these
old names; and the necessary seamlessness of translation will per-
force paper over the multitude of words and passages that are
obscure in the original, subject to philological guesswork. Here
English allows the common reader to remain untroubled by scholarly puzzles and tangles.

But how arresting to learn that Satan appears in the story of Job
not as that demonic figure of later traditions whom we meet in
our translation but as *ha-Satan*, with the definite article attached,
meaning "the Adversary" — the counter-arguer among the angels,
who is himself one of "the sons of God." Satan's arrival in the tale
helps date its composition. It is under Persian influence that he

turns up — via Zoroastrian duality, which pits, as equal contenders, a supernatural power for Good against a supernatural power for Evil. In the Book of Job, the scholars tell us, Satan enters Scripture for the first time as a distinct personality and as an emblem of destructive forces. But note: when the tale moves out of the prose of its fablelike frame into the sovereign grandeur of its poetry, Satan evaporates; the poet, an uncompromising monotheist, recognizes no alternative to the Creator, and no opposing might. Nor does the poet acknowledge any concept of afterlife, though Pharisaic thought in the period of his writing is just beginning to introduce that idea into normative faith.

There is much more that textual scholarship discloses in its search for the Job-poet's historical surround: for example, the abundance of words and phrases in Aramaic, a northwestern Semitic tongue closely related to Hebrew, which was rapidly becoming the lingua franca of the ancient Near East. Aramaic is significantly present in other biblical books as well: in the later Psalms, in Ecclesiastes, Esther, and Chronicles — and, notably, in the Dead Sea Scrolls. The Babylonian Talmud is written in Aramaic; it is the language that Jesus speaks. Possibly the Job-poet's everyday speech is Aramaic — this may account for his many Aramaisms — but clearly, for the literary heightening of poetry, he is drawn to the spare beauty and noble diction of classical Hebrew (much as Milton, say, in constructing his poems of Paradise, invokes the cadences of classical Latin).

And beyond the question of language, the scholars lead us to still another enchanted garden of context and allusion: the flowering, all over the Levant, of a form known as "wisdom literature." A kind of folk-philosophy linking virtue to prudence, and pragmatically geared to the individual's worldly success, it intends instruction in levelheaded judgment and in the achievement of rational contentment. The biblical Proverbs belong to this genre, and, in a more profoundly reflective mode, so do Ecclesiastes and portions of Job; but wisdom literature can also be found in Egyptian, Babylonian, Ugaritic, and Hellenistic sources. It has no overriding national roots and deals with personal rather than collective conduct, and with a commonsensical morality guided by principles of resourcefulness and discretion. A great part of the Book of Job finds its ancestry in the region's pervasive wisdom literature (and its descendants in today's self-improvement bestsellers). But what genuinely seizes the heart are those revolutionary passages in Job that violently contradict what all the world, yesterday and today, takes for ordinary wisdom.

However seductive they are in their insight and learning, all these scholarly excavations need not determine or deter our own reading. We, after all, have in our hands neither the Hebrew original nor a linguistic concordance. What we do have — and it is electrifying enough — is the Book of Job as we readers of English encounter it. And if we are excluded from the sound and texture of an elevated poetry in a tongue not ours, we are also shielded from problems of structure and chronology, and from a confrontation with certain endemic philological riddles. There is riddle enough remaining — a riddle that is, besides, an elemental quest, the appeal for an answer to humankind's primal inquiry.

So there is something to be said for novice readers who come to Job's demands and plaints unaccoutered: we will perceive God's world exactly as Job himself perceives it. Or put it that Job's bewilderment will be ours, and our kinship to his travail fully unveiled, only if we are willing to absent ourselves from the accretion of centuries of metaphysics, exegesis, theological polemics. Of the classical Jewish and Christian theologians (Saadia Gaon, Rashi, ibn Ezra, Maimonides, Gersonides, Gregory, Aquinas, Calvin), each wrote from a viewpoint dictated by his particular religious perspective. But for us to be as (philosophically) naked as Job will mean to be naked of bias, dogma, tradition. It will mean to imagine Job solely as he is set forth by his own words in his own story.

His story, because it is mostly in dialogue, reads as a kind of drama. There is no proscenium; there is no scenery. But there is the dazzling spiral of words — extraordinary words, Shakespearean words; and there are the six players, who alternately cajole, console, contradict, contend, satirize, fulminate, remonstrate, accuse, deny, trumpet, succumb. Sometimes we are reminded of *Antigone,* sometimes of *Oedipus* (Greek plays that are contemporaneous with Job), sometimes of *Othello.* The subject is innocence and power; virtue and injustice; the Creator and His Creation; or what philosophy has long designated as theodicy, the Problem of Evil. And the more we throw off sectarian sophistries — the more we attend humbly to the drama as it plays itself out — the more clearly we will see Job as he emerges from the venerable thicket of theodicy into the heat of our own urgency. Or call it our daily breath.

Job's story — his fate, his sentence — begins in heaven, with Satan as prosecuting attorney. Job, Satan presses, must be put to trial. Look at him: a man of high estate, an aristocrat, robust and in his prime, the father of sons and daughters, respected, affluent, conscientious, charitable, virtuous, God-fearing. God-fearing? How effortless to be always praising God when you are living in such ease! Look at him: how he worries about his lucky children and their feasting, days at a time — was there too much wine, did they slide into blasphemy? On their account he brings sacred offerings in propitiation. His possessions are lordly, but he succors the poor and turns no one away; his hand is lavish. Yet look at him — how easy to be righteous when you are carefree and rich! Strip him of his wealth, wipe out his family, afflict him with disease, and *then* see what becomes of his virtue and his piety!

So God is persuaded to test Job. Invasion, fire, tornado, destruction, and the cruelest loss of all: the death of his children. Nothing is left. Odious lesions creep over every patch of Job's skin. Tormented, he sits in the embers of what was once his domain and scratches himself with a bit of shattered bowl. His wife despairs: after all this, he still declines to curse God! She means for him to dismiss God as worthless to his life, and to dismiss his ruined life as worthless. But now a trio of gentlemen from neighboring lands arrives — a condolence call from Eliphaz, Bildad, and Zophar, Job's distinguished old friends. The three weep and are mute. Job's broken figure appalls: pitiable, desolate, dusted with ash, scraped, torn.

All the foregoing is told in the plain prose of a folktale: a blameless man's undoing through the conniving of a mischievous sprite. A prose epilogue will ultimately restore Job to his good fortune, and, in the arbitrary style of a fable, will even double it; but between the two halves of this simple narrative of loss and restitution the coloration of legend falls away, and a majesty of outcry floods speech after speech. And then Job's rage ascends — a rage against the loathsomeness of "wisdom."

When the horrified visitors regain their voices, it is they who appear to embody reasonableness, logic, and prudence, while Job — introduced in the prologue as a man of steadfast faith who will

never affront the Almighty — rails like a blasphemer against an
unjust God. The three listen courteously as Job bewails the day he
was born, a day that "did not shut the doors of my mother's womb,
nor hide trouble from my eyes." In response to which Eliphaz
begins his first attempt at solace: "Can mortal man be righteous
before God? Can a man be pure before his Maker? . . . Behold,
happy is the man whom God reproves; therefore despise not the
chastening of the Almighty." Here is an early and not altogether
brutal hint of what awaits Job in the severer discourse of his
consolers: the logic of punishment, the dogma of requital. If a man
suffers, it must be because of some impiety he has committed. Can
Job claim that he is utterly without sin? And is not God a merciful
God, "for He wounds, but binds up; He smites, but His hands
heal"? In the end (Eliphaz reassures Job), all will be well.

   Job is not comforted; he is made furious. He has been accused,
however obliquely, of having sinned, and he knows with his whole
soul that he has not. His friends show themselves to be as incon-
stant as a torrential river, icy in winter, vanishing away in the heat.
Rather than condole, they defame. They root amelioration in
besmirchment. But if Job's friends are no friends, then what of
God? The poet, remembering the psalm — "What is man that thou
are mindful of him?" — has Job echo the very words. "What is
man," Job charges God, that "thou dost set thy mind upon him,
dost visit him every morning, and test him every moment? . . . If
I sin, what do I do to thee, thou watcher of men?" And he dreams
of escaping God in death: "For now I shall lie in the earth; thou
wilt seek me, but I shall not be."

   Three rounds of increasingly tumultuous debate follow, with
Eliphaz, Bildad, and Zophar each having a turn, and Job replying.
Wilder and wilder grow the visitors' accusations; wilder and wilder
grow Job's rebuttals, until they are pitched into an abyss of bitterness. Job's would-be comforters have become his harriers; men of
standing themselves, they reason from the conventional doctrines
of orthodox religion, wherein conduct and consequence are mor-
ally linked: goodness rewarded, wickedness punished. No matter
how hotly Job denies and protests, what greater proof of Job's
impiety can there be than his deadly ordeal? God is just; he metes
out just deserts. Is this not the grand principle on which the world
rests?

   Job's own experience refutes these arguments; and his fever-ish condemnation of God's injustice refutes religion itself. "I am blameless!" he cries yet again, and grimly concludes: "It is all one: therefore I say, He destroys both the blameless and the wicked. When disaster brings sudden death, He mocks the calamity of the innocent. The earth is given into the hand of the wicked; He covers the face of its judges." Here Job, remarkably, is both believer and atheist. God's presence is incontrovertible; God's moral integrity is nil. And how strange: in the heart of Scripture, a righteous man impugning God! Genesis, to be sure, records what appears to be a precedent. "Wilt thou destroy the righteous with the wicked?" Abraham asks God when Sodom's fate is at stake; but that is more plea than indictment, and anyhow there is no innocence in Sodom. Yet how distant Job is from the Psalmist who sings "The Lord is upright . . . there is no unrighteousness in Him," who pledges that "the righteous shall flourish like the palm tree" and "the workers of iniquity shall be destroyed forever." The Psalmist's is the voice of faith. Job's is the voice of a wounded lover, betrayed.

Like a wounded lover, he envisions, fleetingly, a forgiving afterlife, the way a tree, cut down to a stump, can send forth new shoots and live again — while man, by contrast, "lies down and rises not again." Or he imagines the workings of true justice: on the one hand, he wishes he might bring God Himself to trial; on the other, he ponders man-made law and its courts and declares that the transcript of his testimony ought to be inscribed permanently in stone, so that some future clansman might one day come as a vindicator, to proclaim the probity of Job's case. (Our translation famously renders the latter as "I know that my Redeemer lives," a phrase that has, of course, been fully integrated into Christian hermeneutics.) Throughout, there is a thundering of discord and clangor. "Miserable comforters are you all!" Job groans. "Surely there are mockers about me" — while Eliphaz, Bildad, and Zophar press on, from pious apologies to uncontrolled denunciation. You, Job, they accuse, you who stripped the naked of their clothing, gave no water to the weary, withheld bread from the hungry!

And Job sees how the tenets of rectitude, in the mouths of the zealous, are perverted to lies.

But now, abruptly, a new voice is heard: a fifth and so far undisclosed player strides onstage. He is young, intellectually ingenious, confident, a bit brash. Unlike the others, he bears a name with a Hebrew ring to it: Elihu. "I also will declare my opinion," he announces. He arrives as a supplanter, to replace stale wisdom with fresh, and begins by rebuking Job's haranguers for their dogma of mechanical tit for tat. As for Job: in his recalcitrance, in his litanies of injured innocence, in his prideful denials, he has been blind to the *uses* of suffering; and doesn't he recognize that God manifests Himself in night visions and dreams? Suffering educates and purifies; it humbles pride, tames the rebel, corrects the scoffer. "What man is like Job, who drinks up scoffing like water?" Elihu points out — but here the reader detects a logical snag. Job has become a scoffer only as a result of gratuitous suffering: then how is such suffering a "correction" of scoffing that never was? Determined though he is to shake Job's obstinacy, Elihu is no wiser than his elders. Job's refusal of meaningless chastisement stands.

So Elihu, too, fails as comforter. Yet as he leaves off suasion, his speech metamorphoses into a hymn in praise of God's dominion. "Hear this, O Job," Elihu calls, "stop and consider the wondrous work of God" — wind, cloud, sky, snow, lightning, ice! Elihu's sumptuous limning of God's power in nature is a fore-echo of the sublime climax to come.

Job, gargantuan figure in the human imagination that he is, is not counted among the prophets. He is not the first to be reluctant to accept God's authority: Jonah rebelled against sailing to Nineveh in order to prophesy; yet he did go, and his going was salvational for a people not his own. But the true prophets are self-starters, spontaneous fulminators against social inequity, and far from reluctant. Job, then, has much in common with Isaiah, Jeremiah, Micah, and Amos: he is wrathful that the wicked go unpunished, that the widow and the orphan go unsuccored, that the world is not clothed in righteousness. Like the noblest of the prophets, he assails injustice; and still he is unlike them. They accuse the men and women who do evil; their targets are made of flesh and blood. It is human transgression they hope to mend. Job seeks to rectify God. His is an ambition higher, deeper, vaster, grander than theirs; he is possessed by a righteousness more frenzied than theirs; the scale of his justice-hunger exceeds all that precedes him, all that was ever conceived; he can be said to be the consummate prophet. And at the same time he is the consummate violator. If we are to understand him at all, if we are rightly to enter into his passions at their pinnacle, then we ought to name him prophet; but we may not. Call him, instead, anti-prophet. His teaching, after all, verges on atheism: the rejection of God's power. His thesis is revolution.

Eliphaz, Bildad, and Zophar are silenced. Elihu will not strut these boards again. Job's revolution may be vanity of vanities, but his adversaries have lost confidence and are scattered. Except for Job, the stage is emptied.

Then God enters — not in a dream, as Elihu theorized, not as a vision or incarnation, but as an irresistible Eloquence.

Here I am obliged to remark on the obvious. In recapitulating certain passages, I have reduced an exalted poem to ordinary spoken sentences. But the ideas that buttress Job are not merely "expressed in," as we say, language of high beauty; they are inseparable from an artistry so far beyond the grasp of mind and tongue that one can hardly imagine their origin. We think of the Greek plays; we think of Shakespeare; and still that is not marvel enough. Is it that the poet is permitted to sojourn, for the poem's brief life, in the magisterial Eye of God? Or is it God who allows Himself to peer through the poet's glass, as through a gorgeously crafted kaleidoscope? The words of the poem are preternatural, unearthly. They may belong to a rhapsodic endowment so rare as to appear among mortals only once in three thousand years. Or they may belong to the Voice that hurls itself from the whirlwind.

God has granted Job's demand: "Let the Almighty answer me!" Now here at last is Job's longed-for encounter with that Being he conceives to be his persecutor. What is most extraordinary in this visitation is that it appears to be set apart from everything that has gone before. What is the Book of Job *about*? It is about gratuitous affliction. It is about the wicked who escape whipping. It is about the suffering of the righteous. God addresses none of this. It is as if He has belatedly stepped into the drama without having consulted the script — none of it: not even so much as the prologue. He does not remember Satan's mischief. He does not remember Job's calamities. He does not remember Job's righteousness.

As to the last: Job will hardly appeal for an accounting from God without first offering one of his own. He has his own credibility to defend, his own probity. "Let me be weighed in a just balance," he insists, "and let God know my integrity!" The case for his integrity takes the form of a bill of particulars that is unsurpassed as a compendium of compassionate human conduct: no conceivable ethical nuance is omitted. It is as if all the world's moral fervor, distilled from all the world's religions, and touching on all the world's pain, is assembled in Job's roster of loving-kindness. Job in his confession of integrity is both a protector and a lover of God's world.

But God seems alarmingly impatient; His mind is elsewhere. Is this the Lord whom Job once defined as a "watcher of men"? God's answer, a fiery challenge, roils out of the whirlwind. "Where were *you*," the Almighty roars, in supernal strophes that blaze through the millennia, "when I laid the foundation of the earth?" And what comes crashing and tumbling out of the gale is an exuberant ode to the grandeur of the elements, to the fecundity of nature: the sea and the stars, the rain and the dew, the constellations in their courses, the lightning, the lion, the raven, the ass, the goat, the ostrich, the horse, the hawk — and more, more, more! The lavishness, the extravagance, the infinitude! An infinitude of power; an infinitude of joy; an infinitude of love, even for the ugly hippopotamus, even for the crocodile with his terrifying teeth, even for creatures made mythical through ancient lore. Even for Leviathan! Nothing in the universe is left unpraised in these glorious stanzas — and one thinks: had the poet access to the electrons, had he an inkling of supernovas, had he parsed the chains of DNA, God's ode to Creation could not be richer. Turn it and turn it — God's ode: everything is in it.

Everything but the answer to the question that eats at Job's soul: why God permits injustice in the fabric of a world so resplendently woven. Job is conventionally judged to be a moral violator because he judges God Himself to be a moral violator. Yet is there any idea in the history of human thought more exquisitely tangled, more furiously daring, more heroically courageous, more rooted in spirit and conscience than Job's question? Why does God not praise the marrow of such a man as Job at least as much as He praises the intricacy of the crocodile's scales? God made the crocodile; He also made Job.

God's answer to Job lies precisely in His not answering; and Job, with lightning insight, comprehends. "I have uttered what I did not understand," he acknowledges, "things too wonderful for me, which I did not know."

His new knowledge is this: that a transcendent God denies us a god of our own devising, a god that we would create out of our own malaise, or complaint, or desire, or hope, or imagining; or would manufacture according to the satisfaction of our own design. We are part of God's design: can the web manufacture the spider? The Voice out of the whirlwind warns against god-manufacture — against the degradation of a golden calf surely, but also against god-manufacture even in the form of the loftiest visions. Whose visions are they? Beware: they are not God's; they are ours. The ways of the true God cannot be penetrated. The false comforters cannot decipher them. Job cannot uncover them. "The secret things belong to the Lord our God," Job's poet learned long ago, reading Deuteronomy. But now: see how Job cannot draw Leviathan out with a hook — how much less can he draw out God's nature, and His purpose!

So the poet, through the whirlwind's answer, stills Job.

But can the poet still the Job who lives in us? God's majesty is eternal, manifest in cell and star. Yet Job's questions toil on, manifest in death camp and hatred, in tyranny and anthrax, in bomb and bloodshed. Why do the wicked thrive? Why do the innocent suffer? In brutal times, the whirlwind's answer tempts, if not atheism, then the sorrowing conviction of God's indifference.

And if we are to take the close of the tale as given, it is not only Job's protests that are stilled; it is also his inmost moral urge. What has become of raging conscience? What has become of lovingkindness? Prosperity is restored; the dead children are replaced by twice the number of boys, and by girls exceedingly comely. But where now is the father's bitter grief over the loss of those earlier sons and daughters, on whose account he once indicted God? Cushioned again by good fortune, does Job remember nothing, feel nothing, see nothing beyond his own renewed honor? Is Job's lesson from the whirlwind finally no more than the learning of indifference?

So much for the naked text. Perhaps this is why — century after century — we common readers go on clinging to the spiritualizing mentors of traditional faith, who clothe in comforting theologies this God-wrestling and comfortless Book.

Yet how astoundingly up to date they are, those ancient sages — redactors and compilers — who opened even the sacred gates of Scripture to philosophic doubt!

DAVID QUAMMEN

Planet of Weeds

FROM HARPER'S MAGAZINE

HOPE IS A DUTY from which paleontologists are exempt. Their
job is to take the long view, the cold and stony view, of triumphs
and catastrophes in the history of life. They study the fossil record,
that erratic selection of petrified shells, carapaces, bones, teeth,
tree trunks, leaves, pollen, and other biological relics, and from it
they attempt to discern the lost secrets of time, the big patterns of
stasis and change, the trends of innovation and adaptation and
refinement and decline that have blown like sea winds among
ancient creatures in ancient ecosystems. Although life is their
subject, death and burial supply all their data. They're the coro-
ners of biology. This gives to paleontologists a certain distance, a
hyperopic perspective beyond the reach of anxiety over outcomes
of the struggles they chronicle. If hope is the thing with feathers,
as Emily Dickinson said, then it's good to remember that feathers
don't generally fossilize well. In lieu of hope and despair, paleontologists have a highly developed sense of cyclicity. That's why I
recently went to Chicago, with a handful of urgently grim questions, and called on a paleontologist named David Jablonski. I
wanted answers unvarnished with obligatory hope.

Jablonski is a big-pattern man, a macroevolutionist, who works
fastidiously from the particular to the very broad. He's an expert
on the morphology and distribution of marine bivalves and gastro-
pods — or clams and snails, as he calls them when speaking casually. He sifts through the record of those mollusk lineages, preserved in rock and later harvested into museum drawers, to extract
ideas about the origin of novelty. His attention roams back through

600 million years of time. His special skill involves framing large, resonant questions that can be answered with small, lithified clam-shells. For instance: By what combinations of causal factor and sheer chance have the great evolutionary innovations arisen? How quickly have those innovations taken hold? How long have they abided? He's also interested in extinction, the converse of abid-ance, the yang to evolution's yin. Why do some species survive for a long time, he wonders, whereas others die out much sooner? And why has the rate of extinction — low throughout most of Earth's history — spiked upward cataclysmically on just a few oc-casions? How do those cataclysmic episodes, known in the trade as mass extinctions, differ in kind as well as degree from the gradual process of species extinction during the millions of years between? Can what struck in the past strike again?

The concept of mass extinction implies a biological crisis that spanned large parts of the planet and, in a relatively short time, eradicated a sizable number of species from a variety of groups. There's no absolute threshold of magnitude, and dozens of differ-ent episodes in geologic history might qualify, but five big ones stand out: Ordovician, Devonian, Permian, Triassic, Cretaceous. The Ordovician extinction, 439 million years ago, entailed the disappearance of roughly 85 percent of marine animal species — and that was before there were any animals *on land*. The Devonian extinction, 367 million years ago, seems to have been almost as severe. About 245 million years ago came the Permian extinction, the worst ever, claiming 95 percent of all known animal species and therefore almost wiping out the animal kingdom altogether. The Triassic, 208 million years ago, was bad again, though not nearly so bad as the Permian. The most recent was the Cretaceous extinction (sometimes called the K-T event because it defines the boundary between two geologic periods, with K for Cretaceous, never mind why, and T for Tertiary), familiar even to schoolchil-dren because it ended the age of dinosaurs. Less familiarly, the K-T event also brought extinction of the marine reptiles and the am-monites, as well as major losses of species among fish, mammals, amphibians, sea urchins, and other groups, totaling 76 percent of all species. In between these five episodes occurred some lesser mass extinctions, and throughout the intervening lulls extinction continued, too — but at a much slower pace, known as a background rate, claiming only about one species in any major group every million years. At the background rate, extinction is infrequent enough to be counterbalanced by the evolution of new species. Each of the five major episodes, in contrast, represents a drastic net loss of species diversity, a deep trough of biological impoverishment from which Earth only slowly recovered. How slowly? How long is the lag between a nadir of impoverishment and a recovery to ecological fullness? That's another of Jablonski's research interests. His rough estimates run to 5 or 10 million years. What drew me to this man's work, and then to his doorstep, were his special competence on mass extinctions and his willingness to discuss the notion that a sixth one is in progress now.

Some people will tell you that we as a species, *Homo sapiens,* the savvy ape, all 5.9 billion of us in our collective impact, are destroying the world. Me, I won't tell you that, because "the world" is so vague, whereas what we are or aren't destroying is quite specific. Some people will tell you that we are rampaging suicidally toward a degree of global wreckage that will result in our own extinction. I won't tell you that either. Some people say that the environment will be the paramount political and social concern of the twenty-first century, but what they mean by "the environment" is anyone's guess. Polluted air? Polluted water? Acid rain? A frayed skein of ozone over Antarctica? Greenhouse gases emitted by smokestacks and cars? Toxic wastes? None of these concerns is the big one, paleontological in scope, though some are more closely entangled with it than others. If the world's air is clean for humans to breathe but supports no birds or butterflies, if the world's waters are pure for humans to drink but contain no fish or crustaceans or diatoms, have we solved our environmental problems? Well, I suppose so, at least as environmentalism is commonly construed. That clumsy, confused, and presumptuous formulation "the environment" implies viewing air, water, soil, forests, rivers, swamps, deserts, and oceans as merely a milieu within which something important is set: human life, human history. But what's at issue in fact is not an environment; it's a living world.

Here instead is what I'd like to tell you: The consensus among conscientious biologists is that we're headed into another mass extinction, a vale of biological impoverishment commensurate with the big five. Many experts remain hopeful that we can brake that descent, but my own view is that we're likely to go all the way down. I visited David Jablonski to ask what we might see at the bottom.

On a hot summer morning, Jablonski is busy in his office on the second floor of the Hinds Geophysical Laboratory at the University of Chicago. It's a large open room furnished in tall bookshelves, tables piled high with books, stacks of paper standing knee-high off the floor. The walls are mostly bare, aside from a chart of the geologic time scale, a clipped cartoon of dancing tyrannosaurs in red sneakers, and a poster from a Rodin exhibition, quietly appropriate to the overall theme of eloquent stone. Jablonski is a lean forty-five-year-old man with a dark full beard. Educated at Columbia and Yale, he came to Chicago in 1985 and has helped make its paleontology program perhaps the country's best. Although in not many hours he'll be leaving on a trip to Alaska, he has been cordial about agreeing to this chat. Stepping carefully, we move among the piled journals, reprints, and photocopies. Every pile represents a different research question, he tells me. "I juggle a lot of these things all at once because they feed into one another." That's exactly why I've come: for a little rigorous intellectual synergy.

Let's talk about mass extinctions, I say. When did someone first realize that the concept might apply to current events, not just to the Permian or the Cretaceous?

He begins sorting through memory, back to the early 1970s, when the full scope of the current extinction problem was barely recognized. Before then, some writers warned about "vanishing wildlife" and "endangered species," but generally the warnings were framed around individual species with popular appeal, such as the whooping crane, the tiger, the blue whale, the peregrine falcon. During the 1970s a new form of concern broke forth — call it wholesale concern — from the awareness that unnumbered millions of narrowly endemic (that is, unique and localized) species inhabit the tropical forests and that those forests were quickly being cut. In 1976, a Nairobi-based biologist named Norman Myers published a paper in *Science* on that subject; in passing, he also compared current extinctions with the rate during what he loosely called "the 'great dying' of the dinosaurs." David Jablonski,

then a graduate student, read Myers's paper and tucked a copy
into his files. This was the first time, as Jablonski recalls, that
anyone tried to quantify the rate of present-day extinctions. "Norman was a pretty lonely guy, for a long time, on that," he says. In
1979, Myers published *The Sinking Ark*, explaining the problem
and offering some rough projections. Between the years 1600 and
1900, by his tally, humanity had caused the extinction of about 75
known species, almost all of them mammals and birds. Between
1900 and 1979, humans had extinguished about another 75
known species, representing a rate well above the rate of known
losses during the Cretaceous extinction. But even more worrisome
was the inferable rate of unrecorded extinctions, recent and now
impending, among plants and animals still unidentified by science.
Myers guessed that 25,000 plant species presently stood jeopard-
ized, and maybe hundreds of thousands of insects. "By the time
human communities establish ecologically sound life-styles, the
fallout of species could total several million." Rereading that sentence now, I'm struck by the reckless optimism of his assumption
that human communities eventually will establish "ecologically
sound life-styles."

Although this early stab at quantification helped to galvanize
public concern, it also became a target for a handful of critics, who
used the inexactitude of the numbers to cast doubt on the reality
of the problem. Most conspicuous of the naysayers was Julian
Simon, an economist at the University of Maryland, who argued
bullishly that human resourcefulness would solve all problems
worth solving, of which a decline in diversity of tropical insects
wasn't one.

In a 1986 issue of *New Scientist*, Simon rebutted Norman Myers,
arguing from his own construal of select data that there was "no
obvious recent downward trend in world forests — no obvious
'losses' at all, and certainly no 'near catastrophic' loss." He later
co-authored an op-ed piece in the *New York Times* under the headline "Facts, Not Species, Are Periled." Again he went after Myers,
asserting a "complete absence of evidence for the claim that the
extinction of species is going up rapidly — or even going up at all."
Simon's worst disservice to logic in that statement and others was
the denial that *inferential* evidence of wholesale extinction counts
for anything. Of inferential evidence there was an abundance —

for example, from the Centinela Ridge in a cloud-forest zone of western Ecuador, where in 1978 the botanist Alwyn Gentry and a colleague found thirty-eight species of narrowly endemic plants, including several with mysteriously black leaves. Before Gentry could get back, Centinela Ridge had been completely deforested, the native plants replaced by cacao and other crops. As for inferential evidence generally, we might do well to remember what it contributes to our conviction that approximately 105,000 Japanese civilians died in the atomic bombing of Hiroshima. The city's population fell abruptly on August 6, 1945, but there was no one-by-one identification of 105,000 bodies.

Nowadays a few younger writers have taken Simon's line, pooh-poohing the concern over extinction. As for Simon himself, who died earlier this year, perhaps the truest sentence he left behind was, "We must also try to get more reliable information about the number of species that might be lost with various changes in the forests." No one could argue.

But it isn't easy to get such information. Field biologists tend to avoid investing their precious research time in doomed tracts of forest. Beyond that, our culture offers little institutional support for the study of narrowly endemic species in order to register their existence *before* their habitats are destroyed. Despite these obstacles, recent efforts to quantify rates of extinction have supplanted the old warnings. These new estimates use satellite imaging and improved on-the-ground data about deforestation, records of the many human-caused extinctions on islands, and a branch of ecological theory called island biogeography, which connects documented island cases with the mainland problem of forest fragmentation. These efforts differ in particulars, reflecting how much uncertainty is still involved, but their varied tones form a chorus of consensus. I'll mention three of the most credible.

W. V. Reid, of the World Resources Institute, in 1992 gathered numbers on the average annual deforestation in each of sixty-three tropical countries during the 1980s and from them charted three different scenarios (low, middle, high) of presumable forest loss by the year 2040. He chose a standard mathematical model of the relationship between decreasing habitat area and decreasing species diversity, made conservative assumptions about the crucial constant, and ran his various deforestation estimates through the model. Reid's calculations suggest that by the year 2040, between 17 and 35 percent of tropical forest species will be extinct or doomed to be. Either at the high or the low end of this range, it would amount to a bad loss, though not as bad as the K-T event. Then again, 2040 won't mark the end of human pressures on biological diversity or landscape.

Robert M. May, an ecologist at Oxford, co-authored a similar effort in 1995. May and his colleagues noted the five causal factors that account for most extinctions: habitat destruction, habitat fragmentation, overkill, invasive species, and secondary effects cascading through an ecosystem from other extinctions. Each of those five is more intricate than it sounds. For instance, habitat fragmentation dooms species by consigning them to small, islandlike parcels of habitat surrounded by an ocean of human impact and by then subjecting them to the same jeopardies (small population size, acted upon by environmental fluctuation, catastrophe, inbreeding, bad luck, and cascading effects) that make island species especially vulnerable to extinction. May's team concluded that most extant bird and mammal species can expect average life spans of between 200 and 400 years. That's equivalent to saying that about a third of one percent will go extinct each year until some unimaginable end point is reached. "Much of the diversity we inherited," May and his co-authors wrote, "will be gone before humanity sorts itself out."

The most recent estimate comes from Stuart L. Pimm and Thomas M. Brooks, ecologists at the University of Tennessee. Using a combination of published data on bird species lost from forest fragments and field data gathered themselves, Pimm and Brooks concluded that 50 percent of the world's forest-bird species will be doomed to extinction by deforestation occurring over the next half century. And birds won't be the sole victims. "How many species will be lost if current trends continue?" the two scientists asked. "Somewhere between one third and two thirds of all species — easily making this event as large as the previous five mass extinctions the planet has experienced."

Jablonski, who started down this line of thought in 1978, offers me a reminder about the conceptual machinery behind such estimates. "All mathematical models," he says cheerily, "are wrong.

They are approximations. And the question is: Are they usefully wrong, or are they meaninglessly wrong?" Models projecting present and future species loss are useful, he suggests, if they help people realize that *Homo sapiens* is perturbing Earth's biosphere to a degree it hasn't often been perturbed before. In other words, that this is a drastic experiment in biological drawdown we're engaged in, not a continuation of routine.

Behind the projections of species loss lurk a number of crucial but hard-to-plot variables, among which two are especially weighty: continuing landscape conversion and the growth curve of human population.

Landscape conversion can mean many things: draining wetlands to build roads and airports, turning tallgrass prairies under the plow, fencing savanna and overgrazing it with domestic stock, cutting second-growth forest in Vermont and consigning the land to ski resorts or vacation suburbs, slash-and-burn clearing of Madagascar's rain forest to grow rice on wet hillsides, industrial logging in Borneo to meet Japanese plywood demands. The ecologist John Terborgh and a colleague, Carel P. van Schaik, have described a four-stage process of landscape conversion that they call the land-use cascade. The successive stages are: 1) *wildlands,* encompassing native floral and faunal communities altered little or not at all by human impact; 2) *extensively used areas,* such as natural grasslands lightly grazed, savanna kept open for prey animals by infrequent human-set fires, or forests sparsely worked by slash-and-burn farmers at low density; 3) *intensively used areas,* meaning crop fields, plantations, village commons, travel corridors, urban and industrial zones; and finally 4) *degraded land,* formerly useful but now abused beyond value to anybody. Madagascar, again, would be a good place to see all four stages, especially the terminal one. Along a thin road that leads inland from a town called Mahajanga, on the west coast, you can gaze out over a vista of degraded land — chalky red hills and gullies, bare of forest, burned too often by graziers wanting a short-term burst of pasturage, sparsely covered in dry grass and scrubby fan palms, eroded starkly, draining red mud into the Betsiboka River, supporting almost no human presence. Another showcase of degraded land — attributable to fuelwood gathering, overgrazing, population density, and decades of apartheid — is the Ciskei homeland in South Africa. Or you might look at overirrigated crop fields left ruinously salinized in the Central Valley of California.

Among all forms of landscape conversion, pushing tropical forest from the *wildlands* category to the *intensively used* category has the greatest impact on biological diversity. You can see it in western India, where a spectacular deciduous ecosystem known as the Gir forest (home to the last surviving population of the Asiatic lion, *Panthera leo persica*) is yielding along its ragged edges to new mango orchards, peanut fields, and lime quarries for cement. You can see it in the central Amazon, where big tracts of rain forest have been felled and burned, in a largely futile attempt (encouraged by misguided government incentives, now revoked) to pasture cattle on sun-hardened clay. According to the United Nations Food and Agriculture Organization, the rate of deforestation in tropical countries has increased (contrary to Julian Simon's claim) since the 1970s, when Myers made his estimates. During the 1980s, as the FAO reported in 1993, that rate reached 15.4 million hectares (a hectare being the metric equivalent of 2.5 acres) annually. South America was losing 6.2 million hectares a year. Southeast Asia was losing less in area but more proportionally: 1.6 percent of its forests yearly. In terms of cumulative loss, as reported by other observers, the Atlantic coastal forest of Brazil is at least 95 percent gone. The Philippines, once nearly covered with rain forest, has lost 92 percent. Costa Rica has continued to lose forest, despite that country's famous concern for its biological resources. The richest of old-growth lowland forests in West Africa, India, the Greater Antilles, Madagascar, and elsewhere have been reduced to less than a tenth of their original areas. By the middle of the next century, if those trends continue, tropical forest will exist virtually nowhere outside of protected areas — that is, national parks, wildlife refuges, and other official reserves.

How many protected areas will there be? The present worldwide total is about 9,800, encompassing 6.3 percent of the planet's land area. Will those parks and reserves retain their full biological diversity? No. Species with large territorial needs will be unable to maintain viable population levels within small reserves, and as those species die away their absence will affect others. The disappearance of big predators, for instance, can release limits on medium-size predators and scavengers, whose overabundance can drive still other species (such as ground-nesting birds) to extinction. This has already happened in some habitat fragments, such as Panama's Barro Colorado Island, and been well documented in the literature of island biogeography. The lesson of fragmented habitats is Yeatsian: things fall apart.

Human population growth will make a bad situation worse by putting ever more pressure on all available land.

Population growth rates have declined in many countries within the past several decades, it's true. But world population is still increasing, and even if average fertility suddenly, magically, dropped to 2.0 children per female, population would continue to increase (on the momentum of birth rate exceeding death rate among a generally younger and healthier populace) for some time. The annual increase is now 80 million people, with most of that increment coming in less-developed countries. The latest long-range projections from the Population Division of the United Nations, released earlier this year, are slightly down from previous long-term projections in 1992 but still point toward a problematic future. According to the U.N.'s middle estimate (and most probable? hard to know) among seven fertility scenarios, human population will rise from the present 5.9 billion to 9.4 billion by the year 2050, then to 10.8 billion by 2150, before leveling off there at the end of the twenty-second century. If it happens that way, about 9.7 billion people will inhabit the countries included within Africa, Latin America, the Caribbean, and Asia. The total population of those countries — most of which are in the low latitudes, many of which are less developed, and which together encompass a large portion of Earth's remaining tropical forest — will be more than twice what it is today. Those 9.7 billion people, crowded together in hot places, forming the ocean within which tropical nature reserves are insularized, will constitute 90 percent of humanity. Anyone interested in the future of biological diversity needs to think about the pressures these people will face, and the pressures they will exert in return.

We also need to remember that the impact of *Homo sapiens* on the biosphere can't be measured simply in population figures. As the population expert Paul Harrison pointed out in his book *The*

Third Revolution, that impact is a product of three variables: population size, consumption level, and technology. Although population growth is highest in less-developed countries, consumption levels are generally far higher in the developed world (for instance, the average American consumes about ten times as much energy as the average Chilean, and about a hundred times as much as the average Angolan), and also higher among the affluent minority in any country than among the rural poor. High consumption exacerbates the impact of a given population, whereas technological developments may either exacerbate it further (think of the automobile, the air conditioner, the chain saw) or mitigate it (as when a technological innovation improves efficiency for an established function). All three variables play a role in every case, but a directional change in one form of human impact — upon air pollution from fossil-fuel burning, say, or fish harvest from the seas — can be mainly attributable to a change in one variable, with only minor influence from the other two. Sulfur-dioxide emissions in developed countries fell dramatically during the 1970s and '80s, due to technological improvements in papermaking and other industrial processes; those emissions would have fallen still farther if not for increased population (accounting for 25 percent of the upward vector) and increased consumption (accounting for 75 percent). Deforestation, in contrast, is a directional change that *has* been mostly attributable to population growth.

According to Harrison's calculations, population growth accounted for 79 percent of the deforestation in less-developed countries between 1973 and 1988. Some experts would argue with those calculations, no doubt, and insist on redirecting our concern toward the role that distant consumers, wood-products buyers among slow-growing but affluent populations of the developed nations, play in driving the destruction of Borneo's dipterocarp forests or the hardwoods of West Africa. Still, Harrison's figures point toward an undeniable reality: more total people will need more total land. By his estimate, the minimum land necessary for food growing and other human needs (such as water supply and waste dumping) amounts to one-fifth of a hectare per person. Given the UN's projected increase of 4.9 billion souls before the human population finally levels off, that comes to another billion hectares of human-claimed landscape, a billion hectares less forest

— even without allowing for any further deforestation by the current human population, or for any further loss of agricultural land to degradation. A billion hectares — in other words, 10 million square kilometers — is, by a conservative estimate, well more than half the remaining forest area in Africa, Latin America, and Asia. This raises the vision of a very exigent human population pressing snugly around whatever patches of natural landscape remain.

Add to that vision the extra, incendiary aggravation of poverty. According to a recent World Bank estimate, about 30 percent of the total population of less-developed countries lives in poverty. Alan Durning, in his 1992 book *How Much Is Enough? The Consumer Society and the Fate of the Earth,* puts it in a broader perspective when he says that the world's human population is divided among three "ecological classes": the consumers, the middle-income, and the poor. His consumer class includes those 1.1 billion fortunate people whose annual income per family member is more than $7,500. At the other extreme, the world's poor also number about 1.1 billion people — all from households with less than $700 annually per member. "They are mostly rural Africans, Indians, and other South Asians," Durning writes. "They eat almost exclusively grains, root crops, beans, and other legumes, and they drink mostly unclean water. They live in huts and shanties, they travel by foot, and most of their possessions are constructed of stone, wood, and other substances available from the local environment." He calls them the "absolute poor." It's only reasonable to assume that another billion people will be added to that class, mostly in what are now the less-developed countries, before population growth stabilizes. How will those additional billion, deprived of education and other advantages, interact with the tropical landscape? Not likely by entering information-intensive jobs in the service sector of the new global economy. Julian Simon argued that human ingenuity — and by extension, human population itself — is "the ultimate resource" for solving Earth's problems, transcending Earth's limits, and turning scarcity into abundance. But if all the bright ideas generated by a human population of 5.9 billion haven't yet relieved the desperate needfulness of 1.1 billion absolute poor, why should we expect that human ingenuity will do any better for roughly 2 billion poor in the future?

Other writers besides Durning have warned about this deepening class rift. Tom Athanasiou, in *Divided Planet: The Ecology of Rich and Poor,* sees population growth only exacerbating the division, and notes that governments often promote destructive schemes of transmigration and rain-forest colonization as safety valves for the pressures of land hunger and discontent. A young Canadian policy analyst named Thomas F. Homer-Dixon, author of several calm-voiced but frightening articles on the linkage between what he terms "environmental scarcity" and global sociopolitical instability, reports that the amount of cropland available per person is fall-ing in less-developed countries because of population growth and because millions of hectares "are being lost each year to a combi-nation of problems, including encroachment by cities, erosion, depletion of nutrients, acidification, compacting and salinization and waterlogging from overirrigation." In the cropland pinch and other forms of environmental scarcity, Homer-Dixon foresees po-tential for "a widening gap" of two sorts — between demands on the state and its ability to deliver, and more basically between rich and poor. In conversation with the journalist Robert D. Kaplan, as quoted in Kaplan's book *The Ends of the Earth,* Homer-Dixon said it more vividly: "Think of a stretch limo in the potholed streets of New York City, where homeless beggars live. Inside the limo are the air-conditioned post-industrial regions of North America, Eu-rope, the emerging Pacific Rim, and a few other isolated places, with their trade summitry and computer information highways. Outside is the rest of mankind, going in a completely different direction."

That direction, necessarily, will be toward ever more desperate exploitation of landscape. When you think of Homer-Dixon's stretch limo on those potholed urban streets, don't assume there will be room inside for tropical forests. Even Noah's ark only managed to rescue paired animals, not large parcels of habitat. The jeopardy of the ecological fragments that we presently cherish as parks, refuges, and reserves is already severe, due to both internal and external forces: internal, because insularity itself leads to ecological unraveling; and external, because those areas are still under siege by needy and covetous people. Projected forward into a future of 10.8 billion humans, of which perhaps 2 billion are starving at the periphery of those areas, while another 2 billion are living in a fool's paradise maintained by unremitting exploitation of whatever resources remain, that jeopardy increases to the point of impossibility. In addition, any form of climate change in the midterm future, whether caused by greenhouse gases or by a natural flip-flop of climatic forces, is liable to change habitat conditions within a given protected area beyond the tolerance range for many species. If such creatures can't migrate beyond the park or reserve boundaries in order to chase their habitat needs, they may be "protected" from guns and chain saws within their little island, but they'll still die.

We shouldn't take comfort in assuming that at least Yellowstone National Park will still harbor grizzly bears in the year 2150, that at least Royal Chitwan in Nepal will still harbor tigers, that at least Serengeti in Tanzania and Gir in India will still harbor lions. Those predator populations, and other species down the cascade, are likely to disappear. "Wildness" will be a word applicable only to urban turmoil. Lions, tigers, and bears will exist in zoos, period. Nature won't come to an end, but it will look very different.

The most obvious differences will be those I've already mentioned: tropical forests and other terrestrial ecosystems will be drastically reduced in area, and the fragmented remnants will stand tiny and isolated. Because of those two factors, plus the cascading secondary effects, plus an additional dire factor I'll mention in a moment, much of Earth's biological diversity will be gone. How much? That's impossible to predict confidently, but the careful guesses of Robert May, Stuart Pimm, and other biologists suggest losses reaching half to two-thirds of all species. In the oceans, deepwater fish and shellfish populations will be drastically depleted by overharvesting, if not to the point of extinction then at least enough to cause more cascading consequences. Coral reefs and other shallow-water ecosystems will be badly stressed, if not devastated, by erosion and chemical runoff from the land. The additional dire factor is invasive species, fifth of the five factors contributing to our current experiment in mass extinction.

That factor, even more than habitat destruction and fragmentation, is a symptom of modernity. Maybe you haven't heard much about invasive species, but in coming years you will. The ecologist Daniel Simberloff takes it so seriously that he recently committed himself to founding an institute on invasive biology at the University of Tennessee, and Interior Secretary Bruce Babbitt sounded the alarm last April in a speech to a weed-management symposium in Denver. The spectacle of a cabinet secretary denouncing an alien plant called purple loosestrife struck some observers as droll, but it wasn't as silly as it seemed. Forty years ago, the British ecologist Charles Elton warned prophetically in a little book titled *The Ecology of Invasions by Animals and Plants* that "we are living in a period of the world's history when the mingling of thousands of kinds of organisms from different parts of the world is setting up terrific dislocations in nature." Elton's word "dislocations" was nicely chosen to ring with a double meaning: species are being moved from one location to another, and as a result ecosystems are being thrown into disorder.

The problem dates back to when people began using ingenious new modes of conveyance (the horse, the camel, the canoe) to travel quickly across mountains, deserts, and oceans, bringing with them rats, lice, disease microbes, burrs, dogs, pigs, goats, cats, cows, and other forms of parasitic, commensal, or domesticated creature. One immediate result of those travels was a wave of island-bird extinctions, claiming more than a thousand species, that followed oceangoing canoes across the Pacific and elsewhere. Having evolved in insular ecosystems free of predators, many of those species were flightless, unequipped to defend themselves or their eggs against ravenous mammals. *Raphus cucullatus,* a giant cousin of the pigeon lineage, endemic to Mauritius in the Indian Ocean and better known as the dodo, was only the most easily caricatured representative of this much larger pattern. Dutch sailors killed and ate dodos during the seventeenth century, but probably what guaranteed the extinction of *Raphus cucullatus* is that the European ships put ashore rats, pigs, and *Macaca fascicularis,* an opportunistic species of Asian monkey. Although commonly known as the crab-eating macaque, *M. fascicularis* will eat almost anything. The monkeys are still pestilential on Mauritius, hungry and daring and always ready to grab what they can, including raw eggs. But the dodo hasn't been seen since 1662.

The European age of discovery and conquest was also the great age of biogeography — that is, the study of what creatures live where, a branch of biology practiced by attentive travelers such as Carolus Linnaeus, Alexander von Humboldt, Charles Darwin, and

Alfred Russel Wallace. Darwin and Wallace even made biogeography the basis of their discovery that species, rather than being created and plopped onto Earth by divine magic, evolve in particular locales by the process of natural selection. Ironically, the same trend of far-flung human travel that gave biogeographers their data also began to muddle and nullify those data, by transplanting the most ready and roguish species to new places and thereby delivering misery unto death for many other species. Rats and cats went everywhere, causing havoc in what for millions of years had been sheltered, less competitive ecosystems. The Asiatic chestnut blight and the European starling came to America; the American muskrat and the Chinese mitten crab got to Europe. Sometimes these human-mediated transfers were unintentional, sometimes merely shortsighted. Nostalgic sportsmen in New Zealand imported British red deer; European brown trout and coastal rainbows were planted in disregard of the native cutthroats of Rocky Mountain rivers. Prickly-pear cactus, rabbits, and cane toads were inadvisedly welcomed to Australia. Goats went wild in the Galápagos. The bacterium that causes bubonic plague journeyed from China to California by way of a flea, a rat, and a ship. The Atlantic sea lamprey found its own way up into Lake Erie, but only after the Welland Canal gave it a bypass around Niagara Falls. Unintentional or otherwise, all these transfers had unforeseen consequences, which in many cases included the extinction of less competitive, less opportunistic native species. The rosy wolfsnail, a small creature introduced onto Oahu for the purpose of controlling a larger and more obviously noxious species of snail, which was itself invasive, proved to be medicine worse than the disease; it became a fearsome predator upon native snails, of which twenty species are now gone. The Nile perch, a big predatory fish introduced into Lake Victoria in 1962 because it promised good eating, seems to have exterminated at least eighty species of smaller cichlid fishes that were native to the lake's Mwanza Gulf.

The problem is vastly amplified by modern shipping and air transport, which are quick and capacious enough to allow many more kinds of organisms to get themselves transplanted into zones of habitat they never could have reached on their own. The brown tree snake, having hitchhiked aboard military planes from the New Guinea region near the end of World War II, has eaten most of the native forest birds of Guam. Hanta virus, first identified in Korea, burbles quietly in the deer mice of Arizona. Ebola will next appear who knows where. Apart from the frightening epidemiological possibilities, agricultural damages are the most conspicuous form of impact. One study, by the congressional Office of Technology Assessment, reports that in the United States 4,500 nonnative species have established free-living populations, of which about 15 percent cause severe harm; looking at just 79 of those species, the OTA documented $97 billion in damages. The lost value in Hawaiian snail species or cichlid diversity is harder to measure. But another report, from the UN Environmental Program, declares that almost 20 percent of the world's endangered vertebrates suffer from pressures (competition, predation, habitat transformation) created by exotic interlopers. Michael Soulé, a biologist much respected for his work on landscape conversion and extinction, has said that invasive species may soon surpass habitat loss and fragmentation as the major cause of "ecological disintegration." Having exterminated Guam's avifauna, the brown tree snake has lately been spotted in Hawaii.

Is there a larger pattern to these invasions? What do fire ants, zebra mussels, Asian gypsy moths, tamarisk trees, melaleuca trees, kudzu, Mediterranean fruit flies, boll weevils, and water hyacinths have in common with crab-eating macaques or Nile perch? Answer: They're *weedy* species, in the sense that animals as well as plants can be weedy. What that implies is a constellation of characteristics: They reproduce quickly, disperse widely when given a chance, tolerate a fairly broad range of habitat conditions, take hold in strange places, succeed especially in disturbed ecosystems, and resist eradication once they're established. They are scrappers, generalists, opportunists. They tend to thrive in human-dominated terrain because in crucial ways they resemble *Homo sapiens:* aggressive, versatile, prolific, and ready to travel. The city pigeon, a cosmopolitan creature derived from wild ancestry as a Eurasian rock dove *(Columba livia)* by way of centuries of pigeon fanciers whose coop-bred birds occasionally went AWOL, is a weed. So are those species that, benefiting from human impacts upon landscape, have increased grossly in abundance or expanded their geographical scope without having to cross an ocean by plane or by boat — for instance, the coyote in New York, the raccoon in

Montana, the white-tailed deer in northern Wisconsin or western Connecticut. The brown-headed cowbird, also weedy, has enlarged its range from the eastern United States into the agricultural Midwest at the expense of migratory songbirds. In gardening usage the word "weed" may be utterly subjective, indicating any plant you don't happen to like, but in ecological usage it has these firmer meanings. Biologists frequently talk of weedy species, meaning animals as well as plants.

Paleontologists, too, embrace the idea and even the term. Jablonski himself, in a 1991 paper published in *Science*, extrapolated from past mass extinctions to our current one and suggested that human activities are likely to take their heaviest toll on narrowly endemic species, while causing fewer extinctions among those species that are broadly adapted and broadly distributed. "In the face of ongoing habitat alteration and fragmentation," he wrote, "this implies a biota increasingly enriched in widespread, weedy species — rats, ragweed, and cockroaches — relative to the larger number of species that are more vulnerable and potentially more useful to humans as food, medicines, and genetic resources." Now, as we sit in his office, he repeats: "It's just a question of how much the world becomes enriched in these weedy species." Both in print and in talk he uses "enriched" somewhat caustically, knowing that the actual direction of the trend is toward impoverishment.

Regarding impoverishment, let's note another dark, interesting irony: that the two converse trends I've described — partitioning the world's landscape by habitat fragmentation, and unifying the world's landscape by global transport of weedy species — produce not converse results but one redoubled result, the further loss of biological diversity. Immersing myself in the literature of extinctions, and making dilettantish excursions across India, Madagascar, New Guinea, Indonesia, Brazil, Guam, Australia, New Zealand, Wyoming, the hills of Burbank, and other semiwild places over the past decade, I've seen those redoubling trends everywhere, portending a near-term future in which Earth's landscape is threadbare, leached of diversity, heavy with humans, and "enriched" in weedy species. That's an ugly vision, but I find it vivid. Wildlife will consist of the pigeons and the coyotes and the white-tails, the black rats *(Rattus rattus)* and the brown rats *(Rattus norvegicus)* and a few other species of worldly rodent, the crab-eating macaques and the cockroaches (though, as with the rats, not *every* species — some are narrowly endemic, like the giant Madagascar hissing cockroach) and the mongooses, the house sparrows and the house geckos and the houseflies and the barn cats and the skinny brown feral dogs and a short list of additional species that play by our rules. Forests will be tiny insular patches existing on bare sufferance, much of their biological diversity (the big predators, the migratory birds, the shy creatures that can't tolerate edges, and many other species linked inextricably with those) long since decayed away. They'll essentially be tall woody gardens, not forests in the richer sense. Elsewhere the landscape will have its strips and swatches of green, but except on much-poisoned lawns and golf courses the foliage will be infested with cheatgrass and European buckthorn and spotted knapweed and Russian thistle and leafy spurge and salt meadow cordgrass and Bruce Babbitt's purple loosestrife. Having recently passed the great age of biogeography, we will have entered the age *after* biogeography, in that virtually everything will live virtually everywhere, though the list of species that constitute "everything" will be small. I see this world implicitly foretold in the UN population projections, the FAO reports on deforestation, the northward advance into Texas of Africanized honeybees, the rhesus monkeys that haunt the parapets of public buildings in New Delhi, and every fat gray squirrel on a bird feeder in England. Earth will be a different sort of place — soon, in just five or six human generations. My label for that place, that time, that apparently unavoidable prospect, is the Planet of Weeds. Its main consoling felicity, as far as I can imagine, is that there will be no shortage of crows.

Now we come to the question of human survival, a matter of some interest to many. We come to a certain fretful leap of logic that otherwise thoughtful observers seem willing, even eager, to make: that the ultimate consequence will be the extinction of us. By seizing such a huge share of Earth's landscape, by imposing so wantonly on its providence and presuming so recklessly on its forgivingness, by killing off so many species, they say, we will doom our own species to extinction. This is a commonplace among the environmentally exercised. My quibbles with the idea are that it seems ecologically improbable and too optimistic. But it bears examining, because it's frequently offered as the ultimate argument against proceeding as we are.

Jablonski also has his doubts. Do you see *Homo sapiens* as a likely survivor, I ask him, or as a casualty? "Oh, we've got to be one of the most bomb-proof species on the planet," he says. "We're geographically widespread, we have a pretty remarkable reproductive rate, we're incredibly good at coopting and monopolizing resources. I think it would take really serious, concerted effort to wipe out the human species." The point he's making is one that has probably already dawned on you: *Homo sapiens* itself is the consummate weed. Why shouldn't we survive, then, on the Planet of Weeds? But there's a wide range of possible circumstances, Jablonski reminds me, between the extinction of our species and the continued growth of human population, consumption, and comfort. "I think we'll be one of the survivors," he says, "sort of picking through the rubble." Besides losing all the pharmaceutical and genetic resources that lay hidden within those extinguished species, and all the spiritual and aesthetic values they offered, he foresees unpredictable levels of loss in many physical and biochemical functions that ordinarily come as benefits from diverse, robust ecosystems — functions such as cleaning and recirculating air and water, mitigating droughts and floods, decomposing wastes, controlling erosion, creating new soil, pollinating crops, capturing and transporting nutrients, damping short-term temperature extremes and longer-term fluctuations of climate, restraining outbreaks of pestiferous species, and shielding Earth's surface from the full brunt of ultraviolet radiation. Strip away the ecosystems that perform those services, Jablonski says, and you can expect grievous detriment to the reality we inhabit. "A lot of things are going to happen that will make this a crummier place to live — a more stressful place to live, a more difficult place to live, a less resilient place to live — before the human species is at any risk at all." And maybe some of the new difficulties, he adds, will serve as incentive for major changes in the trajectory along which we pursue our aggregate self-interests. Maybe we'll pull back before our current episode matches the Triassic extinction or the K-T event. Maybe it will turn out to be no worse than the Eocene extinction, with a 35 percent loss of species.

"Are you hopeful?" I ask.

Given that hope is a duty from which paleontologists are exempt, I'm surprised when he answers, "Yes, I am."

I'm not. My own guess about the midterm future, excused by no exemption, is that our Planet of Weeds will indeed be a crummier place, a lonelier and uglier place, and a particularly wretched place for the 2 billion people comprising Alan Durning's absolute poor. What will increase most dramatically as time proceeds, I suspect, won't be generalized misery or futuristic modes of consumption but the gulf between two global classes experiencing those extremes. Progressive failure of ecosystem functions? Yes, but human resourcefulness of the sort Julian Simon so admired will probably find stopgap technological remedies, to be available for a price. So the world's privileged class — that's your class and my class — will probably still manage to maintain themselves inside Homer-Dixon's stretch limo, drinking bottled water and breathing bottled air and eating reasonably healthy food that has become incredibly precious, while the potholes on the road outside grow ever deeper. Eventually the limo will look more like a lunar rover. Ragtag mobs of desperate souls will cling to its bumpers, like groupies on Elvis's final Cadillac. The absolute poor will suffer their lack of ecological privilege in the form of lowered life expectancy, bad health, absence of education, corrosive want, and anger. Maybe in time they'll find ways to gather themselves in localized revolt against the affluent class. Not likely, though, as long as affluence buys guns. In any case, well before that they will have burned the last stick of Bornean dipterocarp for firewood and roasted the last lemur, the last grizzly bear, the last elephant left unprotected outside a zoo.

Jablonski has a hundred things to do before leaving for Alaska, so after two hours I clear out. The heat on the sidewalk is fierce, though not nearly as fierce as this summer's heat in New Delhi or Dallas, where people are dying. Since my flight doesn't leave until early evening, I cab downtown and take refuge in a nouveau-Cajun restaurant near the river. Over a beer and jambalaya, I glance again at Jablonski's 1991 *Science* paper, titled "Extinctions: A Paleontological Perspective." I also play back the tape of our conversation, pressing my ear against the little recorder to hear it over the lunch-crowd noise.

Among the last questions I asked Jablonski was, What will happen *after* this mass extinction, assuming it proceeds to a worst-case scenario? If we destroy half or two-thirds of all living species, how long will it take for evolution to fill the planet back up? "I don't know the answer to that," he said. "I'd rather not bottom out and see what happens next." In the journal paper he had hazarded that, based on fossil evidence in rock laid down atop the K-T event and others, the time required for full recovery might be 5 or 10 million years. From a paleontological perspective, that's fast. "Biotic recoveries after mass extinctions are geologically rapid but immensely prolonged on human time scales," he wrote. There was also the proviso, cited from another expert, that recovery might not begin until *after* the extinction-causing circumstances have disappeared. But in this case, of course, the circumstances won't likely disappear until *we* do.

Still, evolution never rests. It's happening right now, in weed patches all over the planet. I'm not presuming to alert you to the end of the world, the end of evolution, or the end of nature. What I've tried to describe here is not an absolute end but a very deep dip, a repeat point within a long, violent cycle. Species die, species arise. The relative pace of those two processes is what matters. Even rats and cockroaches are capable — given the requisite conditions, namely, habitat diversity and time — of speciation. And speciation brings new diversity. So we might reasonably imagine an Earth upon which, 10 million years after the extinction (or, alternatively, the drastic transformation) of *Homo sapiens,* wondrous forests are again filled with wondrous beasts. That's the good news.

DAISY EUNYOUNG RHAU

On Silence

FROM THE KENYON REVIEW

> He sitteth alone and keepeth silence, because he hath borne
> it upon him.
> He putteth his mouth in the dust; if so there may be hope.
>
> — Lamentations 3:28–29

WHEN I FINALLY QUIT playing the piano, the first thing I learned to appreciate was the possibility of my own silence. This was difficult. I'd played since I was four, and for almost twelve years I'd filled my life with music, performing and competing to the noise of concert programs, California state competitions. Beneath the pace of fingering practices, lessons in theory, and the lessons in stage presence, remains the youngest form of me, and I barely remember being there. I was a worn stripe down the Los Angeles highway, the girl between school, lessons, competitions, performance. I was the rustle of satin and cotton tights in the photographs that have streaked from a water pipe accident my mother had seven years ago. And now that I am immersed in my own silence, people treat me as though this music were a kind of being away, as if now were the time to question me for the unearthly details. "What did it feel like to perform?" they ask me. "How did you begin?" More confusing, they always ask, "Do you still play?"

About the very beginning, I can say this: there are family stories I have taken as truths and so have swallowed into memory. Even before I was born, I listened to my mother play the piano and sing. She played church pieces mostly, such as "How Great Thou Art," all the Psalter, and the "Gloria Patri." But she liked to play her wedding music also, both marches up and down, and the medita-

tive inserts of *Für Elise* and "The Maiden's Prayer" for ring ex-
changes and for kissing the bride. It was months of listening in the
womb and years of listening as a baby, until one day when I was
not quite four, I climbed onto the bench and played the first
movement of *Für Elise*. And with such feeling, they all marveled.
My mother told me this was proof that gifts from God had nothing
to do with time. That no matter how young, I could play whatever
I wanted. That even while my mother lowered her eyes behind a
veil over thirty years ago, I was already becoming a Destiny.

But the stories I do remember have everything to do with time.
Music begins, it lasts, and then it fades off. But what lasts beyond
that is not simply a matter of memory. I want to tell people: yes,
some people I know do still play. I have heard of others who grew
up like me, painstakingly playing eight hours a day by a direct edict
to maintain focus and virtuosity. But when I turned sixteen, I
betrayed God and quit my piano completely. From where I stand,
this means more than a simple rate of change; it means abnega-
tion. I have heard the stories of musicians elsewhere who have
decided to quit performing, musicians who can now continue to
play as though they were taking a stroll. They take up other
activities, like college, a family, a job. And still, even after years of
dinner parties and football conversations, they can sit at an instrument and simply play a piece, by heart.

But these are saints in my book, if only by the pure factor of
contemplative strength.

I am not like this. It would be easy to say that I can remember
some pieces I have played, but the simplicity of this claim belies
my total loss of whereabouts. To play again, for me, would be like
exercising an arm that has been amputated: I would have to stretch
my mind out toward a part of the body that no longer exists and
reenact the motions of a piece I performed endlessly when I was
eight. After that age, the music I played is unreachable by tactile
memory. When I was the child I'd played out of love, convinced
of my divine touch for beauty and dedication. But I am twenty
years older than that moment, and since grounded by my lesser
virtues. These days, I need the sight of those motions before I can
remember how I'd flourished; call it celestial navigation. The way
my left hand opens over a seventh, for example, or the way both
hands must burst over the opening trills of Debussy's *L'isle Joyeuse*.

In order for me to remember the *Mephisto Waltz*, I would have to place my hands in the opening position, and only then would the flood of cadences thunder in through the tattered manuscript pages, the clean white keys.

It is a different person who knows the music by heart. All I really kept by my heart are the visual stills, the smells museumed into childhood, the artifacts of gesture. To this day, I habitually wring my hands. When I sleep, I sometimes dream that I am full of music again, and that the notes are peeling out of my eyelids and fingers and ears. But these are dreams of the past. In my actual life, I remember mostly the darkness of a closed piano. And stretching back into that time, for me, means facing the weight of velvet curtains drawn over the sounds of stagehands, quiet among the lights. And then the silence of focus also, as a slow submersion of the body beneath the countless repetitions of a difficult phrase. I have evidence of the time I spent on the final movement of Chopin's *Premiere Ballade*. The daily repetitions on the left hand: two hundred at allegretto, three hundred at allegro, four hundred at presto con fuoco. Then the same with the right, with double the repetitions for both hands together. I'd once practiced this way to hit keys three octaves apart at split-second intervals with exactness and nuance. I'd practiced myself into the sacrificial walls of these exercises, working daily over the period of a year to complete a single performance piece to perfection. To this day I have kept those memories only as they are driven into the margins of my music, penciled in Chinese characters of five's running all the way down the page and into themselves. In truth, I can't remember what I was thinking or feeling as I practiced. I can't relive the desire that kept me, eight hours a day, inside those pencil marks. In the end, I remember only the actions themselves, and their silences that bound my heart.

Family stories remind me that I began playing with the urge to throw myself into the performances passionately, and with devotion. But those chronicles of five's remind me mostly of the fear I'd held, that desires could open my soul to all the uncontrollable factors of mistakes. All those self-loves and prides of excitement that closed my eyes spontaneously, blurred eighth notes, and occasionally skipped a note, when performances left no room to make mistakes. There are standards. I believe that my realization of standards led me, at eight years old, to see clearly that God had bought me. I wanted to remain Talented, and there was no avoiding it, just as there was no avoiding history or dreams of heaven. God had bought me, not to do works of charity, but to be bound by the perfection of Mozart. There is a special book dedicated just to blooming prodigies. And bible or no, that book sounded out with commands that were especially for me. They spoke mostly in Italian and commanded delicacy, glissando, and grace. Even the stories and songs issued me toward perfection, taught me that homage sometimes meant living with my mouth in the dust. So every day I prayed to restrain the disorder of myself. I prayed to keep that range of heartfelt meanings from pushing themselves down into the nerves of my fingers, where they could scatter the even touches I'd fought for months to perfect. Because my life always came down to that stage, to that moment rifled with noises of audience members coughing, of the hinged seats shifting, the program pages rattling, and the piano bench beneath you, rocking on the uneven stage, slightly rocking. For if you believe yourself worthy and devout in your desires, just bring yourself to that moment and sit down. Put yourself in that empty place, where there is only one requisite question left to echo through the hallways. Before you can begin, ask: Should you let your fingers fall into their fine molds of practice? Or should you bring your self forward, and play through the unstable memories of your heart? It's always cold in a concert hall. Your hands are sweating. Touch the keys. Feel how easily they could slip.

The fact is, under the gaze of perfection, I simplified. I still wonder if that's what love is about, switching back and forth over the question of what really lies inside your heart, as opposed to what you'll say or do to keep that love going. Even if it means clenching shut on the soul.

While I was performing, I was always younger than most of my competitors: always squeezing past loopholes of the minimum-age requirement, dressed in my mother's hand-me-downs, stitched over with ruffles and lace. Wearing huge orthopedic shoes, I was pushed aside from most discussions backstage; I viewed my competitors from the outside. When I was nine and waiting for my turn at the Los Angeles Young Musicians' Competition, one of the girls who sat beside me reached over with her pen to jab snarls of black ink over my name in all the program notes. She was thirteen, and told me definitively that she'd cast a spell: I was going to trip over myself on the stairs, fall into the symphony pit, and die upon impact before my number was up. Instead, I placed first that year. But when I stepped onstage to accept my trophy at the end of the day, I knew that what she'd said was true. I'd won for that moment, but as the photographers took pictures of me in my Ship'n'Shore blouse and my mother's skirt, I knew that the stakes of perfection had begun to rise in a ballooned silence, beyond the flashing domed ceiling of the concert hall, beyond my control. Perhaps in that one way, I wasn't alone. I could see that audience. I can recall how the congregation was grouped by teachers and judges, and by the mothers who'd dressed their sons and daughters in long black gowns and then sat out there to make notes of their own — their mother-mouths forming hundreds of flat lines across the back row. My mother was not like them, although I didn't know at that time how important it was that she was different. In my mind, there was always history and God to contend with. My mother just stood by the door, looking proud and terrified. She always hugged me beforehand, and brought me Baggies of sliced apples in her purse.

Soon after that year, during Bach festivals and competitions for concertos, I heard whispers of so-and-so taking beta blockers. It seemed to me as though most of the musicians were taking them, had taken them, relied on this heart medicine to perform. I don't know if they got them from their doctors, but pharmacists since have told me it was probably other means; beta blockers are most commonly given to heart attack patients. We were all growing older in those years, and my competitors seemed calmer, listing through the hallways with a kind of focus and aplomb, nodding curtly to the same people who managed to show up at the same competitions. I was still the outsider, the youngest, the girl without her own wallet or duffel bag. But in those piles of adult belongings slumped in the green rooms, I imagined the brown cylinders of propranolol tucked beneath the voluminous contents, like seeds sputtering out the rites of God, beyond earshot. If I had continued playing — that is, if I hadn't quit at the age of sixteen — I might have been a carrier of those bags and purses myself. I might have bought those beta blockers, or any other professional diminution that would have signaled me a veteran, like a large-eyed ballet dancer on diet pills, who chain-smokes Viceroys. Last month, a friend of mine began conducting interaction workshops in a New Mexico clinic for paranoid schizophrenics. He had twenty-some patients milling around the room, not looking at each other, and he said this was easy. But then he had them walk around making eye contact with each other, which was harder. When he asked them to make eye contact with specific people and hold their gaze without aggression, it was almost impossible. The point of this exercise was to make the patients feel attached about being human, without feeling so afraid. But his patients just shuffled through, staying on the level of step number one. It's the medication, he told me. Some of them had been on panic and anxiety suppressors for so long that they had lost most of their feelings, period. It was easier to keep them in line, sure, but their souls were harder to reach. Propranolol, he told me, is one of these medications.

I tell people: you can hope, at a younger age anyway, that the passion of Mozart or Khachaturian might materialize magically in the midst of an expectant audience. You can hope that the anxieties and judges might be the only experiences that are blocked, and that you will be able to play without panic, leaning into the music with perfection. But as it was, even if the passion of concerts had to be imaginatively created by the audience, it was enough. This was a world in which virtuosity could almost always be mistaken for passion. You remember how the Chopin pieces you are playing were once rejected as physically impossible, that left-handed trill, that softest touch. You'd practiced to defy your own weariness from coming through in the melody — instead: lightness, time, precision. This was about ninety-nine percent of it. A past of wearing your fingers into the grooves, of copying the expressions set down by the history of Horowitzes and Bolets. Passion, on the other hand, was so elusive. It was of a moment. It could almost be mistaken for, could almost materialize out of the ghosts in your fingers, if only you did not make a mistake. So it turns out, as the world of outside audiences was going home to watch talk shows and debate issues of self-expression, I was thirteen years old and living inside the silence staked by perfection. Each of my performances, an *hommage*. Not to the passionate musicians who composed this music, but to the air-filled undersong of musicians who ritually suppressed the adrenal gland of their hearts as a way of sacrificing the uncontrollable factors of their lives.

That was what it was like.

In hindsight, then, it doesn't seem unusual that on the day that I decided to stop playing, nothing really happened. There were no emotional family scenes, no cajoling, no announcements. My tutors came and went, and there was no whispering among the adults to figure this one out, or let me be. Perhaps it was because I'd already had a history of long tantrums and compulsive habits. I suffered from hallucinations — a bright orange owl that visited me until I was twelve; simple, large balls of light rolled through the house until I was eighteen. By the time I was seven, I'd already developed a ritual of washing my hands before playing. It took me a half hour to wash my hands, three times with Neutrogena soap under scalding, then very cold water, and then to pat with my lint-free towel before the final air-dry. My parents allowed me to do this every day before I played. They watched me throw the metronome against the wall. The plaster walls crumbled, but the metronome remained intact. I yelled at my mother for the smallest variances in the weather; I methodically tore up my clothes and my bed sheets into long, jagged strips. I often got up to play the piano at three or four in the morning, playing chronically, possessively, for hours at a time before falling asleep in the middle of the afternoon. I complained readily, and cried frequently. I was allowed all these things.

What I was not allowed to do was to ignore my homework, watch television, eat desserts, or neglect my assigned piano pieces for my favorites during practice. And these rules were as steadfast as my parents' tolerance for all my crazed behaviors. Yet on the day I woke up and did not go to my practice room, neither of them said a word. This was the day I remember most clearly, though it seems I hardly did a thing. I spent the day staring, waiting, and wandering aimlessly through the house.

I could show you the practice room to the left of my bedroom. It had been built, soundproofed, and installed with humidity control through payment plans that dissolved my parents' retirement savings and placed mortgages on the house. On the calendar, the upcoming Bach Festival was marked for that same month. I had been preparing for it for over a year. Here were the bills for my lessons, the arts school that allowed excessive absences. Here was the piano itself, with its enormous wing held down by the gravity of silence. And there I was, on the other side of the house, waiting to have my life put in order by my parents or by God. At any moment, I could have sat down at the piano and begun my exercises. Instead, I waited. I wanted to arrest the need for decision. I wanted to avoid confrontation with this moment. Outside the house, children on roller skates rattled down the sidewalk and shouted in bursts. They gave off an iridescent screen-door noise, which zeroed in through the house like a stream of metallic butterflies.

It seemed to have been certain all along that the world would announce itself like this, in the middle of an ordinary afternoon. My only concern had been how I would treat its arrival. How would I decide? Worse, how would I begin again without my life? And yet I, who had been overflowing with neurotic imaginations and agitations, found myself on that day calmly waiting, and choosing not to choose. If God had intervened with his still small voice, I would have continued playing. However passionately or however long doesn't matter, because the fact remains I heard nothing. And this nothingness of conviction illuminated suddenly, the simplest of all possible choices. All those years I had spent perfecting myself into the music had left my heart relying on detachment, on the prayers that had everything to do with good works and nothing to do with knowing. For all I knew, the world outside was made of roses, of traffic white noise sweeping past the house. I had stayed beneath the sounds. I had spent my life lifting the world upside down on myself, and yet I could not bring myself to open the windows and look out. This, perhaps, was the complete surprise. For here was the outside world arriving in the midst of my productions, with all its butterflies and beautiful decisions. Yet how could I possibly respond? It was, as the poet Adelia Prado posits, a metaphysical vertigo: "How would I open the window, unless I am crazy? How would I close it, unless I'm holy?"*

I knew, without ever having belonged out there, that in the middle of this seemingly ordinary afternoon, the rest of south Los Angeles County was continuing. Not in silence, but in some vast and grainy importance of parking meters, littered fast food napkins, and exact change. This was the day I was going to stop

---

*Adelia Prado, "Serenade," *The Alphabet in the Park,* trans. Ellen Watson (Middletown, Conn.: Wesleyan University Press, 1990), p. 22.

washing my hands with ritual, the day that I would read whatever book I wanted. But again, such changes were not so simple. On that day, I spent most of my time sitting by myself and listening to how I was already becoming part of the sounds made by our next-door neighbors.

I could hear them through my window, filing out their side (kitchen?) door, slamming the screen, starting their car, debating loudly over whether they should head toward the Lucky market or just go to the Mas X Menos on the corner of 138th Street. In the form of these vaguely familiar sounds, I heard the footsteps and door sounds made by my own uncontrollable guilt. And the singular difference of my own relief. Here I was sitting at my desk. And though possibly released from playing, I was uninterested in standing up or moving closer to the window, where I could perhaps have seen the neighbors, and maybe even beyond them to the children roller skating back and forth in the street. From certain objective standpoints, one might say that this was an impulse of traumatic detachment, arising on the day that marked Exit into the world out of the numb rhythms of myself.

Except that I would not exit. Jean Tardieu writes, "To advance, I turn upon myself / cyclone invested by stasis."* As I sat there, I was realizing instead that the noises of my world had always said too much, had tried to resurrect too many famous hands, had tried too bitterly to follow perfection. All the music and voices I had heard — either through my window or through the cloaked walls of the green room — I had heard from without. And they pointed indisputably to those high-walled and decaying realms I could never touch. Although it may have been my ears and my nerves poring over this fugue, the music that surrounded me had not been, and never could be, mine. Instead, it made up the staccato of a thousand pasts disappearing, of a self intently separating itself into smaller, even notes, each half-quicker than before. I had lost my sense of destiny. Bordered by too many ideals of ritual and restraint, my heart had never, really, listened to itself.

On the day I stopped, I found that I was stunningly bordered by nothing. That is to say, I was bordered for the first time by the

---

*Jean Tardieu, *Les Témoins Invisibles, The River Underground*, trans. David Kelley (Glasgow: Bell & Bain Ltd., 1991), p. 43.

vivid possibilities of my own silence. And unlike the silence that submerged me in my playing, this silence had no rules of perfection. It made no moves to divide my existence into the two spaces of inside (piano) and outside (the world). I admit, I was half-sunk in guilt and dread over not playing. But if I felt I had no choice whether to open the window, it was because I could not yet begin to consider the practical world: the driving permits, the television demands, the coping. As of that day, there was only the expansion of the moment to consider, the possibility of all possibilities at hand. Tardieu refers to this as an immobility surrounding the cyclone that was being. For me, it meant the cyclone of conscious listening, of dreaming into and beyond the geometrical confines of myself. People in therapy have told me that when a person has not had love, she will go on looking for that love the rest of her life. But this is only half true. I have known all the love that parents and God could give. I have lived to search through five hundred years of music, and have even at moments felt its power fill me to the state of redemption. But silence is an endless hunger. The freedom I have chosen drives me to search endlessly, to find that silence drawing itself out from beneath the weighted doors, where it has begun to cover the room with a single, gloaming window.

SCOTT RUSSELL SANDERS

Beauty

FROM ORION

IN MEMORY, I wait beside Eva in the vestibule of the church to
play my bit part as father of the bride. She hooks a hand on my
elbow while three bridesmaids fuss over her, fixing the gauzy veil,
spreading the long ivory train of her gown, tucking into her bun
a loose strand of hair, which glows the color of honey filled with
sunlight. Clumsy in my rented patent leather shoes and stiff black
tuxedo, I stand among these gorgeous women like a crow among
doves. I realize they're gorgeous not because they carry bouquets
or wear silk dresses, but because the festival of marriage has slowed
time down until any fool can see their glory.

Concerned that we might walk too fast, as we did in rehearsal,
Eva tries in vain to teach me a gliding ballet step to use as we
process down the aisle.

"It's really simple, Daddy," she says, as I botch it over and over.

I fear that I will stagger along beside my elegant daughter like
a veteran wounded in foreign wars.

Eva, meanwhile, seems blissfully confident, not only of being
able to walk gracefully, as she could do in her sleep, but of standing
before this congregation and solemnly promising to share her life
with Matthew Allen, the man who waits in thinly disguised turmoil
at the far end of the aisle. Poised on the dais, wearing a black
ministerial robe and a white stole, is the good friend whom Eva
and I know best as our guide on canoe trips through the Boundary
Waters. He grins so broadly that his full cheeks push up against
the round rims of his spectacles.

"There's one happy preacher," Eva says.

"He believes in marriage," I reply.

"So do I. Remember, Matt and I figured that between you and Mom and his folks, our parents have been married fifty-eight years."

Eva lets go of my arm to lift a hand to her throat, touching the string of pearls she has borrowed from my own bride, Ruth, to whom I've been married thirty years.

Love may last, I want to say, but don't, feeling unsure of my voice. Eva returns her free hand to my arm and tightens her grip. The arm she holds is my left one, close against my racing heart. In her own left arm she balances a great sheaf of flowers — daisies and lilies, marigolds, snapdragons, bee balm, feverfew — and in her left hand she holds a Belgian lace handkerchief, also borrowed from Ruth, in case she cries.

The organ strikes up Bach's "Jesu, Joy of Man's Desiring" for the bridesmaids' entrance, and down the aisle they skim, those gorgeous women in midnight blue. Overawed by the crowd, the flower girls hang back until their mother nudges them along, and then they dash and skip, carrying their fronds of flowers like spears.

Finally, only the bride and the father of the bride remain in the vestibule. Eva whispers, "Remember, now, don't walk too fast." But how can I walk slowly while my heart races? I've forgotten the ballet step she tried to show me. I want events to pause so I can practice the step, so we can go canoeing once more in the wilderness, so we can sit on a boulder by the sea and talk over life's mysteries, so I can make up to my darling for anything she may have lacked in her girlhood. But events do not pause. The organ sounds the first few bars of Purcell's "Trumpet Voluntary," our cue to show ourselves. We move into the open doorway, and two hundred faces turn their lit eyes on us. Eva tilts her face up at me, quirks the corners of her lips into a tight smile, and says, "Here we go, Daddy." And so, lifting our feet in unison, we go.

The wedding took place in Bloomington, Indiana, hometown for Matthew as well as Eva, on a sizzling Saturday in July. Now in early September, I can summon up hundreds of details from that radiant day, but on the day itself I was aware only of a surpassing joy. The glow of happiness had to cool before it would crystallize into memory.

Pardon my cosmic metaphor, but I can't help thinking of the physicists' claim that, if we trace the universe back to its origins in the Big Bang, we find the multiplicity of things fusing into greater and greater simplicity, until at the moment of creation itself there is only pure undifferentiated energy. Without being able to check their equations, I think the physicists are right. I believe the energy they speak of is holy, by which I mean it is the closest we can come with our instruments to measuring the strength of God. I also believe this primal energy continues to feed us, directly through the goods of creation, and indirectly through the experience of beauty. The thrill of beauty is what entranced me as I stood with Eva's hand hooked over my arm while the wedding march played, as it entrances me on these September nights when I walk over dewy grass among the songs of crickets and stare at the Milky Way.

We're seeing the Milky Way, and every other denizen of the sky, far more clearly these days thanks to the sharp eyes of the Hubble Space Telescope, as it orbits out beyond the blur of Earth's atmosphere. From data beamed down by the telescope, for example, I summon onto my computer screen an image of Jupiter wrapped in its bands of cloud like a ball of heathery yarn. Then I call up the Cat's Eye Nebula, incandescent swirls of red looped around the gleam of a helium star, for all the world like the burning iris of a tiger. This fierce glare began its journey toward earth 3,000 years ago, about the time my Assyrian ancestors were in their prime. Pushing back deeper in time, I summon onto my screen the Eagle Nebula, 7,000 light-years away, a trio of dust clouds like rearing horses, their dark bodies scintillating with the sparks of newborn stars. I study images of quasars giving birth to galaxies, galaxies whirling in the shapes of pinwheels, supernovas ringed by strands of luminous debris, and all the while I'm delving back toward that utter beginning when you and I and my daughter and her new husband and the bright heavenly host were joined in the original burst of light.

On these cool September mornings, I've been poring over two sets of photographs, those from deep space and those from Eva's wedding, trying to figure out why such different images — of supernova and shining daughter, of spinning galaxies and trembling bouquets — set up in me the same hum of delight. The feeling is unusually intense for me just now, so soon after the nuptials, but it has never been rare. As far back as I can remember, things seen or heard or smelled, things tasted or touched, have provoked in me an answering vibration. The stimulus might be the sheen of moonlight on the needles of a white pine, or the iridescent glimmer on a dragonfly's tail, or the lean silhouette of a ladder-back chair, or the glaze on a hand-thrown pot. It might be bird song or a Bach sonata or the purl of water over stone. It might be a line of poetry, the outline of a cheek, the savor of bread, the sway of a bough or a bow. The provocation might be as grand as a mountain sunrise or as humble as an icicle's jeweled tip, yet in each case a familiar surge of gratitude and wonder wells up in me.

Now and again some voice raised on the stairs leading to my study, some passage of music, some noise from the street, will stir a sympathetic thrum from the strings of the guitar that tilts against the wall behind my door. Just so, over and over again, impulses from the world stir a responsive chord in me — not just any chord, but a particular one, combining notes of elegance, exhilaration, simplicity, and awe. The feeling is as recognizable to me, as unmistakable, as the sound of Ruth's voice or the beating of my own heart. A screech owl calls, a comet streaks the night sky, a story moves unerringly to a close, a child lays an arrowhead in the palm of my hand, my daughter smiles at me through her bridal veil, and I feel for a moment at peace, in place, content. I sense in those momentary encounters a harmony between myself and whatever I behold. The word that seems to fit most exactly this feeling of resonance, this sympathetic vibration between inside and outside, is beauty.

What am I to make of this resonant feeling? Do my sensory thrills tell me anything about the world? Does beauty reveal a kinship between my small self and the great cosmos, or does my desire for meaning only fool me into thinking so? Perhaps, as biologists maintain, in my response to patterns I'm merely obeying the old habits of evolution. Perhaps, like my guitar, I'm only a sounding box played on by random forces.

I must admit that two cautionary sayings keep echoing in my head. Beauty is only skin deep, I've heard repeatedly, and beauty is in the eye of the beholder. Appealing surfaces may hide ugliness, true enough, as many a handsome villain or femme fatale should remind us. The prettiest of butterflies and mushrooms and frogs include some of the most poisonous ones. It's equally true that our taste may be influenced by our upbringing, by training, by cultural fashion. One of my neighbors plants in his yard a pink flamingo made of translucent plastic and a concrete goose dressed in overalls, while I plant in my yard oxeye daisies and jack-in-the-pulpits and maidenhair ferns, and both of us, by our own lights, are chasing beauty.

Mustn't beauty be shallow if it can be painted on? Mustn't beauty be a delusion if it can blink off and on like a flickering bulb? A wedding gown will eventually grow musty in a mothproof box, flowers will fade, and the glow will seep out of the brightest day. I'll grant that we may be fooled by façades, may be led astray by our fickle eyes. But I've been married to Ruth for thirty years, remember. I've watched my daughter grow for twenty-four years, my son for twenty, and these loved ones have taught me a more hopeful possibility. Season after season I've knelt over fiddleheads breaking ground, studied the wings of swallowtails nectaring on blooms, spied skeins of geese high in the sky. There are books I've read, pieces of music I've listened to, ideas I've revisited time and again with fresh delight. Having lived among people and places and works of imagination whose beauty runs all the way through, I feel certain that genuine beauty is more than skin deep, that real beauty dwells not in my own eye alone but out in the world.

While I can speak with confidence of what I feel in the presence of beauty, I must go out on a speculative limb if I'm to speak about the qualities in the world that call it forth. Far out on that limb, therefore, let me suggest that a creature, an action, a landscape, a line of poetry or music, a scientific formula, or anything else that might seem beautiful, seems so because it gives us a glimpse of the underlying order of things. The swirl of a galaxy and the swirl of a gown resemble one another not merely by accident, but because they follow the grain of the universe. That grain runs through our own depths. What we find beautiful accords with our most profound sense of how things *ought* to be. Ordinarily, we live in a tension between our perceptions and our desires. When we encounter beauty, that tension vanishes, and outward and inward images agree.

*

Before I climb out any farther onto this limb, let me give biology its due. It may be that in pursuing beauty we're merely obeying our genes. It may be that the features we find beautiful in men or women, in art or landscape or weather, are ones that improved the chances of survival for our ancestors. Put the other way around, it's entirely plausible that the early humans who did *not* tingle at the sight of a deer, the smell of a thunderstorm, the sound of running water, or the stroke of a hand on a shapely haunch, all died out, carrying with them their oblivious genes.

Who can doubt that biology, along with culture, plays a crucial role in tuning our senses? The gravity that draws a man and woman together, leading each to find the other ravishing, carries with it a long history of sexual selection, one informed by a shrewd calculation of fertility and strength. I remember how astonished I was to realize, one rainy spring day in seventh grade, that the girl sitting in the desk beside me was suddenly, enormously *interesting*. My attention was riveted on Mary Kay's long blond hair, which fell in luxuriant waves over the back of her chair, until it brushed against a rump that swelled, in a way I had never noticed before, her green plaid skirt. As a twelve-year-old, I would not have called Mary Kay beautiful, although I realize now that that is what she was. And I would have balked at the suggestion that my caveman ancestors had any say in my dawning desire, although now I can hear their voices grunting. Go for the lush hair, the swelling rump.

If we take a ride through the suburbs and study the rolling acres of lawn dotted with clumps of trees and occasional ponds, what do we see but a faithful simulation of the African savanna where humans first lived? Where zoning laws permit, the expanse of green will often be decorated by grazing animals, docile and fat, future suppers on the hoof. The same combination of watering holes, sheltering trees, and grassland shows up in paintings and parks the world over, from New Delhi to New York. It is as though we shape our surroundings to match an image, coiled in our DNA, of the bountiful land.

Perhaps in every case, as in our infatuation with lover or landscape, a sense of biological fitness infuses the resonant, eager, uplifting response to the world that I am calling beauty. Yet I persist in believing there is more to this tingle than an evolutionary reflex. Otherwise, how could a man who is programmed to lust after every nubile female nonetheless be steadily attracted, year after year, to the same woman? Why would I plant my yard with flowers that I cannot eat?

As far back as we can trace our ancestors, we find evidence of a passion for design — decorations on pots, beads on clothes, pigments on the ceilings of caves. Bone flutes have been found at human sites dating back more than 30,000 years. So we answer the breathing of the land with our own measured breath; we answer the beauty we find with the beauty we make. Our ears may be finely tuned for detecting the movements of predators or prey, but that does not explain why we should be so moved by listening to Gregorian chants or Delta blues. Our eyes may be those of a slightly reformed ape, trained for noticing whatever will keep skin and bones intact, but that scarcely explains why we should be so enthralled by the lines of a Shaker chair or a Dürer engraving, or by photographs of Jupiter.

As it happens, Jupiter is the brightest light in the sky on these September evenings, blazing in the southeast at dusk. Such a light must have dazzled our ancestors long before telescopes began to reveal the planet's husk of clouds or its halo of moons. We know that night-watchers in many cultures kept track of the heavenly dance because the records of their observations have come down to us. Did they watch so faithfully because they believed the stars and planets controlled their fate, or because they were mesmerized by the majesty of the night? I can't speak for them. But when I look at Jupiter, with naked eye or binoculars, or in the magnified images broadcast down from the Hubble Telescope, I am not looking for a clue to the morning's weather or to the mood of a deity, any more than I am studying the future of my genes when I gaze at my daughter. I am looking for the sheer bliss of looking.

In a wedding scene that has cooled into memory from the red glow of happiness, I keep glancing at Eva's face as we process down the aisle, trying to match my gawky stride to her graceful one. The light on her skin shimmers through the veil. A ripple of voices follows us toward the altar, like the sound of waves breaking on cobbles. The walk seems to go on forever, but it also seems to be over far too soon. Ready or not, we take our place at center stage, with the bridesmaids in midnight blue to our left, Matthew and his groomsmen in black to our right. My heart thrashes like a bird in a sack.

The minister, our canoeing guide, gives us both a steadying glance. Then he lifts his voice to inquire of the hushed congregation, "Who blesses this marriage?"

I swallow to make sure my own voice is still there, and say loudly, "The families give their blessing."

I step back, lift Eva's hand from my arm and place it on Matthew's, a gesture that seemed small in rehearsal yesterday but that seems huge today. Then my bit part is over. I leave the stage, carefully stepping around the long train of Eva's dress, and go to my seat beside Ruth, who dabs a handkerchief to her eyes. I grasp her free hand, so deft and familiar. Just one month shy of thirty years after my own wedding. I want to marry her all over again. Despite my heart's mad thrashing, I haven't felt like crying until this moment, as I sit here beside my own bride, while Eva recites her vows with a sob in her throat. When I hear that sob, tears rise in me, but joy rises more swiftly.

Judging from the scientists I know, including Eva and Ruth, and those whom I've read about, you can't pursue the laws of nature very long without bumping into beauty. "I don't know if it's the same beauty you see in the sunset," a friend tells me, "but it *feels* the same." This friend is a physicist, who has spent a long career deciphering what must be happening in the interior of stars. He recalls for me this thrill on grasping for the first time Dirac's equations describing quantum mechanics, or those of Einstein describing relativity. "They're so beautiful," he says, "you can see immediately they have to be true. Or at least on the way toward truth." I ask him what makes a theory beautiful, and he replies, "Simplicity, symmetry, elegance, and power."

Why nature should conform to theories we find beautiful is far from obvious. The most incomprehensible thing about the universe, as Einstein said, is that it's comprehensible. How unlikely, that a short-lived biped on a two-bit planet should be able to gauge the speed of light, lay bare the structure of an atom, or calculate the gravitational tug of a black hole. We're a long way from understanding everything, but we do understand a great deal about how nature behaves. Generation after generation, we puzzle out formulas, test them, and find, to an astonishing degree, that nature agrees. An architect draws designs on flimsy paper, and her buildings stand up through earthquakes. We launch a satellite into orbit and use it to bounce messages from continent to continent. The machine on which I write these words embodies hundreds of insights into the workings of the material world, insights that are confirmed by every burst of letters on the screen, and I stare at that screen through lenses that obey the laws of optics first worked out in detail by Isaac Newton.

By discerning patterns in the universe, Newton believed, he was tracing the hand of God. Scientists in our day have largely abandoned the notion of a Creator as an unnecessary hypothesis, or at least an untestable one. While they share Newton's faith that the universe is ruled everywhere by a coherent set of rules, they cannot say, as scientists, how these particular rules came to govern things. You can do science without believing in a divine Legislator, but not without believing in laws.

I spent my teenage years scrambling up the mountain of mathematics. Midway up the slope, however, I staggered to a halt, gasping in the rarefied air, well before I reached the heights where the equations of Einstein and Dirac would have made sense. Nowadays I add, subtract, multiply, and do long division when no calculator is handy, and I can do algebra and geometry and even trigonometry in a pinch, but that is about all that I've kept from the language of numbers. Still, I remember glimpsing patterns in mathematics that seemed as bold and beautiful as a skyful of stars.

I'm never more aware of the limitations of language than when I try to describe beauty. Language can create its own loveliness, of course, but it cannot deliver to us the radiance we apprehend in the world, any more than a photograph can capture the stunning swiftness of a hawk or the withering power of a supernova. Eva's wedding album holds only a faint glimmer of the wedding itself. All that pictures or words can do is gesture beyond themselves toward the fleeting glory that stirs our hearts. So I keep gesturing.

"All nature is meant to make us think of paradise," Thomas Merton observed. Because the Creation puts on a nonstop show, beauty is free and inexhaustible, but we need training in order to perceive more than the most obvious kinds. Even 15 billion years or so after the Big Bang, echoes of that event still linger in the form of background radiation, only a few degrees above absolute zero. Just so, I believe, the experience of beauty is an echo of the order and power that permeate the universe. To measure background radiation, we need subtle instruments; to measure beauty, we need alert intelligence and our five keen senses.

Anyone with eyes can take delight in a face or a flower. You need training, however, to perceive the beauty in mathematics or physics or chess, in the architecture of a tree, the design of a bird's wing, or the shiver of breath through a flute. For most of human history, the training has come from elders who taught the young how to pay attention. By paying attention, we learn to savor all sorts of patterns, from quantum mechanics to patchwork quilts.

This predilection brings with it a clear evolutionary advantage, for the ability to recognize patterns helped our ancestors to select mates, find food, avoid predators. But the same advantage would apply to all species, and yet we alone compose symphonies and crossword puzzles, carve stone into statues, map time and space. Have we merely carried our animal need for shrewd perceptions to an absurd extreme? Or have we stumbled onto a deep congruence between the structure of our minds and the structure of the universe?

I am persuaded the latter is true. I am convinced there's more to beauty than biology, more than cultural convention. It flows around and through us in such abundance, and in such myriad forms, as to exceed by a wide margin any mere evolutionary need. Which is not to say that beauty has nothing to do with survival: I think it has everything to do with survival. Beauty feeds us from the same source that created us. It reminds us of the shaping power that reaches through the flower stem and through our own hands. It restores our faith in the generosity of nature. By giving us a taste of the kinship between our own small minds and the great Mind of the Cosmos, beauty reassures us that we are exactly and wonderfully made for life on this glorious planet, in this magnificent universe. I find in that affinity a profound source of meaning and hope. A universe so prodigal of beauty may actually need us to notice and respond, may need our sharp eyes and brimming hearts and teeming minds, in order to close the circuit of Creation.

MARK SLOUKA

Hitler's Couch

FROM HARPER'S MAGAZINE

> This was the Angel of History! We felt its wings flutter through the room.
> — Schwerin von Krosigk

I

IF STEPHEN DEDALUS, that fearful Jesuit, was right, if history, in the century of Bergen-Belsen and Nanking and Democratic Kampuchea, is a nightmare from which we are all — even the most effectively narcotized among us — trying to awake, how then do we explain the dream that foreshadows the event, the actual nightmare that precedes the waking one?

When he was eight years old, my father was visited by a nightmare so powerful that half a century later the mere retelling of it would stipple his skin with gooseflesh and lift the hair on the back of his arms. He himself would wonder at his own bristling body, the shameless atavism of fear. "Look at this," he'd say when I was young, shoving one big arm across the table. "It never fails." And seeing the coarse, familiar fur rise as by some conjurer's trick to the memory of a dream decades gone, I'd know that the immaterial world was a force to be reckoned with.

In the dream (although nothing translates as badly as dreams — no grief, no scent, no earthly grammar), my eight-year-old father hurries, clockwise, down a white spiral staircase. The stairwell has no windows, no central shaft; its sides are as smooth as a chambered nautilus. Just ahead, the left-hand wall continuously extends itself, emerging out of the seam.

He stops, suddenly aware of a sound coming from far below. He can make it out clearly now: the heavy scrape of footsteps, as harsh as steel on marble; behind these, what he assumes at first is the suck and hiss of a factory steam engine, then realizes is actually the sound of huge, stentorian breathing. The man coming up the stairs, he knows, is gargantuan, grotesquely fat; he fills the stairwell plug-tight, like a moving wall of flesh. Getting past him is impossible; the corridor is sealed. Resistance is inconceivable; if my father remains where he is, he'll be crushed.

Turning, my father starts back up the stairs he just descended. He begins to run. Whenever he stops to catch his breath, he can hear the metronome tread, the fat man's breathing. He rushes on, confident of his speed. The man is slow, after all, barely moving. He'll simply outrun him, or keep ahead forever. The stairs unwind like a ribbon in the wind, rising into the dark. It's then that he remembers there is no exit; the stairwell ends in solid stone. Having entered the dream already descending the stairs, he can only return to where he began. Instantly sick with terror, my father turns toward the unseen thing heaving itself up the stairs behind him, toward the enormous bellows of the lungs, already filling the corridor with their sound, and his own scream wrenches him awake. The year is 1932.

II

Seven years later, on March 18, 1939, my father, not yet sixteen, stood with his friend, Cyril Brana, peering excitedly through the heavy blue curtains of his friend's second-floor apartment onto Veveří Street, in Brno, Czechoslovakia. It had rained the night before. The dripping cables of the trolley cars, catching the light, looped thin and delicate across the city's drab pigment. Even though it was a weekday, my father said, there were no cars passing in the street below, no umbrellas hurrying down the cobbled walks or stepping over puddles as if they were fissures into the earth, nor any crowding the midstreet islands to the clanging of the trolley bell, their number suddenly doubled like inkblots on an opened paper.

Three days earlier, in an official radio message that must have seemed as unbelievable to those listening to it as the formal announcement of their own deaths, Czechoslovakia had ceased to exist. The message was delivered, as all subsequent communications would be delivered, in the declarative, staccato tones of an authority accustomed to ruling by decree, to establishing fact by fiat: Bohemia and Moravia were now the Protektorat Böhmen and Mähren, under the control of the Reichsprotektor; Slovakia, henceforth, would be an "independent" state under the German-backed Catholic clergyman Jozef Tiso.

Although the exact route the Führer's motorcade was to take through Brno had not been divulged, it was easy enough to figure out by the placement of the soldiers, my father said. Already that morning, in the drizzling half-light of dawn, long lines of dark forms could be seen along certain streets and avenues, slowly coalescing into human shapes.

The motorcade was to pass through Brno around eleven that morning. By eight, a deep, unnatural silence had settled over the city; all public transportation had been stopped, all automobile traffic forbidden. People lingered in the hallways of their apartment buildings, saying little. Military loudspeakers echoed outside, announcing that all windows onto the street were to remain closed until 2:00 P.M. By nine-thirty, Brno was deserted.

Tired of waiting, Cyril and my father went to the kitchen for a snack. Taking turns holding a crusty loaf tight against their stomachs, they cut thick slices that they then covered with butter and a generous sediment of sugar. Half an hour later, realizing that no one would stop them — neither Cyril's father, standing strangely still a step back from the curtains of the second window, nor his mother, sitting by the piano, soundlessly crying into a red handkerchief — they made themselves some more.

Returning to the window, the two boys looked through the crack in the curtains toward the square. In the building opposite, all the curtains were drawn. Directly in front of the bookseller's shop, a German soldier in a gray-green uniform stood beside a box of small German flags on round wooden sticks. There had been no one to distribute them to. *"Tak neplač"* — don't cry — said Cyril's father at one point, without turning around, so that for a moment, my father said, he seemed to be speaking to the city before him as much as to the woman behind.

"Už jedou" — here they come — said Cyril. The motorcade

passed quickly, my father recalled, headed north, fifteen or even twenty black limousines surrounded by twice as many motorcycles, as tight as a swarm. Hitler's personal limousine, an open car, perhaps fifth in line, rode slightly apart from the others. Hitler himself, when my father saw him, was just sitting down, his features from that second-floor window — except for a quick glimpse of jaw and mustache — almost completely obscured under the visor of his military cap. He had been standing, though to what purpose, and for whose benefit, in that dead, unmoving city, one can only guess.

III

Adolf Hitler sat down. The motorcade passed, disappearing into the curtain's edge. My father took a bite of bread. Over the next six years, nearly 50 million souls would disappear into a furnace so profound it would forever wither any attempts to reckon its magnitude, caking the brain, leaving only a still, unsounded dust for which there could be no analogies, no accounting, out of which could emerge no saving truth. All that remained were apparent facts, recorded dates, accounts of events and motivations so jarring, so emotionally dissonant that they seemed to refer to some other world, a realm from which both humanity and sense had been seamlessly removed.

During the last days of the Third Reich, for example, as the concussions of Russian heavy artillery jingled the crystal in the cabinets of the Reichschancellery in Berlin, Propaganda Minister Goebbels would while away the long after-dinner hours reading to Hitler from Thomas Carlyle's history of Frederick the Great. Imagine the scene: Hitler, perhaps, at one end of a plum-colored damask sofa, his head tilted to his right hand, absentmindedly running his middle finger along the center of his brow; Goebbels in a comfortable chair opposite, one leg draped over the other, the fire companionably puffing and spitting . . .

And there, in one of the well-furnished rooms of the armor-plated, concrete-reinforced bunker beneath the Chancellery (only six years after passing through the line of sight of a fifteen-year-old boy standing behind a thick blue curtain), Adolf Hitler wept, touched by Carlyle's apostrophe to the long-dead king in the moment of his greatest trial: "Brave King! Wait yet a little while, and the days of your suffering will be over. Already the sun of your good fortune stands behind the clouds and soon will rise upon you."

Sixty feet over their heads, the nine-hundred-room Chancellery, with its polished marble halls and hundred-pound chandeliers, was methodically being pounded into dust and rubble: stacks and columns of books taken from the Chancellery libraries blocked the tall windows looking out onto the wrecked Wilhelmstrasse, short, ugly barrels of machine guns poking between the spines; bulky crates of crosses and oak leaves barricaded the main entrance. A month earlier, Anglo-American armies had crossed the Rhine.

None of this mattered, apparently. Sensing a promise, an omen of redemption in Carlyle's description of Frederick's deliverance, Hitler and Goebbels sent a guard to retrieve the Reich's official horoscopes. And there it was: proof that, just as Prussia had been saved in the darkest hours of the Seven Years' War by the miraculous death of the czarina, so the Third Reich would survive her harshest trials. History would save her. "Even in this very year a change of fortune shall come," Goebbels proclaimed in an eleventh-hour message to the retreating troops. "The Führer knows the exact hour of its arrival. Destiny has sent us this man so that we . . . [can] testify to the miracle. . . ."

A few days later, Goebbels had his miracle, his czarina. Returning to Berlin late on the night of April 12, the capital around him rising in flames, he was approached by a secretary with urgent news: Franklin Roosevelt was dead. Phoning the news to Hitler in the bunker beneath the burning Chancellery, Goebbels was ecstatic. Here, blazingly revealed at last, was the power of Historical Necessity and Justice. The news, he felt, would revive the spirit of hope in the German people. His feelings seem to have been shared by most of the German Supreme Command. "This," wrote Finance Minister Schwerin von Krosigk in his diary, "was the Angel of History! We felt its wings flutter through the room."

Less than two weeks later, in the cramped air-raid shelter of the Ministry of the People's Enlightenment and Propaganda, Goebbels's six children lay dead, their lips, eyes, arms, and legs turned blue from the potassium cyanide pills given to them by their father. Goebbels's wife, Magda, who had apparently dressed her children in their lace nightgowns and curled their hair for the occasion, was also dead, shot by her husband, who then poured gasoline on her and set fire to her skirt. Goebbels himself, after killing his family, poured gasoline on his clothes, set fire to a trouser leg, then turned the gun to his temple. Across the Wilhelmplatz, German gunners lay buried beneath the crumbled barricades of books, the high-ceilinged rooms behind them wavering in the heat of raging fires. In a small room in the bunker below, having rejected poison after watching the agonized deaths of the Chancellery dogs, Adolf Hitler sat down on a deep-cushioned, brocade sofa next to the body of his bride, Eva Braun, put a gun in his mouth, and pulled the trigger. Blood flowed down and coagulated on the brocade. The Angel of History fluttered its wings.

IV

Thirty-four years later, on one of those drizzling October afternoons in New York City when dusk sets in at noon, they fluttered again. An undergraduate at Columbia College at the time, I'd found myself that fall more than usually broke, and, reaching the limits of my inventiveness on the hot plate, I decided to find a job. In a small office off the claustrophobic circular hallway in the basement of Low Library, I answered an ad for something called Student Help for the Elderly. After filling out a long questionnaire, I was given the name of one Beatrix Turner, an address on Sixty-ninth Street off Broadway, and told when to appear. The job paid $3.50 an hour.

I didn't want it. Between classes and sleeping with a young woman I'd met at Barnard that fall (or rather not sleeping, never sleeping), I felt exhausted, perpetually late to everything, always sprinting bleary-eyed up Claremont Avenue or leaping puddles on the way to some overheated classroom where a professor whose name I couldn't remember would already be discussing whatever author — Hobbes or Locke, Nietzsche or Kant — I'd failed to finish reading the night before. When I added to this the hundred-block walk down Broadway and back (I begrudged the bus fare), the fact that it always seemed to be raining on the days I had to go, and, finally, that I'd be skipping two classes a week (I'd had to lie on my application to get the job), it seemed like a bad deal. I took the job anyway.

I don't remember Beatrix Turner very well, just a small, well-kept woman in a bone-white dress given to straight talk and strong opinions. I remember that her apartment, small even by dormitory standards, was very cluttered, very still. Everything sounded louder there: the door down the hall, the spoon in the cup, the tiny steps of the minute hand drawing its harvest of days on the mantle. She showed me how to make tea for her with whole cinnamon, cloves, and ginger, and for years afterward, though I'd never particularly enjoyed being there (she was cranky and irritable; I, no doubt, sullen and impatient), these smells were my mildly unpleasant madeleines, dragging me, willy-nilly, back to that apartment on Sixty-ninth Street, my unmourned Combray by the Hudson.

And so, on the misty, gray afternoon of October 2, I started down Broadway to Beatrix Turner's apartment, moving quickly through the crowd, dodging trucks on 110th Street, checking out the nickel-and-dime bodegas where I bought the odds and ends I needed for my dormitory room. To compensate for my jeans and sneakers, I'd thrown on my one good jacket. Ten blocks north of Sherman Square, with the rain beginning to come down in earnest and umbrellas opening all around me like strange black blooms, I took it off, folded it under my arm, and sprinted for 69th Street.

I found Beatrix Turner in a reflective mood that afternoon. The tea, as I recall, had already been made; the chores, she said, could wait. Toweling off as best I could, I wiped my steaming glasses on a napkin and, balancing my cup and saucer awkwardly on my lap, sat down in the chair she indicated. I looked around the apartment. I'd never noticed the mementos before — the framed letters, the ribbons, the statuary. There was something oddly moving about that crowded menagerie. Everywhere I looked the small faces of men and women (many in British or American World War II uniforms, some with their arms around each other, all very young) smiled down out of the photographs that lined the bookshelves and the walls of that apartment, a tiny eternal audience come to witness the final act of Beatrix Turner's long performance. A pretty young woman in an Air Force cap sat on the hood of a jeep. A rough-looking young man in a black sweater (his teeth closed tight and his brow furrowed as though he were squinting into the sun) looked out from what I took to be the loops and bars of his own overbold signature, written across the sky.

The spiced tea tasted good that afternoon. Every now and again the radiator, as though harboring some furious apartment gnome, would begin to clang and ping and whine. Past the safety grates and the slowly rusting fire escape, I could see the rain. The blinds in the windows across the airshaft were shut. Inexplicably mellow that afternoon (or perhaps just resigned to my ignorance), Beatrix Turner began to talk. Her voice, ordinarily strong, decidedly ungentle, now softened. It seemed to me then, though the details are lost, that she'd been nearly everywhere, done almost everything — drank ouzo with Hemingway, danced with Dos Passos. Some of her accounts, admittedly, were more obscure, and for long stretches I listened to stories of people I'd never heard of, places that held no meaning for me, selfishly grateful that I didn't have to scrub an already spotless sink or look, yet again, for the reading glasses that she had just had a second before; grateful too, I'll admit now, for the fact that I was closing in on $10.50 without yet having done a stitch of work.

But then I started to listen. Beatrix Turner, I realized, had been a war correspondent through much of 1944 and 1945. She'd been with the American First Army when it met the Russians at Torgau on the Elbe River. And on May 3 or 4, traveling on foot, she'd entered Berlin.

The city had fallen the day before. Where the crumbling outlines of foundations and rooms showed through the piled rubble, they seemed, as though escaping their own reality, to hark backward or forward to the very ancient or the purely ephemeral, to some Neolithic civilization, recently unearthed, or to a child's sandcastle, broken by the tide. On the bullet-chipped walls and columns of the Reichstag, now a blackened shell, Russian names, scrawled by the living, memorialized those who had died for victory. Somehow making her way to the Chancellery through that heaped, smoldering city — whether alone or accompanied I don't remember — Beatrix Turner arrived to discover that Russian engineers had already burned the hinges off the heavy steel doors facing the charred and smoking garden.

She leaned forward. "You know, of course, that Adolf Hitler shot himself in his bunker beneath the Chancellery."

I began to say something, but she waved it away.

"Oh, that's all bosh about Paraguay and Argentina," she said. "He shot himself. Eva Braun took arsenic."

I didn't say anything.

Beatrix Turner took a sip of tea. "I was one of the first ones down," she said.

I don't remember if Beatrix Turner told me how she talked her way past the guards that day, nor can I be certain whether the image I have of her descending those endless pitch-black stairs by candlelight or flashlight is based on the description she gave me or the ones I've read since then. In the entry I wrote in my journal later that night, there's no mention of the cold, dank smell of extinguished fires, of the charred picture frames, like overdrawn metaphors, still hanging from the walls, of the black water, ankle deep, that covered the carpets.

But one memory remains as clear as on the night I wrote it down. Sensing my skepticism, perhaps, Beatrix Turner put down her cup and saucer and went to a closet near the front door. "I have something to show you," she said. "A little souvenir." I stood up, thinking to help her, but she was already carrying an ordinary cardboard carton. Placing it on the table, she opened it, removed another, smaller carton, and from this a carefully folded wad of tissue. Unwrapping this bundle, she revealed a fragile piece of cloth with a strange, almost Egyptian-looking pattern, marred by an ugly dark stain.

I looked at the thing, uncomprehending.

"I cut this piece out of the sofa in the bunker," Beatrix Turner said. She pointed. "That's Adolf Hitler's blood."

Before I could say anything, she was leafing through an old issue of *Life* she'd brought out of the closet with her, and suddenly there it was: a photograph of correspondents, one holding a candle, inspecting the richly patterned brocade sofa on which Adolf Hitler and Eva Braun had committed suicide. In the photograph one could see the pattern of the sofa clearly, a repeating motif of male figures dressed in traditional folk garb standing next to huge, orchidlike blooms, or fanciful palms, or exploding fireworks. Each figure held a short leash that dipped in a lazy U to the neck of a prancing stag.

On the right armrest, a dark, vaguely phallic bloodstain had soaked the brocade, obliterating half a leash and half a stag. I looked at the piece of cloth I now held in my hand. The stag was nearly gone; only its hooves and hindquarters remained. The pattern matched.

I left the apartment soon afterward. Waiting for the elevator, I noticed a door at the far end of the hall. I pushed it open. Four flights down a badly lit stairwell brought me to a locked door. Looking around, I saw another, smaller door. Forcing it open, I saw that it let out onto a fire escape. A fixed steel ladder dropped twenty feet to the alley below. I climbed out, soiling my jacket against the rusting frame. Even today I can remember the good strong sting of the rain against my face. At the bottom of the unlit, cluttered alley rising like a canyon to the sky, I pushed open the heavy iron gate to Sixty-ninth Street and started to run.

Coda

Pleasure and pain are immediate; knowledge, retrospective. A steel ball, suspended on a string, smacks into its brothers and nothing happens: no shock of recognition, no sudden epiphany. We go about our business, buttering the toast, choosing gray socks over brown. But here's the thing: just because we haven't understood something doesn't mean we haven't been shaped by it. Although I couldn't understand what I'd seen in Beatrix Turner's apartment that autumn afternoon in 1979, although I ran the way a child will run, stopping up its ears, from something dark and grotesque, something far beyond its years, the deed had been done. That cloth, in its own pathetic way, dealt a featuring blow to my life.

What I reacted to — instinctively, I suppose — was the terrible smallness of the thing, the almost vertiginous compaction of the symbol. Behind that ridiculous cloth with its vaguely shit-brown stain, I could sense the nations of the dead pushing and jostling for space, for room, for a voice; it was as though all the sounds of the world had been drawn into the plink of a single drop, falling from the lip of a loosened drain. One could resist the implicit lesson, recognize the obscenity of linking that worthless piece of fabric to the murder of millions, even note the small irony of it being preserved, like some unholy relic, from the disintegration it implied, and yet still be moved by an inescapable thought, a thought both unjust and unavoidable: that it should come to this, O God asleep in heaven, a tattered piece of cloth in an apartment on Sixty-ninth Street.

But of course it didn't. History resists an ending as surely as nature abhors a vacuum; the narrative of our days is a run-on sentence, every full stop a comma in embryo. But more: like thought, like water, history is fluid, unpredictable, dangerous. It leaps and surges and doubles back, cuts unpredictable channels, surfaces suddenly in places no one would expect. How else can one explain the dream that foreshadows the event? Or a fear immaculately conceived? Or a will to resistance that reemerges, inexplicably, continents and generations from where it fell?

And so, perhaps, it comes down to this: that the irresistible march of events through time — the cup raised, the drink taken, the sudden knock on the door — is the only truth we have and yet, and I don't mean to be clever here, the greatest lie we tell. The empire of facts is irrefutable; death *will* have its dominion. Recognizing the limits of chronology, resisting its unforgiving dictates, is our duty and our right. There is no contradiction.

TOURÉ

What's Inside You, Brother?

FROM HIGH PLAINS LITERARY REVIEW

> You ache with the need to convince yourself that you do exist in the
> real world, that you're a part of all the sound and anguish, and you
> strike out with your fists, you curse and you swear to make them
> recognize you.
>
> — Ralph Ellison, *Invisible Man*

FROM OUTSIDE the circle of spandexed actresses jumping rope,
their ponytails bouncing politely, Body & Soul appears to be a
boxing gym rated G. But push through the circle, past the portly,
middle-age lawyers slugging through leg lunges and past the
dumpy jewelry designers, wearing rouge, giggling as they slap at
the speed bag. Keep pushing into the heart of the circle, toward
the sound of taut leather pap-papping against bone, toward the
odor of violence, and, as often as not, you'll find two men sparring,
their fists stuffed into blue or red or black Everlast gloves, T-shirts
matted down by hot perspiration, heavy breaths shushed through
mouthpieces, moving quick and staccato and with tangible tinges
of fear as they bob and weave and flick and fake, searching for a
taste of another man's blood.

Sometimes Touré will be in the heart of the circle, maybe sparring with Jack, hands up, headgear laced tight, lungs heavy, ribs
stinging after Jack backs him into a corner and slices a sharp left
uppercut through Touré's elbows into the soft, very top section of
his stomach. Then, for Touré, time stops. He loses control of his
body, feels briefly suspended in air, his thoughts seemingly hol-
lered to him from far away. Life is never faster than in the ring,
except when you're reeling from a razing punch. Then, life is

never slower. Sometimes Touré will be in the heart of the circle sparring, but I don't know why: he's not very good.

I've known Touré a long, long time — you could say we grew up together. He's just over five feet ten inches and about one hundred sixty pounds. That's one inch taller and a few pounds lighter than the legendary middleweight Marvelous Marvin Hagler. Touré, however, has neither long arms to throw punches from a distance, which minimizes vulnerability, nor massive strength to chop a man down with a few shots. He has the stamina to stay fresh through five and occasionally six rounds, yet after four years of boxing he still lacks the weapons to put a boxer in real danger, and that puts him in danger. Being a lousy fighter is far different from sucking at, say, tennis. So, if he's not good, why does he continue climbing into the ring? I went to the gym to find out.

"Three men walkin down the deck of a luxury liner," says Carlos, the owner of Body & Soul. He is a yellow-skinned Black man and a chiseled Atlas who always gives his clients good boxing advice and a good laugh. "Italian guy, Jewish guy, Black guy." He begins giggling. "Italian guy pulls out a long cigar," he says and begins walking stiff and tough like Rocky. "He whips out his lighter, lights the cigar, puts it in his pocket, and keeps walking. Jewish guy wants to be as big as him, so he takes out a slightly longer cigar, grabs out his matchbook, and strikes the match on the book. It won't light."

"Oy vay!" a Jewish woman interjects dramatically.

"So the Jewish guy strikes the match on the deck. It lights. He puts the match in the ashtray and keeps steppin. Now the Black guy . . ."

"Aww shit," you say.

". . . The Black guy want to be as big as them — you know how niggas are," he says, and everyone cracks up. "So he takes out the longest cigar and a match and goes to strike it on the matchbook. Won't light. Tries it on the deck. No dice. So finally, he strikes it *on the seat of his pants.* The match lights! He lights the cigar, tosses the match overboard. But when the match goes overboard, the luxury liner is passing an oil slick. The match hits the oil and the boat blows up." He pauses and smiles like the Kool-Aid man. "What's the moral of the story?"

Everyone grins expectantly.

"If a nigga scratch his ass he'll set the world on fire!"

You and Carlos laugh hard, doubling over together.

Nigga scratch his ass he'll set the world on fire, you say to yourself. How ridiculous. More of the silly Black chauvinist — negrovinist? — joking that we waste time with instead of thinking of ways to get ahead. Black is more often lit on fire by the world! How stupid to think that by doing something as crude as scratching your ass you could grab the world's attention, shake it up, maybe even blacken it. That just by being your Black self, you could make the world ours.

As Carlos's audience for the joke disperses, he pulls you close to put on your headgear in the same way that your parents once pulled you close to zip up your snowsuit. Your hands stuffed into large gloves in preparation for combat, you are immobilized, unable to do anything for yourself — not hold a cup of water, not scratch your ass — anything but throw punches. Carlos squeezes the thick leather pillow past your temples, down around your ears, and pulls tight the laces under your chin. The padding bites down on your forehead, your temples, your cheeks. You look into the mirror. Your head and face are buried so deeply in padding you can't tell yourself apart from another head wrapped up in headgear. You can't recognize your face.

The buzzer rings, launching the three-minute round, and you turn to the heavy bag, a large sack of leather and padding that hangs from the ceiling like a giant kielbasa. You approach the bag as you would another fighter, working your rhythms and combinations and strength, sinking in your hooks and jabs and crosses. You begin hitting slowly, paying close attention to each stinging shot, moving in slow, sharp rhythms like an old Leadbelly guitar-and-harmonica blues, each punch slapping the bag and sounding like a dog-eared, mud-splattered, ripped-apart boot stomping the floorboards of a little Alabama juke joint where they chased away the blues with the blues, sung in a key so deep whites thought they could hear it, but Negroes knew only they could. Because slaying the blues was a never-ending gig halted only for one thing, and that was radio dispatches of a Joe Louis bout. That cured the blues in a hurry, hearing the Brown Bomber slaying one or another white boy by fighting so slowly he looked like sepia-toned stop motion, his body stiff and slow like a cobra, hypnotizing his man, until the precise moment for the perfect punch. Then, lightning: a left-right would explode from Louis, and quick as a thunderclap his man would be sprawled on the ground below him, that's right, an Italian or a German with his spine on the canvas as thousands listened on, Louis having done what Negroes dreamed of doing but hardly dared think. Then Louis, the grandson of Booker T. Washington, the grandfather of Colin Powell, humbly retreated to his corner, his face wooden and emotionless, his aura as unthreatening as only the highest of the high-yellows could manage.

So you go on hitting the bag and talking to yourself in body English, the dialect of Joe Louis, talking with a near Tommish lilt as you slink slowly around the bag, but not quite Tommish because after a few racially quiet sentences you slash a few quick, deadly words and leave your opponent counting the sheep on the ceiling. You speak to yourself in the most necessary Black English in America, that of the humble assimilationist, and you move around the bag, trying to hypnotize your opponent, then lashing two, three rocket shots at him, and imagine yourself, like the Brown Bomber, lighting the world on fire, quietly.

The bell ring-ring-rings. The round is over. Fighters wander from their bags over toward Carlos, in the center of the room. Jack, a gruesome-looking, thirty-year-old white dentist, bumps into you, feigning an accident. "Touré! I didn't even see you!" he lies with a laugh. "I can't recognize you without my jab in your face."

People crack up. During breaks the fighting doesn't stop, it just turns oral — a crude variant on the verbal fisticuffs called the dozens takes its place. But instead of attacking your poverty, or your mama, it's your boxing or your looks. The one who makes everyone laugh loudest wins. And as with the dozens, sometimes it hurts, but when it's done by your own, to strengthen you for the onslaught from without, you know that a beatdown is really a buildup and you just keep on. "What's the point in us fighting?" you ask, looking at Jack's flattened nose and honeycombed skin. "That face cain't get ruined no worse." More laughs. This round is a tie.

The bell comes again and you head back to the heavy bag for three minutes more of fervor. You attack the bag savagely now, punching harder with all of the strength in your arms and all the evil in your hands, making the bag suck hard and send back flat, dull beats like the cold, thick drumbeats of raw, gutbucket southern soul, maybe Otis Redding, and now you are speaking Sonny Liston.

This is the body English of the back alley, the backroom, the back corner of the prison's back cell, where Liston, serious criminal, Mob enforcer, learned to box and became a straight-ahead, raw and rugged, black as blue, bruiser nigga. The grandson of Nat Turner, the grandfather of Mike Tyson. The scion and hero of every bully who ever lived. This is not the English of the street, no, too much bustling energy and zooming hustler's pace, no, this is the English of the street *corner.* Home of the long-faced, too-silent, thin-tie, black-black nigguhs who work only at night, who don't read *Ebony,* who have a look that could make death turn around. Liston knocked his man out and strolled over to a neutral corner with a glower that took the whole stadium right back to some alley that ain't seen the sun in decades off some long-forgotten street at the end of the world. You're slamming your hands into the bag, but you're in that same alley, scrapping as you're sidestepping ancient garbage and streams of green water and body parts without bodies, as a single long-broken street lamp looks on, saying nothing. Liston lit the world on fire as the most hated man on the planet, and now here you come fighting ugly, banging the bag, banging like a ram, talking that crude, foul, dirty Liston-ese.

"Hey, Touré!" Jack screams from across the gym as the buzzer ending the second round begins to sound. "What's goin on inside that voodoo-do up on your head?"

The gym goes into hysterics. "Get out my face," you shoot back, "you melanin-*challenged* mothafucka." People double over. This round to you.

Before the third round starts, you stop moving long enough to get your heart back and your head together. This round you're going to put it all together. When the bell sounds you're a flurry of movement and flow, dancing out, then stepping in, weaving your head through the air and sliding in to land two, three, four, five quick punches and then out, dancing and bobbing, then three, four, five more quick shots to the bag on which you play a hot staccato tempo borrowed from high-pace jazz, from the sheets of sound of Coltrane. And now you're talking Muhammad Ali, the

smooth-flowing, fan-dazzling, rhythm poet, the melding of Louis
Armstrong and Malcolm X and Michael Jackson and the zip-bam-
boom, the speed, swagger, swish, rope-a-dope jungle rumbler, Ma-
nila thriller, who turned the ring into an artist's studio, the canvas
his own beautiful body.

Now, in front of the bag is a true African-American, a cool
synthesis, not merely assimilating, not merely rebelling, but blending like jazz, melding what is gorgeous and grotesque about Africa
and America. It's a body English that's the high-tech version of
that spoken by Brer Rabbit, the Negro folktale trickster and blues-
trained hero whose liquid mind and body could find a way past
any so-called insurmountable force on any so-rumored impossible
mission without the force even knowin he been there and gone.
It's a body English filled with signifying, which means you say bad
and mean good or you say bad and mean bad. And either way
everyone who's supposed to know always know and know without
anyone having to explain because everyone who's supposed to
know know about signifying even if they don't know the word.

But you know all that, so you fire through the round in constant,
unstoppable motion, lighting the entire universe on glorious, ecstatic, religious-fervor fire with your Ali-ese, and of Black, and of
beauty. And then, as punches rain from deep within your heart
onto the bag, you see that Carlos was right, a Black man can light
the world on fire, wake it up, change it up, blacken it up, by
something as crude and simple and natural as scratching his ass,
that is, simply by being himself.

The round ends and Jack comes rushing over. You two are about
to spar a few rounds, and he is teasing you now with a half-speed
flurry of pantomimed jabs and hooks. Everyone looks on. "He's
attacking me!" you call out in mock horror. "I sense a bias crime!
Is there a lawyer in the house?" Again, laughter carries the day,
but then the laughter carries you back, back to the laughter of the
playground, back to the beginning of your fight career.

On the playground you sat alone, the only Black face as far as you
could see on the playground of that century-and-a-half-old New
England prep school. Matthew came over. He never liked you. He
was brown-skinned with curly black hair, and Mom always whispered that he had to be part Black, but he never claimed it, never

even admitted to being adopted. He saw you sitting alone in the playground and said, "Hey, Touré, why don't you come over and play?" You don't mean it. "If you get dirty, no one will know." Then he began to laugh.

You sprang at him in a frenzy, flinging tiny fists into his face, one after another without aim or direction, punch after punch flowing overhand and sloppy at his head and face and shoulders. Tears flying as easily as arms, finding room on your cheeks amid the hot sweat breaking into the brisk New England cold, you didn't feel his tiny fists jolting back at you, didn't hear the delighted screams of other children — *Fight! Fight!* — didn't hear the teacher Miss Farrah running to break it up after a few seconds that seemed like a year spent roaring at each other with tiny fists. You weren't even certain who you were as you rolled about in a gale of blows until you crawled inside yourself and found a serenity inside your embattled self, a peace beneath your warring skin, because you were fighting back and that made you certain that you could light the world on fire because there was a fire lit inside of you.

The Body & Soul buzzer screamed. Touré snapped back to attention as Jack came toward him, beginning their first round of sparring. Right away, Jack stepped close and stung Touré with a left jab to his nose, then another and another. Touré backed up and slipped a jab that landed on Jack's nose, pushing his head back sharply, then another jab that Jack blocked. Touré was much better fighting from the outside than the inside. The outside is when there's a few feet between fighters. They stand a polite distance away from each other, moving on their toes, occasionally jabbing or blocking and always looking for openings. When the boxers are outside, relatively speaking, there's a gentlemanly calm and leisurely pace about the fight. Inside, the fighters are just inches away from each other and it's point-blank range for both men and it's at once sexy and dangerous. Over and over again Touré tried to get inside, and finally Jack made him pay for coming into the wrong neighborhood. Touré stepped close to Jack and tried a quick left hook. Then a hard right uppercut caught Touré in the ribs. Jack saw him coming and pulled his trigger faster.

In the locker room of Body & Soul I caught up with Touré. Since we've known each other so long, I felt I could be completely honest. I was wrong.

"Why do you keep boxing?"

"I can't stop," he said without looking up.

"You mean, you won't stop."

"No. I can't. I love it."

"You get in the ring and get knocked down. Aren't you worried about — "

"Yo, man, a punch in the face ain't but a thing."

"Are you trying to take physical punishment to absolve your middle-class-based guilt and be literally banged into the gang of proletarian Blacks who live to give and take lumps every day and . . ."

Then he lunged at me. He swung at me with force and fury, and I fell hard on the ground. I saw my blood then, and for a fleeting second I felt a jolt of adrenaline. I was hot with anger and humiliation, but I was also not at all self-conscious and still wonderfully aware, as wide open as the sky. I was in pain and ecstasy. And from somewhere deep inside, I laughed loud and hard.

He stood over me and roared down, "I don't need to hear yo shit, man. I've sparred a few times. *I beat myself up all the time.*" He paused, then spoke with a soft intensity. "See, before my Moms sent me off to first grade she said, 'You have to be twice as good as those little white kids.' And that shit was real. But not here. In that ring all you got is two gloves and your head. That's a real . . . what's the word . . ."

"Meritocracy?"

"Boxocracy? Fightocracy? Whatever. I can do whatever I want and be whoever I want to be. All fighters live until the day they die. That's not a thing all men can say. But while he's alive, a fighter lives."

Then I looked away and my mind floated back and I saw myself in college, junior year, at a party. As things broke up, a group of juniors stood talking, fifteen or so others within easy earshot. A small argument began, quickly turned hot. Then, finally, The Whisper was stated — The Whisper that had begun my freshman year when I arrived on campus and, after a decade-plus in a white prep school, I didn't join the Black community but pledged a white fraternity and vacationed with white boys and dated white girls. I was branded a traitor then, a Black Judas, and The Whisper started, followed me sophomore year, when I consciously and conspicu-

ously turned away from my white friends to party and protest with
Black students. It chased me into junior year, when I moved into
the Black house and became a campus political figure. And that
night, as things broke up, The Whisper stepped from the shadows.
"Touré, *you ain't Black.*"

And I said nothing. I stood in the middle of a circle of my Black
classmates and heard the silence screaming in my ears and saw my
chance to answer The Whisper, and I said nothing. I just turned
slowly and walked away. I went to bed and promised myself never
to tell the story of that night, not even to myself. I locked the
memory away, closed my eyes. But the memory seeped out and
kept me awake. And worse than the public humiliation was my
nonanswer: I had taken the knockdown sitting down.

The memory obsessively replayed again and again, as I crossed
the quad, ate lunch, sat bored in class, furtively took sex, sometimes adding something I should have done — a witty retort, a
tough reply, a physical attack — sometimes not. And it germinated
in me and festered and burned and with time turned inventively
malignant, burning new each time, a tumor inside my personal
history, throbbing, reaching out around the corners of my mind,
grabbing toward my self-image, threatening my internal balance.
Then, realizing the power of my conscience, my sense of regret,
the fire inside me began burning hotter.

"No matter what," Touré said, looking directly at me, "I've got
to fight, always fight, even in the face of sure defeat, because no
one can hurt me as badly as I can."

I knew exactly what he meant. And he bent down and helped
me up.

GEORGE W. S. TROW

Folding the Times

FROM THE NEW YORKER

The New York Newspaper

ONE OF THE THINGS my father taught me when I was young which has proved almost useless is how to fold a folio newspaper, a large-format newspaper like the *Times,* so that it could be read in close quarters on the subway in New York. It was assumed that you would read a large-format newspaper, and that you'd be sitting close to your neighbors on the subway, and you had to know how to do it: how to follow the story over from page 1 to page 32, folding the newspaper while existing in a small, confined space. This skill — which I don't think I have anymore — resembled origami, Japanese paper folding. It really was fairly complicated. My father did it beautifully; he could read contentedly for an hour on the subway, folding and following and moving back and forth. In any case, the variety of what I'm calling the folio newspapers in New York in 1950 has been forgotten, and we have to remember that the television mind hadn't yet been formed; that the newspaper mind was dominant in New York City, and that, unquestionably, New York City, as it had been for some time, was the dominant city in the country as to culture, especially as to mass culture, certainly as to media.

Naturally, a moment matters. Was New York interesting in 1865? Of course it was: the city of Astor, Vanderbilt, and Washington Irving, say. In some ways, New York had never been more powerful than it was then. And on February 1, 1929? You bet: the rock-and-roll financial life, the booze, Broadway. To a large extent, we've been working our way back to that legendary electricity ever since. What of media life? Was it more intelligent in 1865 than in 1950? Well, yes. Was media life more frenetic, more charged with energy, on February 1, 1929, than it was twenty-one years later? Well, yes, it was. However, the moment — I mean the world moment — was different. In 1950, America was about to reach the height of her power. An interesting moment: Victoria assumes the throne, in a way; Napoleon is about to dismember the Holy Roman Empire, in a way. We were about to have our most pervasive influence. The world waited for what America would say, and paid attention to whatever America did say.

New York in 1950 was a gray city. From a boy's point of view, it was a masculine city, a maritime city, a serious place — shot through with a bit of pastel-feminine color. The newspapers then seemed to be the oracles of the city. They, too, were gray, and even the tabloids seemed serious — like a U.S.O. show. Even our entertainment — even our gossip — had a warrior vector; or so it seemed to me.

When I was seven, in 1950, I was told by my father that you couldn't be a real Trow without knowing how to read a newspaper. My father came from a brownstone New York family and had long been obsessed with Franklin Roosevelt. His grandmother, my great-grandmother, had been a brownstone Progressive dedicated to Theodore Roosevelt right into his Bull Moose days, and so by 1950 we were into our fiftieth year, more or less, of our family obsession with the Necessary Correctness of the Roosevelts. You may not know what the Black Nobility used to be in Rome. It's a vanished phenomenon, just as the phenomenon I am describing within my family is a vanished phenomenon. The Black Nobility was mostly descended from or related to the Italian popes, and it was felt within those families that a certain thread of church life was maintained only within those families; the thread, of course, was blood loyalty. It was all of a piece, my father indicated to me in the strongest terms: gentlemanliness, my family's history in New York City, New York City itself, the liberal arts — and the New York newspaper. My father had this notion, and he took it as Job 1 to pass it on to me. Not for me were any of the freedoms whose promises had drawn ordinary Americans into the Roosevelt fold. My job was

to be Black Roosevelt — tinged so deep that no amount of change
could change my color.

By the age of four, although I could not read, I knew what a
headline was, what a lead story was, which columnists were respectable and which were not (I learned to loathe Westbrook Pegler
before I was in kindergarten). I learned what the *Times* represented and what the *Daily News* represented, and the difference
between the *News* and the *Mirror,* and who Old Man Hearst was,
and what was wrong with Roy Howard (the head of the Scripps-
Howard chain). I was told that not to read the *Times* was to con-
demn oneself to second-class citizenship. And I was told that the
Sun was in trouble, and that our newspaper was the *Herald Tribune.*

In 1950, the *Herald Tribune* was continuous with what my father
was saying Wasp civilization was. My grandmother, my father's
mother, was a devotee of Clementine Paddleford, who wrote the
food column; it was my grandmother's firm opinion that the only
person writing for the public who could give you a really good
recipe was Clementine Paddleford, and all through my childhood
I ate spaghetti sauce made by my grandmother from Clementine
Paddleford's recipe. We were, it is safe to say, in our souls a *Herald
Tribune* family. But that was over, or was about to be over.

The *Herald Tribune* was Heartbreak House. It was losing reader-
ship and losing authority, and for no particular reason. That it
didn't report the news as fully as the *Times* did was the obvious
one, but my personal experience was that people who switched
from the *Herald Tribune* to the *Times* in the 1950s did it for Zeitgeist
reasons: they did it to escape Heartbreak House. The heaping feast
of information in the *Times* was picked at, not read completely; the
move was made because one wanted to associate oneself with the
secular, scientific, factual approach of the *Times.* The *Herald Tribune*
still reported the news a little in the spirit of one who had seen
you at St. James Church on Sunday, of someone who was suspicious
of Mammon and was reluctant to give you sensational information
of any kind, lest it damage your soul.

I didn't like the *World-Telegram* (as of January 1950, it became
the *World-Telegram & Sun*). There was a deadness around that paper. It was the paper read by a certain kind of person working in
the advertising business, or on Wall Street. Such people read the
World-Telegram pretty thoroughly. It wasn't like the *Herald Tribune.*
There was no fine and pretty stuff from old-time Waspdom, and

there wasn't the endless factuality and relative high-mindedness of the *Times*. The *World-Telegram* was for Wasps who understood that their education and their background were dominance weapons.

The *Journal-American* was read by the people who were moving toward a dominant position in the culture — the Irish and also the Italians, the Roman Catholics of the city. They wanted to be appealed to, and coaxed, and beguiled, and they wanted some piece of information from previous avatars of the dominant culture. There was a bit of what we'll call real social authority in the *Journal-American*, and it came in two parts: Broadway-Hollywood and Café Society. The *Journal-American*, in part because of its link through ownership with William Randolph Hearst, who was one of the gaudiest creatures of this century, reported something like the real deal in those two departments. It wasn't going to offend Mr. Hearst to give you the real deal about how it was at El Morocco; that was a world he wasn't intimidated by. And Mr. Hearst, who had been in long association with motion pictures, expected to see something like the real deal from that world reported in his papers. The Hearsts also ran the most negligible of all the news-gathering services, the International News Service, which, nevertheless, gave you a feeling that the Hearst ownership had a kind of world view and world access. The final element was "Puck — The Comic Weekly," the best comics section in New York. With Mr. Hearst you have a bus-and-truck Winston Churchill — the Winston Churchill who didn't keep much to ancient, honorable rituals but partied with you.

I don't think there can have been many people reading those papers from the point of view I was developing in the 1950s. After all, a newspaper is something that you read — or not. No one is there to force you to read it, and usually you read just one — the one that appeals to you. But when my father pointed out this Whole to me — America, New York City, the New York newspaper, Franklin Roosevelt, and us Trows — he said that all of it was important, and all of it fitted together. I took him at his word, and agreed to look at things that way. I was daunted by the *Times*, but I could see the other papers in relation — each as one part of a functioning world. The old Wasps were on the way out; the new Wasps were flat and status-conscious; the tabloids had their own netherworld of strident liveliness.

Now, however, I see the whole thing as a tragic dysfunction —

as horses pulling in different directions and running roughshod over what really needed to be said. The newspapers represented different parts of what I have come to call an Assumed Dominant Mind. And the very existence of that Assumed Dominant Mind, with its narrowness — even at the *Times* — meant trouble: it meant creeping catatonia, and creeping illiteracy, and those have come to pass.

Following a Story — Now and Then

Today, if you know how a newspaper is edited, you can read it quite quickly. The better the newspaper, the faster you can read it, because you can trust the consistent mind of the editors.

There isn't much real news. Most news has to do with what a government (or a unit of government) is willing to let you know about what it is saying or doing in relation to another government or unit of government. You could spend your whole life reading about the Middle East. You don't want to do that. But if there is a car bombing in Tel Aviv you may want to read about that for reasons of your own. And then what you must do is see what Arafat says the next day. You have to get to know the reporter. What does he think is going to happen? The clue is in his style, in his selection of quotes. Does he quote the mainstream professor who thinks that the peace process will stay on track anyway, or does he take you into a violent neighborhood and show you a picture of hopelessness? I dislike all talk about "bias" and "lack of objectivity" in a reporter. He is there to clue you in to his best assessment — his reading of the code of events. He has no way to be objective (other than not to have a personal stake in the argument); he doesn't know the real facts — or, if he does, it's so rare as not to be worth the mentioning. He can't read Arafat's mind, or Assad's, or anybody's. In a way, what you value most about him is his appropriate subjectivity, his feel for events.

I read every word in the paper about Algeria, Ukraine, and Belarus: these are the underreported zones. You should get a sense of what is underreported and what is overreported. Overreported is Newt Gingrich. One-tenth of one percent of what has been written about Newt would have done you just fine. You also need to read every word about Shanghai, Chinese billionaires, and the Russian mafia. Also currency trading. Stories are boiling (or seem to be boiling) here. If you have a personal reason to take an interest in a Baby Bell reaching out to yet another media conglomerate, sure, read it, but be aware that the deal will ravel or unravel, happen or not happen, be consummated or not consummated, be important or not important, and that you will have just read ten thousand words.

I read nothing about the Equal Rights Amendment during the time it was in the news, for instance. Either it was going to get to be an amendment or it wasn't. There are a lot of stories like that: years in the making; infinite detail; you have no say as to the outcome; it will happen or it won't.

Do yourself a favor. Just wait to see if Al Gore is nominated. Wake up the day after the next Democratic Convention and ask a friend, "Did Gore make it?" My guess is that he will have made it. Take the fifty-thousand-word investment you were prepared to make on Gore's election prospects and follow another story.

Television will not allow you to follow a story. Each broadcast is self-contained; television newspeople are embarrassed if they ever have to remind you that the story existed yesterday as well. The only exception is Big Human Interest. If it has the quality of a soap opera — O. J. Simpson, or the plane that exploded mysteriously — then they trust it as a story that will have had the dramatic elements necessary for their formula. It's reliable. It won't let them down. Television hates stories that turn out to be — you know — disappointing. No cum shot.

Take Belarus. This guy who runs Belarus may turn out to be our next big-time bad guy. We don't know now that he will; and, until he does, who cares? There are no rules in TV journalism; there is no American Medical Association to revoke your license; there are no rules of engagement. If the Belarus guy does turn out to be what we will call a real factor, we just do an In-Depth Segment, and fast. Dan flies to Minsk and does an interview, and CBS's ass is covered retroactively.

The best example of what I'm talking about concerning following a story was the *Times*'s coverage of the Kabila phenomenon in what was then called Zaire. I read every word. You could see the reporter struggling with it. At first, it was confusing. The first three

stories I read two or three times. There were rebels, and there were
refugees. The relationship wasn't clear, it wasn't clear in the reporter's style just who was who — even if, perhaps, it was clear in
his mind.

The more the reporter came to understand the subtext and the
history, however, the more the text of the story became legible to
him, and to the reader; and the more elaborate the story became,
the simpler it was to read. One day, there was a cum shot: he
understood the story; the story made its way into Katanga, and
back to Patrice Lumumba and into the question of Zaire's mineral
wealth, and South Africa's role, and so forth. With the reporter's
full participation, the story achieved critical mass. It made this
reader happy.

The *Times* and the *Washington Post* are the only newspapers you
can follow a story in now. Political news in the *Post* is still interesting, because Watergate was, and is, a visceral experience there. The
Times believes in its soul that foreign news still matters (even if the
reader happens not to agree). The *Times*, by my perception, is a
little ashamed, at just this minute, that it still carries this old belief
around. But it shouldn't be ashamed.

In the *Times* of February 1, 1950, however, every story is a story
that demands to be followed. Almost every story chills the bones,
for it takes one back into the past and unfolds the "F" of Future.

In going through the paper (I went to the State Library in
Albany and looked at it on microfilm), I was able to read — and,
finally, understand — this mystical object that had puzzled me as
a boy. I saw an advertisement for an appliance-store chain in the
paper. Vim, that chain of stores was called. "Vim Vim Vim Vim Vim
for Value" was its radio slogan. That was the kind of message I was
really capable of absorbing as a boy. An advertisement for an
appliance-store chain. A picture of a television set — available at
Vim — with a corny cowboy on the screen.

Almost fifty years later, as I looked at the front page of the paper,
what I saw was a kind of soap opera for Edwardians. These stories
all referred back to the world of Bismarck. Readers of the paper
had been born in 1910 or 1900 or 1890. They had been present
for Act I (the First World War), for the disastrous entr'acte, for Act
II (the Second World War), and here was . . . Well, let me try to
give you a sense of the paper that day.

Critics since 1950 have complained, with increasingly loud voices, to this day, about the power of the *Times*. "The *New York Times* represents the establishment. . . . The State Department calls the *New York Times* and suggests that they do this or they do that" and "The people at the New York *Times* are much too much in touch with the government." Well, all this may be true, but the *Times* is now about ten percent as representative of the ruling mind of America as it was in 1950, and, moreover, the ruling mind of America has split up now, into a hundred pieces, and even if you put those hundred pieces together you wouldn't have what you had then.

If we look at the front page of the *Times* of February 1, 1950 — at the juxtaposition of the headlines — we're looking at an important piece of theater. This theater has certain qualities. It is oblique. It uses a newspaper template of reportage. If you could imagine your own personal life put into a *Times* template — the announcement of your domestic problems, the paying off of your mortgage, whatever it is — it would be oblique. There would be a formality, a system of arrangement, that would give the information about your personal life but would not give, perhaps, the visceral quality you know your life has. That is what a newspaper template of the *Times* type does; it drains out the visceral.

In the *Times* of 1950, there are eight columns, which are more columns than we have now, and Column 8 is the column of the lead story — it's way over on the right-hand side, to which the eye drifts naturally, top right — and the second lead is Column 1, and that itself is an interesting bit of theater, because to get to know that Column 1 is the second lead requires a little knowledge, a little self-discipline. And that was the nature of the *Times*-reading mind of February 1, 1950: the natural drift of the eye was acknowledged, but a little bit of self-discipline was assumed as well. A certain amount of insider's information about how the *Times* was edited was assumed; well, that's not assumed by the editors of the *Times* today. In fact, the *Times* today is terrified that its reader's mind is a mystery.

In any case, the second lead in the *Times* of February 1, 1950, is "PRESIDENT SEEKS 70 DAY COAL TRUCE, FACT FINDING BOARD." There was a coal strike, and the coal miners were powerful and militant; they felt that they were any man's equal, that they didn't like their rate of pay, and that the president was in

opposition to them. The miners represented the decent working people of this country who'd met their test, time after time,
including service in the Second World War, and were dissatisfied.

Next to the second lead is a serialization of Winston Churchill's
work *The Second World War.* And the installment of February 1,
1950, came from Volume III, *The Grand Alliance; Book I: Germany
Drives East.* Churchill wasn't in office in 1950, but he was, uncate-
gorically, the No. 1 guy in the world. He'd been proved right.
People remembered that they, perhaps, had not wanted to go to
war against Germany. And Americans were aware, too, that they
had been, in a way, submissive to Churchill in the war. Churchill
represented one possibility for our soap opera, since he was very
powerful at that moment. But he was destined to become unpow-
erful almost immediately. The strange fact being that Winston
Churchill's reelevation to office in 1951 represented something of
a defeat for him, because his mind — his glorious, old-fashioned
mind — was suddenly, and obviously, not sufficient to deal with our
postwar world.

The lead story is "TRUMAN ORDERS HYDROGEN BOMB
BUILT FOR SECURITY PENDING AN ATOMIC PACT; CON-
GRESS HAILS STEP; BOARD BEGINS JOB." Its second headline
is "HISTORIC DECISION"; a third is "PRESIDENT SAYS HE
MUST DEFEND NATION AGAINST POSSIBLE AGGRESSOR." I
remember that moment. The A-bomb had been viewed for a time
as an unparalleled thing. And, for a time, it was, because we had
it and no one else did. After the end of the Second World War, we
were the one superpower, because we were the country that had
this weapon. It was an uncomfortable situation in some ways but
comfortable in other ways. We were confident that we weren't
going to drop the A-bomb again so we felt, in our own hearts, that
nuclear war was not actually a possibility. Well, of course, then the
Russians developed an A-bomb, and that shattered us all to the
core (just as it would shatter us all to the core now if we were
suddenly to cease, once again, to be the world's only superpower).
The H-bomb told us, "Oh, God, not only is this what we have, it's
what we're gonna have, and we can't see the end of it. Is there
gonna be an I-bomb after an H-bomb? We don't know." It's one
of those moments in which you suddenly discover that the unparalleled thing that pushed you over the frontier isn't the limit —

you're going to march on. The lead stories on the front page of the *Times* were almost impossible to reconcile with each other, almost impossible to bring together. The H-bomb had nothing to do with Winston Churchill, with English-language dominance, or with morals; it had nothing to do with coal miners, with the dissatisfaction of the working people of America. This was about mechanization taking on a life of its own.

There's one other story on the front page — in the fourth column — that strikes a chord with me: it's "FRANCE PROTESTS SOVIET RECOGNITION OF HO CHI MINH RULE." Need I say more?

There is no story on the front page of the *Times* of February 1, 1950, however, that is related in any way, shape, or form to the world that is being reported on today by the panels of communications experts you can watch on C-span or CNN. You might as well be talking about a different country. In the *Times* of February 1, 1950, the country we were going to have appears on a back page. It appears in a section called "Programs on the Air," which is itself divided into four sections, and the fourth section is a combination of television and FM radio. There isn't much in it.

It's striking, as one looks at the paper of February 1, 1950, to see what was destined to be of paramount importance and what was going to go away. Churchill was simply going to go away, and fast — certainly by 1956. Coal miners? Well, the coal mines were going to shut down. The H-bomb? It looks as though, for a time, we have put it away. I hope that's true. In any case, when it comes to developing a national mind sufficient to encompass the meaning of the H-bomb, we have never tried to do it, and probably it's impossible to imagine doing it. But those tiny television listings were the seeds out of which our new national culture was to grow.

While I was learning to read the papers, television — an ignorant little snippet of a medium — was in the wings. It had no real standing in February 1950, but out of all the cultural avatars I encountered in New York as a boy it was what was going to be left standing. Looking back at the *Times* of 1950, I wonder if our current culture of irony and anger and freneticism — our TV culture — doesn't have its essential qualities because the culture as a whole in America in 1950 felt in its bones a contradiction. Having just climbed the pinnacle, stretching our cultural fabric to the limit along the way, we were condemned by the nature of the moment — technology interacting with our fundamental war-weariness and our need for distraction — to embrace a foolish child's reaction to a world situation that demanded a mind more remarkably adult than any of us had in fact achieved.

My view of the civilization as it was presented in the *Times* of February 1950 is that in the Second World War the Germans lost and television won.

Overview

There are four kinds of newspapers. (And that's all there are.)

(1) Let's take the tabloid first. The tabloid sensibility knows only one job: to make the world safe for the moment in which it had its hit — the 1920s, the age of Broadway Brevities, the gangster, the flagpole sitter. Consider the former Soviet Union today. Journalists are simple creatures, and the "scoop" has left Russia, so all that is left is ordinary work — you know, inventory, facts, and that hardest job of all, interesting the reader and getting him to follow the story. In the bad old days, Russia wouldn't let us in, and that was a big part of every story reported out of Russia — how journalism in the Soviet Union was under the thumb of the state, and how foreign journalists were spied on, and so forth. Well, it's different now, and we get less, not more.

Recently, I heard on the radio a story out of Russia. A young man is going to drive from Moscow to Vladivostok in his Yugo automobile. First gear. That was the hook. He's a flagpole sitter, this young man with the Yugo automobile, a marathon dancer, a jazz baby in the making; and if you'll just think about this man in the Yugo you'll understand all you need to understand about the tabloid model, which owns the aesthetic of the World As We Know It Today. Now it has a Yugo racing across the tundra in first gear.

(2) Information for and by the Dominant Mind in a limited sphere. The *Racing Form* is the best newspaper in America, in a way. The part of the public that follows horse racing knows a lot

about horse racing, and the people at the *Racing Form* know more. Readers of the *Times* are now a little vague about Winston Churchill — who he was and whether we still like him or not — but the readers of the *Racing Form* are not vague about Churchill Downs, where the Kentucky Derby is run. Events on the world stage as of 1943 are no longer before us in clarity, but readers of the *Racing Form*, many of them, will recall that Count Fleet won the Triple Crown in that year.

The *Wall Street Journal* would like you to believe that it is the *Racing Form* for business and finance, and indeed it used to be, but it isn't anymore. It missed a big beat: the game changed — the mudders began to win on dry tracks, and so forth — and the *Journal* never told us the reason. You can't follow a story in the *Journal* — this despite the fact that its old-timey appearance makes it look as if it had been published (and thought over) at the Morgan Library. The *Wall Street Journal* can and will tell you that Citicorp has gobbled up whomever, but what banking is, and how one thing got to be another — all that is apparently as mysterious to the people at the *Journal* as it is to poor us, their readers.

The *Washington Post* is a paper for a company town. People complain that the *Post* is too much like the *Racing Form*. They shouldn't. What they should complain about is that the paper of the moment in the mid-seventies had twenty years to make itself our national newspaper, and didn't do it. Most "good" newspapers — the *Boston Globe*, the *Los Angeles Times*, the *Miami Herald*, etc. — fall into the *Post* category, except that they never will have a chance to be our national newspaper.

(3) The *Times*. Our national treasure. Our Marilyn. Our Elvis. In other words: What We Have. People who complain murderously about the *Times* ought to be shot. We all ought to pray for the continued financial well-being of the Sulzbergers.

(4) Papers of the Assumed Dominant Mind. In 1950, the job of owning the Assumed Dominant Mind fell to newspaper people. Let me go back for a minute to the physical city of New York in 1950. It was old and gray. There hadn't been much building since the Depression. Rockefeller Center and the Waldorf-Astoria seemed almost new. He was an Old Man, New York was: powerful, but a little weary; victorious, but in need of a rest. He spoke through the papers. Now the Assumed Dominant Mind belongs to

television and other visual people. *USA Today* is back-formed from the Assumed Dominant Mind of television. There is nothing oracular about *USA Today.* It is a printout, a downloading of the mind you already have. What seems oracular in our new national newspaper is that marvelous, all-in-color weather page.

Biographical Notes

ANDRÉ ACIMAN is the author of *Out of Egypt: A Memoir* (Farrar, Straus & Giroux/Riverhead). He was born in Alexandria and has lived in Egypt, Italy, and France. Educated at Harvard, he has taught at Princeton and now teaches at Bard College. He is the recipient of a Whiting Writers' Award and a Guggenheim Fellowship. A contributor to the *New York Times, The New Yorker, The New Republic, The New York Review of Books,* and *Commentary,* he is currently working on a love novel entitled *Over the Footbridge. Letters of Transit* (New Press), his edition of essays by five authors on exile, was published in May 1999. *Spirit of Place* (Farrar, Straus & Giroux), a collection of essays on exile, travel, and memory, is due to appear in 2000.

CHARLES BOWDEN has written fourteen books, including *Blood Orchid: An Unnatural History of America; Blue Desert; Juarez: The Laboratory of Our Future;* and (with Michael Binstein) *Trust Me: Charles Keating and the Missing Billions.* A contributing editor of *Esquire* and *Harper's Magazine,* he lives in Tucson, Arizona, with a malevolent tortoise and a witch.

FRANKLIN BURROUGHS teaches English at Bowdoin College and is the author of *Billy Watson's Crocker Sack* and *The River Home.* An essay from the former was included in *The Best American Essays 1989.*

MICHAEL W. COX's personal essays have appeared in the *New York Times Magazine,* the *St. Petersburg Times,* and *New Letters,* which awarded him the 1997 Literary Award in the Essay. His fiction has appeared in *Columbia, ACM, Other Voices, Cimarron Review,* and other literary journals. His criticism has appeared in *Aethlon* and the *Explicator,* and he has co-authored several scientific articles on the epidemiology of children's cancer.

JOAN DIDION has written five novels, the most recent of which is *The Last Thing He Wanted,* and several books of essays and reporting, including *Slouching Towards Bethlehem, The White Album, Salvador,* and *Miami.* She contributes to *The New York Review of Books* and *The New Yorker.* Her most recent collection of essays is *After Henry.*

ANNIE DILLARD is the author of *For the Time Being, The Living, An American Childhood, Teaching a Stone to Talk,* and other books. *Pilgrim at Tinker Creek* won the Pulitzer Prize in general nonfiction for 1975.

BRIAN DOYLE is the editor of *Portland Magazine* at the University of Portland in Oregon. He and his father, Jim Doyle, are the authors of *Two Voices,* a collection of their essays. Brian's collection of essays on Catholic matters, *Credo,* will be published in the fall of 1999. Doyle's essays and poems have appeared in *The American Scholar, Commonweal, Orion, Yankee,* and other magazines.

IAN FRAZIER is the author of two works of nonfiction, *Family* and *Great Plains,* as well as several collections of humorous essays: *Dating Your Mom; Nobody Better, Better Than Nobody;* and *Coyote v. Acme.* His writing has appeared in *The New Yorker, The Atlantic Monthly, Outside,* and many other magazines. A book of nonfiction, *On the Rez,* is forthcoming. He lives in Missoula, Montana.

DAGOBERTO GILB is the author of *The Magic of Blood* and *The Last Known Residence of Mickey Acuna,* both published by Grove Press. He has been the recipient of Guggenheim and NEA fellowships and a Whiting Writers' Award. Recent work of his has appeared in *The New Yorker, The Nation, DoubleTake,* and *The Best American Essays 1997.* He is living in Austin, Texas.

MARY GORDON's novels — *Final Payments, The Company of Women, Men and Angels, The Other Side, Spending* — have been bestsellers. She has published a memoir, *The Shadow Man;* a book of novellas, *The Rest of Life;* a collection of stories, *Temporary Shelter;* and a book of essays, *Good Boys and Dead Girls.* Her most recent collection of essays, *Seeing Through Places,* will be published in January 2000. She has received the Lila Acheson Wallace Reader's Digest Award and a Guggenheim Fellowship. She is a professor of English at Barnard College.

PATRICIA HAMPL's most recent book is *I Could Tell You Stories: Sojourns in the Land of Memory.* She is also the author of the memoirs *A Romantic*

Education and *Virgin Time.* She is Regents' Professor at the University of Minnesota and is a member of the permanent faculty of the Prague Summer Seminars.

BARBARA HURD, author of *Objects in This Mirror,* a collection of poems, was a winner of the Sierra Club's Nature Writing Award and a finalist for the Annie Dillard Award for Nonfiction and the PEN/Jerard Award. "The Country Below" is part of her collection of essays on swamps and imagination. A four-time winner of Maryland State Arts Council Awards for Poetry, she teaches creative writing at Frostburg State University in Frostburg, Maryland.

JOHN LAHR is the author of fifteen books, including *Notes on a Cowardly Lion,* a biography of his father, the comedian Bert Lahr, and *Prick Up Your Ears: The Biography of Joe Orton.* He has written two novels, *The Autograph Hound* (1973) and *Hot to Trot* (1974). Mr. Lahr has twice won the George Jean Nathan Award for Dramatic Criticism, most recently in 1995 for his work at *The New Yorker,* where he has been writing about theater and popular culture since 1992.

HILARY MASTERS grew up in Kansas City, Missouri. His eight novels include the Harlem Valley Trio, *Clemmons, Cooper,* and *Strickland,* and, most recently, *Home Is the Exile.* He is also the author of a family memoir, *Last Stands: Notes from Memory,* and two collections of short fiction. A collection of his personal essays, *In Montaigne's Tower,* will be published in 1999 by the University of Missouri Press. He teaches at Carnegie Mellon University in Pittsburgh.

JOHN MCNEEL was born in Hillsboro, West Virginia, and attended Davis-Elkins College and Antioch College. He served in an antiaircraft battalion in seven campaigns in Sicily, Italy, France, and Germany. For many years a newspaper editor and reporter in the New York area and a staff writer for trade and consumer publications, he wrote *The Brain of Man* (G. P. Putnam's Sons) for high school reading in science. He now lives in New York and is working on a novel.

BEN METCALF was born in Illinois and raised in that state and in Virginia. He currently makes his home in New York City, where he is a senior editor of *Harper's.*

ARTHUR MILLER grew up in Harlem and Brooklyn and is a graduate of the University of Michigan. His first Broadway production, *The Man Who Had All the Luck* (1944), was followed by *All My Sons* (1947), which won the Drama Critics' Circle Award; *Death of a Salesman* (1949), which won a Pulitzer Prize; *The Crucible* (1953); *A View from the Bridge* (1955);

After the Fall (1964); *Incident at Vichy* (1964); *The Price* (1968); and many other award-winning plays, including most recently *Broken Glass* (1994) and *Mr. Peters' Connections* (1998). A long-time advocate of PEN International, he is the author of several screenplays, an autobiography, *Time Bends: A Life,* as well as many essays and works of fiction.

JOYCE CAROL OATES is the author most recently of the novel *My Heart Laid Bare* and the story collection *The Collector of Hearts.* She teaches at Princeton University and is a member of the American Academy of Arts and Letters.

CYNTHIA OZICK is the author of three collections of essays — *Art & Ardor, Metaphor & Memory,* and *Fame & Folly* — three collections of short stories, and five novels, the most recent being *The Puttermesser Papers.* She is the recipient of numerous awards, including four O. Henry first prizes, a Guggenheim Fellowship, and the Rea Award for the Short Story. She was the 1998 guest editor of this series and is a member of the American Academy of Arts and Letters. A fourth collection of essays is in preparation.

DAVID QUAMMEN is the author of *The Song of the Dodo* and seven other books of nonfiction and fiction, including a spy novel, *The Soul of Viktor Tronko.* For fifteen years he wrote a natural science column for *Outside* magazine. His most recent book is *Wild Thoughts from Wild Places,* a collection of essays; another collection, *The Boilerplate Rhino,* is forthcoming. Quammen lives in Montana and travels frequently on assignment to jungles and swamps. His current book project involves crocodiles, lions, and bears.

DAISY EUNYOUNG RHAU has published poems and essays in *The Kenyon Review, New Letters,* and *North American Review.* She lives in the San Francisco area, where she is working on a memoir.

SCOTT RUSSELL SANDERS is the author of fifteen books, including *Secrets of the Universe, Writing from the Center,* and *Staying Put.* "Beauty" became a chapter in *Hunting for Hope,* published in 1998. In his latest book, *The Country of Language,* he tells the story of his lifelong romance with words. He has won Guggenheim and National Endowment for the Arts fellowships in support of his writing, and for his nonfiction he has received the Lannan Literary Award. He teaches literature and writing at Indiana University, in Bloomington, where he lives with his wife, and where his two grown children currently study.

MARK SLOUKA's essays and fiction have appeared in *Harper's Magazine, Esquire, Story, Epoch,* and *The Georgia Review.* His collection of stories, *Lost Lake,* appeared in 1998. He teaches at Columbia University.

TOURÉ was born in Boston in 1971 and now lives in Brooklyn. He studied at Columbia University's Graduate School of Creative Writing and has written for *The New Yorker, The New York Times Magazine, Rolling Stone, Playboy,* and *The Village Voice.* Not long after writing this piece for a collection called *Personals,* edited by Thomas Beller, he quit boxing. He now plays guerrilla tennis.

GEORGE W. S. TROW is the author of *Within the Context of No Context,* an attempt to make sense of media civilization in terms of autobiography and classical social history. He is also the author of *Bullies,* a collection of satiric stories, and *The City in the Mist,* a novel. In 1985 he was awarded the Jean Stein Prize by the American Academy and Institute of Arts and Letters. He is on the staff of *The New Yorker.* Long ago he was a founding editor of *National Lampoon.* "Folding the Times" appears in his 1999 collection, *My Pilgrim's Progress: Media Studies, 1950–1998.*

Notable Essays of 1998

SELECTED BY ROBERT ATWAN

PAUL ZIMMER
  The Blind World, Atomic
    Battlefields. *The Georgia Review,*
    Winter.
HOWARD ZINN
  The Massacres of History. *The*
    Progressive, August.

HILLER B. ZOBEL
  The Undying Problem of the Death
    Penalty. *American Heritage,* January.

Issues of *Five Points,* with the essays "Thread" by Stuart Dybek and "The Third Servant" by Margo Livesey, arrived too late to be considered for this year's volume.

Readers will also find many essays of interest in the following special issues of periodicals published in 1998: "A View from the Divide (Creative Nonfiction on Health and Science)," *Creative Nonfiction,* no. 11, Lee Gutkind, editor; "Whiteness: What Is It?" *Hungry Mind Review,* Spring, Bart Schneider, editor; "Personal Narratives," *Prairie Schooner,* Fall, Hilda Raz, editor; "American Families," *Witness,* vol. 12, no. 2, Peter Stine, editor.

DATE DUE